Pamela Rice Hahn
Dennis E. Hensley, Ph.D.

W9-BAB-597

Alpha
Teach Yourself

Grammar and
Style

in 24 hours

Pearson Education, Inc.
201 West 103rd Street
Indianapolis, IN 46290

Alpha Teach Yourself Grammar and Style in 24 Hours

International Standard Book Number: 0-02-863899-9
Library of Congress Catalog Card Number: Available upon request.

Printed in the United States of America

First printing: 2000

03   02   4   3   2

Trademarks

SENIOR ACQUISITIONS EDITOR
Renee Wilmeth

DEVELOPMENT EDITOR
Doris Cross

PRODUCTION EDITOR
JoAnna Kremer

COPY EDITOR
Amy Lepore

INDEXER
Lisa Wilson

COVER DESIGNER
Alan Clements

BOOK DESIGNER
Gary Adair

PRODUCTION
Terri Edwards
Donna Martin
Tim Osborn
Mark Walchle

MANAGING EDITOR
Cari Luna

PRODUCT MANAGER
Phil Kitchel

PUBLISHER
Marie Butler-Knight

Dedicated in loving memory to RJ Corradino (1979-2000), gifted poet and one of the best friends anybody could ever have. I miss your kind spirit and unselfish nature. Thank you for all of those moments you enriched my life.

Pam

This book is affectionately dedicated to my wife, Rose, for believing in me, oh, those many years ago when I decided I wanted to be a writer. Thanks, hon, for the encouragement, nudging, and loyalty. I wouldn't have made it otherwise.

Dennis

Overview

Introduction   xxiii

PART I Grappling with Grammar   1

HOUR 1 Understanding Grammar   3

HOUR 2 Mastering the Basic Parts of a Sentence   19

PART II Getting Grounded in Grammar   35

HOUR 3 Elementary Sentence Components I: Nouns   37

HOUR 4 Elementary Sentence Components II: Pronouns   55

HOUR 5 Elementary Sentence Components III: Verbs   71

HOUR 6 Expanding Sentences with Articles, Adjectives, and Adverbs   87

HOUR 7 Reaching Agreements   103

HOUR 8 Other Considerations   115

HOUR 9 Phrases   129

HOUR 10 Main and Subordinate Clauses   145

HOUR 11 Controlling the Comma and the Semicolon   161

HOUR 12 Other Forms of Punctuation   177

PART III Setting Your Style   **191**

    HOUR 13 The Importance of Knowing the Rules   193

    HOUR 14 Forego the Fluff   207

    HOUR 15 Getting the Job Done   221

    HOUR 16 Leads and Closings   237

PART IV Putting Your Style into Practice   **253**

    HOUR 17 Developing Ideas   255

    HOUR 18 Managing Your Research   269

    HOUR 19 The Ins and Outs of Italics, Parentheses, Quotation Marks, and More   289

    HOUR 20 Remain on Task   303

    HOUR 21 Getting Beyond Your First Draft   315

    HOUR 22 Putting Your Style into Practice I   329

    HOUR 23 Putting Your Style into Practice II   347

    HOUR 24 Problem Words and Expressions   361

    APPENDIX A Glossary   375

    APPENDIX B Resources   385

    APPENDIX C Tables   389

    Index   397

Contents

Introduction   **xxiii**

PART I Grappling with Grammar   **1**

HOUR 1 Understanding Grammar   **3**

Chapter Summary 3
Grammar's Six Senses 4
The Logic of Grammar 5
    Context..6
    Function 6
    Pragmatics 6
    Semantics 7
    Wording 7
    Sound Patterns 7
Nuances, Trivia, and Important Stuff 7
    Alliteration...7
    Allusion 8
    Anthropomorphism 8
    Antonyms...8
    Assonance 9
    Clichés 9
    Colloquialisms...9
    Figures of Speech 10
    Gist...10
    Homonyms...10
    Hyperbole 10
    Idioms 10
    Idiomatic Translations 11
    Irony...11
    Task: Try Some Irony 11
    Jargon...11
    Lexicons...12
    Malapropisms 12
    Metaphors 12
    Task: Make a Metaphor...12
    Metonymy 12

Morphemes 13

Onomatopoeia 13

Puns 13

Rhyme 14

Task: Rhyme Time...14

Rhythm 14

Sarcasm 15

Similes 15

Synonyms 15

Hour's Up! 16

Answers 18

Recap..18

Hour 2 Mastering the Basic Parts of a Sentence 19

Chapter Summary 19

The Subject of the Subject 20

Task: Who's on First? 20

Subjects on the Loose 21

The "Understood You" 21

Making a Statement...22

Subject Positioning 22

Main Clause..22

Subordinate Clause 23

The Predicate Defined 23

Task: Find the Predicate 23

Compound Subjects and Predicates 24

Sentence Types 24

The Simple Sentence..24

The Compound Sentence....................................25

The Complex Sentence 25

The Compound-Complex Sentence...........................25

Task: Find the Flaw 26

Sentence Fragment 26

Parallel Construction 27

Run-On Sentences 28

Fused Sentence Error..28

Comma Splice 28

Interrogative Sentences (Questions) 28

Sentence Variation 29

Sentence Rules 31

Hour's Up! 31

Answers 33

Recap 33

PART II Getting Grounded in Grammar   35

HOUR 3 Elementary Sentence Components I: Nouns   37

Chapter Summary 37

Common Nouns 38

Proper Nouns 38

Mass Nouns 41

Plural Nouns 42

Count Nouns 45

Possessive Nouns 46

Compound Nouns 47

Collective Nouns 48

Noun Gender 48

Gerunds 49

Task: Form Fitting 49

Hour's Up! 51

Answers 53

Recap 53

HOUR 4 Elementary Sentence Components II: Pronouns   55

Chapter Summary 55

Personal Pronouns 55

Pronoun Numbers 56

Possessive Pronouns 56

The Pronoun "Who" 57

Relative Pronouns 58

Contractions 59

Demonstrative Pronouns 59

Indefinite Pronouns 59

Reflexive Pronouns 60

Task: Test Your Reflexives 60

Intensive Pronouns 61

Interrogative Pronouns 61

Reciprocal Pronouns 62

Avoiding Pronoun Pitfalls...62
    Task: Avoid Ambiguity 62
    Task: Maintain Pronoun and Antecedent Agreement 62
Other Agreement Rules...64
Noun or Pronoun Case 64
    Subjective or Objective Pronoun Choice 65
Last Minute Rules and Refreshers 65
    Workshop: Testing Pronoun Choices 66
    Pronoun Chart 66
Hour's Up! 67
    Answers 69
Recap..69

HOUR 5 Elementary Sentence Components III: Verbs   71
Chapter Summary 71
Setting the Mood..72
Understanding Verb Tense 72
    Present Tense 73
Progressive Tense 74
    Present Progressive Tense 74
    Simple Past Tense 74
    Present Perfect Tense..75
    Past Perfect Tense 75
    Past Progressive Tense...75
    Present Perfect Progressive Tense 76
    Past Perfect Progressive Tense 76
    Future Tense 76
    Future Perfect Tense 76
    Future Progressive Tense 76
    Future Perfect Progressive Tense 76
Regular Verbs 77
Irregular Verbs...78
    Irregular Verbs Without Spelling Changes 79
    The Verb "To Be" 79
Action Verbs 79
    Transitive Verbs 80
    Intransitive Verbs 80
Linking Verbs 80
Helping Verbs 81
Verb Voice: Active Versus Passive 81
"To Be," "To Do," and "To Have" as Ordinary Verbs 82
Hour's Up! 83
    Answers 85
Recap...85

Hour 6 Expanding Sentences with Articles, Adjectives, and Adverbs   **87**

Chapter Summary 87
   Indefinite Articles 87
   The Definite Article "The" 87
   The Demonstratives 88
   The Distributives 89
   The Exclamatives 89
   The Numbers 89
   The Possessives 90
   The Quantifiers 91
Adjectives 92
   Adjective Position 92
   Adjective Types 93
   Kinds of Adjectives 93
Adjective Form and Functions 94
Adjective Endings..95
Adverbs 96
   Adverb Position 96
Adjective and Adverb Comparisons 97
   Forming the Comparative and Superlative 97
Hour's Up! 100
   Answers 102
Recap..102

Hour 7 Reaching Agreements   **103**

Chapter Summary 103
   Plural Pronoun with a Compound Antecedent 103
   Indefinite Pronoun Agreement 104
Avoiding Unclear Pronoun Reference 106
   More Than One Possible Antecedent 106
Subject and Verb Agreement..107
   Compound Subjects..107
   Collective Nouns 108
   Confusing Nouns 109
   Quantity Expressions..109
   Averting Word Pattern Difficulties 110
Agreement of Adverbs 110
Q&A 111
Hour's Up! 112
   Answers 114
Recap..114

HOUR 8 Other Considerations   **115**

    Chapter Summary 115

        Prepositional Phrases..116

        Phrasal Verbs 117

    Infinitives 117

    Contractions 118

    Conjunctions 119

    Faulty Parallelism 121

    Participles 122

    Metaphors 122

    Simile 123

    Idioms 123

    Collocation 124

    Clichés...124

    Subjunctives 125

    Hour's Up! 126

        Answers 128

    Recap..128

HOUR 9 Phrases   **129**

    Chapter Summary 129

        Noun Phrases...129

        Adjective Phrases 130

        Absolute Phrases 130

        Appositive Phrases 131

        Vocative Phrases 133

    Verbal Phrases..134

        Gerund Phrases 134

        Participial Phrases 134

    Infinitive Phrases..135

    Phrases and Cases 136

        The Subjective Case 136

        Direct Objects 137

        Indirect Objects 138

        Object Complements 139

        Auxiliary Verbs 140

    Hour's Up! 141

        Answers 143

    Recap..143

HOUR 10 Main and Subordinate Clauses **145**

Chapter Summary 145
   Compound Sentences 146
   Coordinating Conjunctions 146
   Conjunctive Adverbs 147
Subordinate Clauses 147
Complex Sentences..147
Compound-Complex Sentences 148
Noun Clauses 148
   Noun Clauses Used as Subjects 149
   Noun Clauses Used as Direct Objects................................150
   Noun Clauses Used as Indirect Objects 150
   Noun Clauses Used as Object Complements 150
Adjective Clauses 151
   Adjective Clauses as Subjects 151
   Adjective Clauses as Objects 151
   Task: Agree to Agree 152
   Adjective Clauses as Complements 152
   Restrictive Clauses 152
   Adverbial Clauses 153
   Subordinators..153
   Q&A 156
Hour's Up! 157
   Answers 159
Recap..159

HOUR 11 Controlling the Comma and the Semicolon **161**

Chapter Summary 161
   Simple Sentence Divisions 161
   Phrases That End a Sentence...162
   Between Two Main Clauses 162
   After Introductory Subordinate Clauses 163
   Separating a Weak Clause 164
   After Introductory Words and Phrases 164
   The Serial Comma...164
   Separating Coordinate Adjectives Before a Noun..............165
   After -ly Adjectives Used with Other Adjectives 166
   Isolate Words That Interrupt 166
   Separating Nonessential Words 166
   Task: Nonessential Words Test 167
   Emphasize Words in a Direct Address 167

Direct Quotations...168
Rules for Comma Usage with Dates............................168
Geographical Names 168
Geographical Addresses 169
Degrees or Titles 169
Comma Splices 169
A Common Error with Essential Elements.................170
Comma Confusion..171
Semicolon 171
Q&A 173
Hour's Up! 173
Answers 175
Recap...175

HOUR 12 Other Forms of Punctuation   **177**
Chapter Summary 177
Question Mark 178
Exclamation Mark...180
Colon...180
Apostrophe 182
Ellipsis...184
Hyphen 185
Dash 188
Hour's Up! 188
Answers 190
Recap...190

PART III Setting Your Style   **191**

HOUR 13 The Importance of Knowing the Rules   **193**
Chapter Summary 193
What Spell Checks Can't Tell You 193
Mutable Meanings 195
History, Attitudes, and Habits 196
Gender-Sensitive Writing 196
Task: Evaluate Your Audience 197
Nouns and Verbs 198
Verbalizing Nouns 199
Active and Passive Voice.....................................199
Adjective and Adverb Overuse 200
Grammatical Ambiguity 200
Workshop: Logic and Clarity 200

Perspective and Point of View 202
Hour's Up! 203
Answers 205
Recap..205

Hour 14 Forego the Fluff **207**

Chapter Summary 207
The Rules of Effective Communication 207
Use Everyday Language 208
Performance Art 208
Task: Write It Right 209
Can the Clichés...209
Frugal, Yet Forceful 209
Keep It Simple 210
Versatile Variables..210
Practical Paragraphs 211
Word Position to Emphasize Meaning 212
Keep Things Active...212
Clutter-Free Commentary 214
Task: Cut, Don't Paste 214
Conversational Narrative 214
Research, Then Record..215
Task: Get the Picture...216
Find Your Own Voice 216
Pedestrian Patter 217
Timing Your Edits 217
Practical Punctuation 218
Hour's Up! 218
Answers 220
Recap..220

Hour 15 Getting the Job Done **221**

Chapter Summary 221
Task: Adapting to Your Audience 221
Selling Ideas 222
Appealing Presentations 223
Sales Letters...224
Task: Preparing Sales Letters 224
Fundraising Letters 226
Press Releases...228
Preparing a Personal Biography 230

Task: Reflect Your Personality 231
Add Flesh to the Skeleton..232
    Establish Your Voice 232
    Aim for Simplicity, Not Simple 232
Hour's Up! 233
    Answers 234
Workshop 234
Recap...235

HOUR 16 Leads and Closings   **237**

Chapter Summary 237
Solid from Start to Finish 237
Lead Me, and Lead Me NOW!..238
Task: Take It from the Movies 238
Leads for Nonfiction Writing 239
In Fiction, Lead with Your Write 241
    Establish the Locale...241
    Set Up the Story Setting 242
    Introduce the Main Characters 242
    Set the Tone 242
    Get to the Conflict Quickly 243
In the Beginning 243
All's Well That Ends Well 246
The Finishing Touches 247
Hour's Up! 249
    Answers 251
Recap...251

PART IV Putting Your Style into Practice   **253**

HOUR 17 Developing Ideas   **255**

Chapter Summary 255
    Task: Making a List...255
    Task: Mind Mapping 256
Discovering What's News..256
    The Never-Miss Categories 257
    The Fairly-Safe Categories 258
Sources of Idea Stimulators 258
    Discovering the "Gold" Pages...259
    Getting an Expert Opinion 260

Tickle Your Fancy 261
Storyboard It 263
The Tickling Continues. 263
It Works for Fiction Writing, Too...............................264
Workshop: Turning Nonfiction into Fiction 266
Hour's Up! 266
Answers 268
Recap..268

HOUR 18 Managing Your Research   269

Chapter Summary 269
The Range of Research...270
Narrow the Topic 271
Task: Overall Research Planning 271
Getting to Work...272
Taking Your Research Online 273
Other Internet Options...274
Library Speak 274
Media Merit..275
Task: Recording Sources 275
Conducting the Professional Interview..........................276
Task: Organizing the Material 279
Your Lead 280
Sequential Order 281
Cause and Effect 281
Comparison and Contrast 282
The Soapbox 282
Counterpoint and Rebuttal......................................282
Define and Exemplify 282
Process Analysis 282
Proper Documentation 283
Workshop: Hone to the Bone 284
Hour's Up! 284
Answers 287
Recap..287

**HOUR 19 The Ins and Outs of Italics, Parentheses, Quotation Marks,
and More   289**

Chapter Summary 289
Parentheses 290
Brackets..293

The Slash/Virgule 293
Quotation Marks 294
Task: Avoid Incorrect Run-On Quotes 298
Single Quotation Marks 299
And You Can Quote Me on That 299
Hour's Up! 300
    Answers 302
Recap..302

HOUR 20 Remain on Task   **303**

Chapter Summary 303
Words to Remember 304
Why You Need Take-Away Value...304
Task: Guarantee Take-Away Value 305
Workshop: Blueprints and Work Permits 307
    Task: Timetable 307
    Negative Realities 309
Getting Around the Block..309
    Do a Free Write 310
    Work Backward 310
    Close Your Eyes..310
    Draft a Sequence of Events Scenario 311
    Imagine the Sequel 311
Hour's Up! 311
    Answers 313
Recap..314

HOUR 21 Getting Beyond Your First Draft   **315**

Chapter Summary 315
Proofreading Techniques 315
Inadvertent Errors 318
Punch the Puns 318
Editing..319
Workshop: Checking Revisions 323
Learn from Other Writers 323
Reading with a Purpose 324
Hour's Up! 325
    Answers 327
Recap..327

HOUR 22 Putting Your Style into Practice I 329

Chapter Summary 329
   Adapt to Your Audience 329
   Task: Making Sure It Fits 330
   Softening Bad News 330
Presenting Your Information 331
   Use an Outline 331
   Structure Your Data 332
Business Writing 332
   Interoffice Memos and Electronic Mail 333
   Business Letters 335
   Task: Preparing Reports 337
   Proposals 337
   Meetings 338
   Oral Presentations 340
   Brochures and Ad Copy 340
   Press Releases 341
Preparing a Resumé or Curriculum Vitae 341
Task: Using Action Words in Your Resumé 342
Hour's Up! 343
   Answers 345
Recap 345

HOUR 23 Putting Your Style into Practice II 347

Chapter Summary 347
Writing the Essay 348
Writing About Law 349
Writing about Science 350
   Task: Is It Timely, Interesting, and Understandable? ...351
Specialized Science Writing 352
   The Environment 352
   Medicine 353
   Technology 353
Criticism and Reviewing 354
   Book Reviews 355
   Stage and Screen Reviews 355
Seriously Funny 356
Academic Writing 356
Sports Writing 357
Hour's Up! 357
   Answers 359
Recap 359

HOUR 24 Problem Words and Expressions   **361**

Chapter Summary 361

Styles Change 361

Problems When the Rules Keep Changing........................363

   Accents and Other Diacritical Marks 363

   Apostrophes for Plurals..363

Problems That May Not Be Problems 364

   To Split or Not To Split an Infinitive 364

   Turning Nouns into Verbs 365

   Implied Infinitives 365

Problem Words 366

   a while versus awhile 366

   all ready versus already 366

   appendix versus glossary..366

   complement versus compliment 367

   dialogue versus dialog..367

   farther versus further 367

   former and latter 367

   fewer versus less 368

   its versus it's 368

   lay versus lie 368

   moot versus mute..369

   than versus then 370

   their, they're, and there 370

   to, too, and two 370

Problem Expressions...371

   Slang 371

   Ambiguity at Work 371

Hour's Up! 373

   Answers 374

Recap..374

APPENDIX A Glossary   **375**

APPENDIX B Resources   **385**

Dictionaries..385

   Grammar Guides 385

   Style Guides..386

   Vocabulary Guides...387

   Writing Guides 387

Online Resources 387
    Dictionaries 387
    General Reference 388
    Grammar Guides 388
    Style Guides...388

APPENDIX C Tables   **389**
    Irregular Verbs With Spelling Changes 389
    Slang 394

Index   **397**

Introduction

Before speech was created, everybody spoke in sign language. However, that didn't always work too well—especially at distances of several hundred yards or around corners.

People soon realized that they could better communicate using sounds. (Refer to Hour 1, "Understanding Grammar," to see if you can figure out why we believe spoken language started with onomatopoeia.) This made things easier, but it also meant you could no longer ignore somebody just by turning away. Once (and if) people used the same sounds to represent certain things, other people caught on to what was meant; when that happened, language was born.

Okay. Maybe it didn't happen quite like that, but it's close enough for our purposes. Worries about dangling participles, misplaced modifiers, split infinitives, and ending a sentence with a preposition probably weren't priorities when someone was trying to get out of the path of a woolly mammoth or escape from a saber-toothed tiger. Regardless of language's true evolution, when you boil it down to its essence, grammar means using words in a way that other people will understand. Once you communicate in a way that forges this understanding, you can better master your world.

This book teaches the fundamentals of English grammar. The good news is that you probably know most of these rules. You've been speaking and writing since you were a kid. You probably have an inner knack for being able to tell if a sentence is wrong or right; however, if you're like most people, you probably can't say why. This book will teach you how to tell the difference and when it's okay to ignore that difference.

Even if you're new to the English language, you probably speak another one. Therefore, you'll find that, despite all of its exceptions, most of the rules of English actually make sense; you'll probably even find that some of the rules are identical to rules in other languages.

WHAT YOU'LL FIND IN THIS BOOK

Don't be afraid. English grammar can appear daunting, but once you start to get inside it, you find that you absorb the rules quite naturally. We've taken the essentials and broken them down into easy-to-understand segments. Most of the grammar rules appear in the first half of the book.

In **Part I, "Grappling with Grammar,"** we cover the definition, logic, and nuances of grammar and show you exactly what makes up the basic parts of a sentence.

Part II, "Getting Grounded in Grammar," explains the elementary sentence components—nouns, gerunds, pronouns, verbs, articles, adjectives, adverbs, phrases, clauses—and most forms of punctuation.

By **Part III, "Setting Your Style,"** you'll be ready to apply the rules you've learned. We'll show you the steps to add the necessary flair and finesse to take the written and spoken word beyond the mundane and into the realm of efficiency and effectiveness.

Finally, in **Part IV, "Putting Your Style into Practice,"** you're ready to do just that. You'll learn how to come up with and develop ideas, adapt presentations to fit your audience, handle the standard forms of business correspondence, and overcome problem words and expressions.

We wrap up with the appendixes, which provide you with a glossary to verify word and term definitions plus additional (and sometimes alternative) information on the books and other resources you've encountered in "Biblio File" notes throughout the book.

Rome may not have been built in a day, but your better understanding of grammar and style will be—one hour at a time.

EXTRAS

At the end of each hour, you'll find a short quiz to help you support what you've learned. This is where you can pat yourself on the back for a job well done and know that you're ready for the next building block.

Take the quiz again the next time you sit down to read an hour. It will act as a refresher to help you remember what you've learned and to get your mind in gear for the next round of grammar and style. You can also use the glossary in Appendix A as a quick reference guide for terms you're not completely comfortable with yet.

We know you don't have a lot of extra time. You're a hard-working individual whose life is probably spent working for others, whether it's your boss or your family, and you want to do something for yourself. We've created this book for you, to make learning the rules—and the exceptions to those rules—as easy as possible. To that end, along with the general instructions, we've inserted some elements into each hour to help you with your new-found and expanding understanding of grammar and style.

This book contains a lot of miscellaneous cross-references, tips, shortcuts, and warnings as sidebars from the regular text. These odds and ends are given particular names, and here's how they stack up:

e.g.

These are examples of grammar and style rules.

JUST A MINUTE

Here you'll find helpful tips to make learning grammar and style even easier.

PROCEED WITH CAUTION

Watch for these warnings about grammar and style pitfalls.

STRICTLY DEFINED

These are embellished definitions of grammar and style terms.

These are quick references to direct you toward further reading and examples in other sources.

About the Authors

Pamela Rice Hahn is the author of *The Unofficial Guide to Online Genealogy* (IDG Books, 2000) and is lead author on *Master the Grill The Lazy Way* (Alpha Books, Macmillan General Reference, 1999) and *How to Use Microsoft Access 2000* (Macmillan Computer Publishing, July 1999). She has served as editor for a local community-action commission newsletter, *The AMCAC News*, as well as for a number of computer-related and business newsletters. In addition, she has taught business and sales training seminars; her most recent speaking engagements have been about writing opportunities on the Internet. Pam has published several hundred bylined and ghostwritten articles that have appeared in *Glamour, Country Living, Business Venture, Current Notes*, and other national publications. In addition, she works as a tech editor and writer for Macmillan Computer Publishing, Sybex, Osborne, Quessing, and DDC.

Pam is publisher and editor in chief for the online magazine *The Blue Rose Bouquet* at www.blueroses.com, and she maintains several other Web sites, among them her personal site at www.ricehahn.com as well as www.ricehahn.com/grill/, www.ricehahn.com/genealogy/, The Ultimate Chronic Illness Resource Directory at www.ricehahn.com/resource/, and the #Authors on the Undernet chat channel pages at www.blueroses.com/authors/.

Pam is the 1997 winner of The Manny Award for Nonfiction from the MidWest Writers Workshop.

Dennis E. Hensley, Ph.D. is an associate professor of English at the Fort Wayne campus of Taylor University, where he teaches such courses as Corporate Communications, Public Relations, and Business and Technical Writing. He has served as a consultant for more than 20 years with such businesses as Chrysler Corporation, General Motors, North American Van Lines, Indiana & Michigan Power, ITT Corporation, Magnavox, and Spartan Motors, among many others.

He holds four degrees in communications, including a Ph.D. from Ball State University. He was director of public relations at Manchester College from 1978–82 and received the Award for Teaching Excellence from Indiana University in 1990.

Dr. Hensley is the author of 29 books including *Uncommon Sense*; *Positive Workaholism*; *Become Famous, Then Rich*; *How to Manage Your Time*; *Making The Most Of Your Potential*; *How to Fulfill Your Potential*; and *Millennium Approaches*. Dr. Hensley has published more than 3,000 bylined articles in such publications as *Reader's Digest*, *The Writer*, and other local and national publications. He has been a contributing writer for six books published by Writer's Digest Books and has been a regional correspondent for *Writer's Digest* magazine for 24 years. Dr. Hensley is also a frequent speaker and instructor at writing conferences and workshops.

Acknowledgments

First and foremost, I want to thank David L. Hebert and Doris Cross for their help on this project and their friendship; special thanks also go to Sheree Bykofsky, Renee Wilmeth, JoAnna Kremer, Amy Lepore, Keith Giddeon, Stevie Harris, RJ Corradino, Jodi Cornelius, Gail Smith-Sofsky, Diana Rowland, Troy More, Robert Marcom, the entire #Authors crew, Michael, my parents, Andy, Randy, Taylor, Charlie, and the patient librarians at the St. Marys Community Public Library.

Pamela Rice Hahn

I wish to thank the following people for encouraging me in my careers as a writer and teacher: Neil Ringle, Daryl Yost, Ron Sloan, Pam Jordan, Holly G. Miller, Pamela Rice Hahn, Lin Johnson, Frances Rippy, Tom Koontz, Dwight Jessup, and the entire Hensley clan: Ed, Juanita, Pam, Gary, Donna, Andrew, Jeanette, and Nathan.

Dennis E. Hensley

PART I

Grappling with Grammar

Hour 1 Understanding Grammar

Hour 2 Mastering the Basic Parts of a Sentence

HOUR 1
Understanding Grammar

LESSON PLAN:

In this Hour, you'll learn what grammar means and how some of its elements can add "color" to your use of the language.

Among the things we'll cover are

- The different types of grammar.
- Some common terms used in grammar.
- The subtle ways to "flavor" your English usage.
- Some uses for rhymes.

Grammar is the study of sentence structure and the rules that govern it.

Writing is about usage and style. The spoken word relies on the same conventions, just in a less obvious sense.

The most difficult thing about the study of grammar is that, to do it, you have to take the language out of its context—its atmosphere, surroundings, or setting. Rigid *syntax* (sentence structure) without context can cause anxiety (and dry prose).

Traditional schoolbook grammar emphasizes parsing, sentence diagramming, and the identification of parts of speech and parts of a sentence. It is based on a system of rules derived from Latin grammars of the seventeenth and eighteenth centuries.

The traditional standards evolved to encompass usage conventions such as

- Ending a sentence with a preposition (or not). (See Hour 8 for a review of prepositions.)
- Feeling bad versus feeling badly. (See Hour 12 for a review of problem words and expressions.)
- "It is I" versus "It's me." (See Hour 4 for a review of pronouns.)
- Pronoun and antecedent agreement. (See Hour 7 for a review of reaching agreements.)

- Rules for capitalization. (See Hour 3 for a review of proper nouns.)
- Verb tense. (See Hour 5 for a review of verbs.)

Knowledge of grammar alone doesn't make a good writer. The ability to diagram sentences with the best of 'em is no substitute for the gut feeling of how words should appear on a page. The same holds true for having a sense of how to tell a story. However, the ability to do both of these well—to write and speak with the authority necessary to be taken seriously—does develop from the knowledge and application of the "rules."

So if grammar isn't going to be the main thing that helps you master the language, why do you need to learn it?

Because it shows us two things:

1. How the English sentence works
2. How the parts of the sentence work together to express a meaning

Once we learn the rules that govern these things, grammar helps us to

- Identify our shortcomings as writers and speakers.
- Gain a common vocabulary for sentence elements, which helps us learn how to address those shortcomings.

Your best approach to grammar is to see it not as a series of mundane rules to be mastered but as a way of helping yourself look and sound as if you know what you're talking (or writing) about.

GRAMMAR'S SIX SENSES

Grammar is not simply a fixed set of general rules. In fact, the term *grammar* has six distinct senses:

- **Descriptive grammar**　The study that records the description of how people speak and the patterns contained in that speech. Descriptive grammar is the basis for modern *linguistics*—the scientific study of language.
- **Pedagogical grammar**　The name for a textbook specifically written to teach a language. It stresses and clarifies the systematic nature of the sentence in the language it's teaching.
- **Prescriptive grammar**　The rules for how people should speak a language; it contrasts with descriptive grammar because the latter describes the principles people actually follow when they talk.

- **Reference grammar**   Sets forth the rules of grammar in a dictionary format.
- **Theoretical grammar**   The analysis of the components necessary in any human language.
- **Traditional grammar**   The term used to sum up the unscientific approach to grammatical study used 2,000 years ago by the classical Greeks and Romans prior to the advent of linguistic science.

THE LOGIC OF GRAMMAR

Grammar can mean many things. It can be

- The proper way to speak or write.
- The *inflection* or the word ending from which aspects of a word can be determined.
- The way to choose and arrange words.
- The way to organize ideas into words.

Certain conclusions about a word grouping can be made by the context of those words. You make these conclusions by comparing the words to others you've encountered in the past. Oftentimes, you decipher a new definition by forming a *hypothesis,* or theory, about a word based on the context; if your conclusion makes sense, you determine that your hypothesis is correct. Basically, whether you realize it or not, you employ the same methods used by a linguist studying any facet of a language including its grammar. You just do it subconsciously rather than scientifically.

Words may proceed in a seemingly linear fashion, but that fashion can make all the difference in the world. Words mean things. You can't just throw them around in any old way you choose. (And we don't mean restraining those profanities you're mumbling under your breath about your boss.)

e.g.
_____

The cow jumped over the moon.
As improbable as this scenario seems, it's more probable than
The moon jumped over the cow.

Certain words have certain restrictions. As you'll learn in Hour 2, "Mastering the Basic Parts of a Sentence," sentences and sentence order are important.

The words within a sentence are at work on six different levels simultaneously.

Context

Context refers to the time and place in which an utterance occurs.

Cultural context involves the things a person brings to the meaning or the interpretation of that meaning based on such things as national origin or religion.

The *linguistic context* is the setting (words, phrases, and sentences) in which the text occurs.

Social context includes the identity of the speaker and the person or persons to whom he or she is speaking, their relationship, and the speaker's intent or purpose in making the remark. Understanding the context is a major step toward comprehension of any communication.

Function

Function refers to the purpose for which individual words are chosen and how they relate to each other; it is also about how words are used. Language performs a wide range of functions, some of which are

- To command.
- To contrast.
- To deny.
- To emphasize.
- To indicate continuity of actions.
- To indicate continuity of participants.
- To indicate logical relationships such as causality.
- To inform.
- To question.
- To sequence narration of events.

Pragmatics

Pragmatics is the study of language in context. Discourse doesn't occur in a vacuum, so context is necessary to fully understand the meanings of words and structures within an utterance (semantics).

SEMANTICS

[handwritten: Branch of linguistics concerned with meaning]

★ *Semantics* is the study of the meaning of individual words as well as how those words are interrelated through syntax and context.

WORDING

Wording is the word order in a sentence. Wording can alter the meaning of a sentence. (Refer to the "cow" and "moon" example earlier in this Hour.)

SOUND PATTERNS

Phonetics deals with how speech sounds are actually made, transmitted, and received. Those of you who learned to read by being told to "sound out the word" probably had phonics class in grade school.

 FYI See Hour 13, "The Importance of Knowing the Rules," for a review of formal versus informal English usage.

Phonology is the branch of linguistics that deals with sounds and sound changes, the study of all the sounds the human voice is capable of creating. It's partially responsible for some of the spelling variations we struggle to make sense of (blue, blew, bleu) because it traces specifically the ways in which those sounds made it into our languages. Phonology is, in effect, a subcategory of phonetics.

NUANCES, TRIVIA, AND IMPORTANT STUFF

Before we go on to the hard stuff (sentence construction, parts of speech, and so on), here are some style terms and issues that will give you non-liberal-arts majors something to talk about at parties.

ALLITERATION

Alliteration is the repetition of the beginning consonant sound of two or more words that appear close together in speech. Alliteration is used to add poetic pleasantry to a phrase and to grab attention or focus.

e.g.

Freckled frogs frolicked friskily through the forest.

Peter Piper picked a peck of pickled peppers.

Some say sunshine soothes the soul.

Okay, these are extreme examples. But you get the idea. Alter your **alliteration** to **a**ccommodate the **p**articular **p**urpose **p**lanned for your **p**rose.

ALLUSION

An *allusion* is an indirect reference to something else. It is employed by a speaker who assumes his audience will understand what he's saying.

e.g.

When a Southern Baptist minister alludes to the **Good Book,** his congregation knows he means the Bible.

ANTHROPOMORPHISM

Anthropomorphism is a big word that refers to human characteristics being attributed to a nonhuman object.

e.g.

Wind whipped through the trees, causing the **branches to dance** in the moonlight.

The **wind roared** and the **skies screamed** as the fury of the storm blew in.

ANTONYMS

An *antonym* is a word whose meaning is the opposite of another word.

Antonyms

Word	Antonym
afraid	fearless
beautiful	ugly
dark	light
day	night
old	new
sweet	sour

ASSONANCE

Assonance is the repetition of vowel sounds in two or more words that appear close together in speech. Assonance is sometimes used as an alternative to rhyme in verse.

e.g.

Sighing silent cries, Viola divides her prize.

CLICHÉS

A *cliché* is a phrase, saying, or term that has become dated and, due to overuse, lacks the creativity that makes language interesting. A cliché is sometimes referred to as a hackneyed expression, but the adjective "hackneyed" is almost a cliché itself.

e.g.

Trish was **as mad as an old wet hen.**
The group of men stood around **flapping their jaws.**

COLLOQUIALISMS

Colloquialisms are short-lived fad or slang sayings that are best avoided in formal English usage because they can date the speaker or a piece of writing.

Twentieth-Century Colloquialisms

Colloquialism	Meaning
bag	ugly or old woman
bananas	crazy or insane
dive	a seedy nightclub
groovy	nice
threads	clothing

FIGURES OF SPEECH

A *figure of speech* is a nonliteral usage of words employed to achieve an effect beyond the range of ordinary language. Examples include

- Anthropomorphisms.
- Metaphors.
- Similes.

GIST

The *gist* refers to the essence of a text. It is an understanding or synopsis of the core ideas or main points.

HOMONYMS

A *homonym* is one of two or more words pronounced the same but spelled differently.

brake	break
hair	hare
we'd	weed

HYPERBOLE

Hyperbole is an exaggeration for emphasis or effect, and its meaning is not meant to be taken literally. Examples of hyperbole are in bold type in the following examples:

e.g.

Everybody who was anybody was there.

All the king's horses and all the king's men couldn't put Humpty Dumpty back together again. (Unless it was the normal practice at the time for all of them to try.)

IDIOMS

An *idiom* is an expression that is unique to a language and cannot be understood simply from the meaning of its individual words. (See Hour 8, "Other

Considerations," for additional information on idioms.) In other words, the total meaning of an idiom is not the sum of its individual parts:

- Down in the dumps
- Fell off the wagon
- Had a cow
- Hit the sack
- Pulling your leg
- Skating on thin ice
- Spilled her guts

IDIOMATIC TRANSLATIONS

An *idiomatic translation* is one in which the meaning of the original is translated into forms that best preserve the meaning of the original form.

IRONY

Irony is criticism or ridicule in which words mean the opposite of what they state.

e.g.
_____

Her car broke down on the freeway, she had a run in her stocking, and now she was an hour late for the interview. **Mandy was having a wonderful day.**

TASK: TRY SOME IRONY

In speech, irony is often conveyed by voice inflection. Many times, a speaker states something that under normal circumstances could be considered a compliment, but because of the sarcastic tone of voice, it actually is an underhanded or subtle insult. (Example: Yeah, right.)

Come up with five ironic statements of your own.

JARGON

Jargon refers to a specialized vocabulary unique to a certain segment of a population for reasons such as trade, occupation, technology, medical science, and academic discipline.

e.g.

> The **Web, uniform resource locators,** and **zip drives** are all examples of computer jargon.

LEXICONS

A *lexicon* is the dictionary and vocabulary used by people speaking a particular language.

MALAPROPISMS

A *malapropism* is a word that sounds like another word with a totally different meaning, used by someone who has mistaken the sound-alike words.

e.g.

> For all **intensive** (intents and) purposes, it looked to be a good day.

METAPHORS

A *metaphor* is a word, phrase, or figure of speech that denotes one kind of object or idea in place of another; it suggests a likeness or an analogy between them. In a metaphor, a word or phrase that usually labels one thing is used to designate another.

TASK: MAKE A METAPHOR

Metaphors don't allow for literal translation; doing so causes the figurative meaning to be lost, and that meaning is most often the intended meaning. Here are two clichéd examples to illustrate the concept: Ken is **drowning in work.** Barbara is a **workhorse.**

Make up five metaphors of your own.

METONYMY

Metonymy is figurative language in which a word or phrase is substituted for another with which it is closely associated and with which the "audience" is familiar:

e.g.

Bishop is hoping for tenure at **the university.**

The family plans to spend the day at **the park.**

In the preceding examples, the speaker assumes the audience knows which **university, family,** or **park.**

MORPHEMES

A *morpheme* is the smallest unit of meaning in a language. If a word has only one meaning part, the morpheme is the definition of the word; if each word part has separate meanings, each meaning part is a morpheme. The study of the morphemes of a language is called *morphology.*

e.g.

Michael's screen**play** isn't quite finished. ("Play" is one of the two smallest units of meaning in the word screenplay.)

ONOMATOPOEIA

Onomatopoeia is the ability of a word's sound to suggest its meaning.

The following are some examples of onomatopoeia:

- Achoo
- Bang
- Buzz
- Cuckoo
- Drip
- Ring
- Splat

PUNS

A *pun* is the use of a word—usually with humorous intent—in such a way as to suggest two or more of its meanings or the meaning of another word similar in sound. (See Hour 21, "Getting Beyond Your First Draft," for an additional discussion on puns.)

Puns can take many forms. They can be used as a substitute for another similar-sounding or -rhyming word to give new meaning to a sentence or phrase:

These are the times that **fry** men's **rolls.**

A pun also is often used as the source for a *double entendre* (implied risqué meaning):

innuend**o** and out the other

RHYME

Rhyme is a series of word endings that repeats the same, or similar, sounds.

Old Mother **Hubbard** went to her **cupboard ...**

Rhymes can be used to add a whimsical, yet effective, touch to ad copy:

e.g.
_____

You can always trust our milk, so buy some **now.**
The only stuff fresher is still in the **cow.**

TASK: RHYME TIME

Rhymes increase a child's attention span because the child soon learns to listen for the repeated, familiar sound patterns. You can use this to your advantage if you have a youngster in the car with you during a long trip.

Example: Through the **fog,** the little green **frog** in a **soggy** wet **bog** jumped from **log** to **log** before the **dog** could **hog** all the **grog.**

Play a game to see how many rhyming words you can use in a sentence. This stuff is allowed to be fun, too. (Don't forget to let the kid win!)

RHYTHM

Rhythm is the repetition of stressed and unstressed syllable patterns rather than sounds. Here are two *iambic* (one short syllable followed by one long syllable or one unstressed syllable followed by one stressed syllable) sentence examples:

e.g.

The lonely pirate filled his fraying sack with coins of shining gold.

Your Mountain Dew is chilled and poured inside a frosted mug.

SARCASM

Sarcasm, while similar to irony, is more intense and is intended to have a negative impact. Sarcasm is another example of the use of words by a speaker or author who does not intend them to be taken literally.

Sarcasm is often intended to insult; however, just because something is sarcastic doesn't mean it can't include a level of humor. Consider this review reportedly written by the late Dorothy Parker:

"This is not a book to be set aside lightly; it should be thrown with great force."

SIMILES

A *simile* is a figure of speech that indicates a comparison. The existence of the comparison is explicitly signaled by a word such as "as" or "like" to present a contrast between two subjects or items.

LIKE, AS
AS..., AS
AS THOUGH,
THAN

e.g.

Marvin has muscles as strong as **iron.**

Fog shrouded the countryside like a **blanket.**

Rita's words cut like a **knife.**

SYNONYMS

A *synonym* is a word that means the same thing as another word. Theoretically, no word is a complete synonym or has exactly the same meaning as another. There are usually subtle distinctions between the words (nuances), but the meanings are close enough to consider them the "same" in this instance.

Synonyms

Word	Synonym
cry	weep
died	expired
eat	dine
sleep	snooze
talk	speak

PROCEED WITH CAUTION

Be careful not to confuse a synonym with a *euphemism,* which is a word or phrase whose intent is to "soften" the meaning of the original word. For example, some euphemisms for "died" are **bit the dust, bought the farm, cashed in his chips, checked out, kicked the bucket,** and **went to his reward.**

HOUR'S UP!

1. What form of speech makes a direct comparison, saying that it is like something else?

   a. metaphor *— ANALOGY*

   b. simile *← LIKE, AS COMPARISON*

   c. gerund *— NOUN ENDING IN ING*

   d. onomotopoeia *— SOUNDS LIKE THE SOUND IT IS TRYING TO DESCRIBE*

2. What do you call the repetition of the beginning consonant sound of two of more words that appear close together in speech?

   a. ellipses

   b. participle

   c. alliteration

   d. punctuation

3. What is it called when you refer to something indirectly, assuming that people will understand the actual meaning?

    (a.) allusion

    b. semantics

    c. nuance

    d. conjugation

4. What is it called when a word means the same as another word?

    a. metaphor

    b. morpheme

    c. idiom

    (d.) synonym

5. What is it called when you exaggerate for emphasis or effect?

    a. irony

    (b.) hyperbole

    c. jargon

    d. colloquialism

6. What is it called when a series of word endings repeat the same, or similar, sounds?

    a. cliché

    b. sarcasm

    (c.) rhyme

    d. gist

7. What is it called when you apply human characteristics to inanimate objects?

    a. altruism

    (b.) anthropomorphism

    c. metonymy

    d. pragmatics

8. What is a word whose meaning is the opposite of another word?

    (a.) antonym

    b. rhythm

    c. context

    d. innuendo

QUIZ

9. What is the study that records the description patterns contained in speech?

   a. lexicon

   b. pedagogical grammar

   c. phonology

   d. descriptive grammar

10. What is the study that examines how the sounds of words are used in a language?

    a. phonetics

    b. malapropism — INCORRECT WORDS

    c. semantics — STUDY OF WORD MEANING).

    d. assonance — REPEATED VOWELS

ANSWERS

1. b	**6.** c
2. c	**7.** b
3. a	**8.** a
4. d	**9.** d
5. b	**10.** a

RECAP

This Hour covered the meaning of grammar and some of the elements that help give our language its nuances and distinctions. Now that you have a basic understanding of the meaning of grammar, you're ready to begin putting it into practice by learning about sentences in Hour 2, "Mastering the Basic Parts of a Sentence."

HOUR 2

Mastering the Basic Parts of a Sentence

CHAPTER SUMMARY

LESSON PLAN:

In this Hour, you'll learn the basic structure of a sentence, the foundation on which you build your written and spoken statements. You'll learn what a sentence is and how it works, putting you on the path to communicating more effectively in every area of your life and work.

Among the things we'll cover are

- How to determine the parts of a simple sentence.
- How to recognize the subject and predicate.
- The basic rules for creating longer sentences.
- How to avoid basic sentence problems.

You may be wondering why we're starting off with sentences before we cover the parts of speech used to construct a sentence. It's like building a house. You start with the foundation, but before you do that, you have to clear the ground and measure its dimensions. And even before that point, lots of "groundwork" goes on such as hiring an architect to draw up the house plans and getting a contractor to build it based on those plans. As you go through all the steps leading up to the actual construction, you learn a lot of the terms and procedures of the construction process. And, equally important, you have the advantage of having seen other houses—you most likely lived in one before you started building your own home.

Using the same logic, we're going to go out on a limb here and guess that, before you picked up this book, you'd already seen and heard sentences and had even written and spoken millions or trillions of them—probably without any conscious thoughts about what a sentence is.

Just because you're using sentences doesn't mean that you're necessarily doing so correctly. In order to ensure that you do that, you need to learn some of the basics.

Let's start with the fact that every sentence has two essential parts:

1. A complete subject
2. A complete predicate

To give you an idea of what the function of a subject is, take another look at some sentences from the opening paragraph of this Hour, only this time with the subjects left out:

> may be wondering why starting off with sentences before cover the parts of speech used to construct a sentence. 's like building a house. start with the foundation, but before do that, have to clear the ground and measure its dimensions.

Now see what some of the opening sentences look like without predicates:

> You why we're we. It'. You. you, you. that. Lots of "groundwork" such as hiring an architect to draw up the house plans and getting a contractor to build it based on those plans.

The preceding has given you an idea of what subjects and predicates do. Let's take a closer look.

THE SUBJECT OF THE SUBJECT

The *complete subject* is the *simple subject* (a noun or pronoun) plus any words or groups of words modifying the simple subject that tell what or who the sentence is about:

e.g.

The pain from a headache generally persists about a day.

TASK: WHO'S ON FIRST?

To figure out which words make up the complete subject in the preceding sentence, ask yourself

1. Who or what persists? ("Persists" is the verb in that sentence.) Once you've figured out the answer, you've found the complete subject.

2. What generally persists about a day?

3. What is the simple subject?

The simple subject is the essential noun, pronoun, or group of words in the sentence. If you omit the simple subject, the sentence lacks its true meaning because there's not a word within the sentence to perform or receive the action from the verb. We know that the verb in the example is "persists."

- Once you strip away most of the other words in the sentence—the complements and modifiers that you'll learn more about as you progress through this book—you're left with the simple subject: **pain.**
- In its simplest form, our sentence is: **pain persists.**
- In the example sentence, anything that isn't the predicate ("generally persists about a day") is the complete subject: **the pain from a headache.**

The Parts of the Example Sentence

Sentence Word(s)	Function in the Sentence
The	article
pain	simple subject
from a headache	prepositional phrase
generally persists about a day.	predicate

SUBJECTS ON THE LOOSE

Life might be easier if the subject always appeared at the beginning of a sentence, but sentences would be boring. You'd be boring. Embrace change. It adds variety to your life.

The following section covers some examples of changes in word order. The "predicate" we refer to is dealt with in detail later in the chapter.

THE "UNDERSTOOD YOU"

An *imperative sentence* is one that issues a command or makes a request. Often, in an imperative sentence, the subject isn't actually in the sentence; it's implied. At such times, that invisible subject (you) is known as the *understood you:*

e.g.

Embrace change. Save that work until later.

MAKING A STATEMENT

A *declarative sentence* is one that makes a statement.

e.g.

Lunch will be served at noon. Bob asked if anyone had seen the game.

SUBJECT POSITIONING

The subject most often appears before the verb; however, it can also appear after the verb in

- Sentences that start with an *expletive*—an empty word that pretty much just gets the sentence underway—such as **there.**

e.g.

Verb then subject: There is **a cold front** coming in from Canada.

Subject then verb: **A cold front** is coming in from Canada.

- Sentences inverted for effect.

e.g.

Predicate then subject: Athletic is **the winner** of the gold medal in an Olympic event.

Subject then predicate: **The winner** of the gold medal in an Olympic event is athletic.

MAIN CLAUSE

In Hour 10, "Main and Subordinate Clauses," you'll learn more about the *main clause*—a group of words that contains both a subject and a verb and expresses a complete thought. A main clause, sometimes referred to as an *independent clause,* can stand alone because it is a sentence:

Leslie threw some shrimp on the barbie.

As the main clause in the sentence, "**Leslie threw some shrimp**" can be placed anywhere within a sentence: beginning, middle, or end.

SUBORDINATE CLAUSE

A *subordinate clause* is a group of words that does not express a complete thought, even though it contains a subject and a verb. Therefore, a subordinate clause, sometimes referred to as a *dependent clause*, cannot be a sentence:

While Leslie threw some shrimp on the barbie, Troy made the salad.

"While Leslie threw some shrimp on the barbie" becomes a subordinate clause because, due to the addition of the word "while," the clause can no longer stand alone as a sentence.

(See Hour 10 for a review of subordinate clauses and their uses within sentences.)

THE PREDICATE DEFINED

The *complete predicate* is the verb plus its objects, complements, and adverbial modifiers that tell what the complete subject does or is. The predicate is where the action is.

TASK: FIND THE PREDICATE

Earlier in this hour, we established that "(The) pain" is the subject of the example sentence. To figure out which words make up the complete predicate

1. Examine the sentence: "The pain from a headache generally persists about a day."

2. Ask yourself what the subject (The pain) does.

   The answer is the pain "generally persists about a day." That is the complete predicate.

3. Make up a sentence with a subject and a complete predicate.

The *simple predicate* is the essential verb or verb phrase without which the sentence would be incomplete. To check for the simple predicate

1. Determine what cannot be left out of the complete predicate: "generally persists about a day."

2. Try removing each word until you identify which one is necessary to the sentence.

If the sentence makes sense with just the word you identified, you have found your simple predicate.

The answer is: The pain from a headache … **persists** ….

3. Make up your own sentence with a subject and a simple predicate.

COMPOUND SUBJECTS AND PREDICATES

The examples so far have contained only one subject and one verb. A sentence can contain a compound subject, a compound predicate, or both.

A *compound subject* has two or more subjects that use the same verb and are joined by a conjunction such as "and" or "or":

Taylor and Charlie played with their toys.

A *compound predicate* has two or more verbs that have the same subject and are joined by a conjunction such as "and" or "or":

Troy **asked** for a fork, **ate** his Australian-style meat pie, and **endured** the stares of other men in the restaurant.

Bethany **can choose** from the standard menu or **order** a la carte.

(See Hour 3, "Elementary Sentence Components I: Nouns," and Hour 7, "Reaching Agreements," for a review of agreement between the subject and the verb.)

SENTENCE TYPES

Sentences can be simple, compound, complex, or compound-complex.

THE SIMPLE SENTENCE

A *simple sentence* only has one main clause, contains no subordinate clauses, and is limited to one subject and one predicate. The sentence, however, may contain modifying words or phrases:

e.g.

Assignment deadlines are important.

Washington is the capital **of the nation.**

THE COMPOUND SENTENCE

A *compound sentence* has two or more main clauses joined by a coordinating conjunction or a semicolon. (See Hour 8, "Other Considerations," for a review of coordinating conjunctions and Hour 11, "Controlling the Comma and the Semicolon," for a review of semicolons.)

AND
BUT
;

e.g.

Darren went on vacation, **and** Leslie traveled with him.

Darren visited the seashore, **but** he felt the waves were disappointing.

Leanne enjoyed the trip; she doesn't like waves.

THE COMPLEX SENTENCE

A *complex sentence* has one main clause and one or more subordinate clauses. In the following examples, subordinate clauses are in bold and main clauses are in italics:

e.g.

As Sean sat in his cubicle, *he fell asleep at his desk.*

Sean falls asleep at his desk **when he is in his cubicle.**

THE COMPOUND-COMPLEX SENTENCE

A *compound-complex sentence* contains two or more main clauses and one or more subordinate clauses. (It is a compound sentence and a complex sentence joined together.)

SUBORDINATE CLAUSE

e.g.

Kelly wears clothes she created, **which are often rather shocking,** but that she believes give her a more glamorous presence.

After Rachel left for Ireland, Jay decided he really wanted to join her, but Rachel did not want him along because he snores, and they'd be sharing the same room.

TASK: FIND THE FLAW

Now that you know that a group of words containing a subject and a predicate and expressing a complete thought is called a sentence or a main clause, it's time to look at some common sentence errors.

It's easy to see at first glance that there's something wrong with each of the following sentences, but can you specify the error in every case?

1. When he left the house. Ronnie failed to lock the door.
2. Rick enjoys boating, to fish, and swimming.
3. Rick likes to boat, fishing, and to swim.
4. Dan said that everyone planning to attend should get the tickets early, realize there is going to be an hour wait before game time, and be packing his or her own lunch.
5. Darren went on vacation he traveled with Leslie.

You can find out how well you did in the following sections.

SENTENCE FRAGMENT

A *sentence fragment* is an incomplete sentence. Either it lacks a subject or a predicate, or it is a sentence that is written in an attempt to use a subordinate clause or another incomplete thought as a complete sentence.

When he left the house. Ronnie failed to lock the door.

A sentence fragment that is a subordinate clause can be fixed by

- Combining it with another sentence to make a complete thought: **When he left the house,** Ronnie failed to lock the door.
- Removing the subordinate marker: He left the house.

Fragment usage is generally not acceptable for formal English or academic writing, and you should avoid using fragments as sentences except for the occasional exclamation (What a day!), to emphasize or elaborate on a preceding sentence (They had money. Lots of it.), or to answer a question (Where did she see the cat? In the garden.).

The sentences in parentheses are examples of the very few ways in which it is considered permissible to use sentence fragments as literary devices. Unless you're a newspaper or magazine journalist or a fiction writer, the rule is to set strict limits on how, and how often, you use them.

PARALLEL CONSTRUCTION

Parallel structure is the use of the same pattern in words, phrases, or clauses to show that two or more concepts have the same level of importance. A parallel structure must continue and end with the same form with which it begins: clauses are used with other clauses, phrases with phrases, infinitives with infinitives, and like words with like words. Changing to another pattern or changing the voice of the verb (from active to passive or vice versa) will break the parallelism. Parallel structure is usually created with the use of coordinating conjunctions such as "and" or "or":

- Words and phrases ending in the -ing form:

    Parallel: Rick enjoys **boating, fishing,** and **swimming.**

    Form error: Rick enjoys *boating,* **to fish,** and *swimming.*

- Infinitive phrases:

    Parallel: Rick likes **to boat, to fish,** and **to swim.**

    Also parallel: Rick likes **to boat, fish,** and **swim.** (This is preferred by many because it avoids redundant words.)

    Form error: Rick likes *to boat,* **fishing,** and *to swim.*

- Clauses:

    Parallel: Dan said that everyone planning to attend **should get** the tickets early, **should expect** an hour wait before game time, and **should bring** his or her own lunch.

    Parallel: Dan said that everyone planning to attend should **get** the tickets early, **expect** an hour wait before game time, and **bring** his or her own lunch.

    Form error: Dan said that everyone planning to attend should get the tickets early, realize there is going to be an hour wait before game time, and **be packing** his or her own lunch.

RUN-ON SENTENCES

A *run-on sentence* contains two or more complete sentences (main clauses) joined to read as an improperly punctuated single sentence:

Run-on: Darren went on vacation he traveled with Leslie.

Correct two-sentence format: Darren went on vacation. He traveled with Leslie.

Correct one-sentence format: Darren went on vacation, and he traveled with Leslie.

Correct one-sentence format: Darren went on vacation; he traveled with Leslie.

FUSED SENTENCE ERROR

A *fused sentence error* is when a sentence has two or more main clauses that are not separated by any form of punctuation. Yep! This is just another way of saying you have a run-on sentence. Therefore, a period or semicolon (or sometimes a colon) can be inserted into the sentence to separate it into the correct number of sentences. (Refer to the preceding examples shown for the run-on sentence.)

COMMA SPLICE

A *comma splice error* is the improper use of a comma between two main clauses. That makes a comma splice another label for a run-on or fused sentence improperly punctuated with a comma instead of with the form of punctuation that would correctly divide it into the appropriate number of sentences.

INTERROGATIVE SENTENCES (QUESTIONS)

Almost every simple question in English is based on the structure of: **How are you?**

Simple Question Structure

Question Word	Verb	Subject	Punctuation
How	are	you	?

An *interrogative sentence (question)* is one that asks for information.

SENTENCE VARIATION

Sentence variety can be accomplished by

- **Coordination:** Join short, choppy, complete sentences, clauses, and phrases with coordinators (coordinating conjunctions):

  and, but, or, nor, yet, for, so

  Example: Debra woke up. Debra made coffee. Debra ate breakfast.

  Coordination: Debra woke up, made coffee, and ate breakfast.

- **Subordination:** Link two related sentences to each other so that one contains the main idea and the other is no longer a complete sentence. Instead, it takes on a lesser value (subordination) within the sentence. Use the appropriate connector to show the relationship:

  after, although, as, as if, because, before, even if, even though, if, if only, rather than, since, that, though, unless, until, when, where, whereas, wherever, whether, which, while

  Example: This country continues to have the same problems. People keep electing the same type of unreliable politicians to office.

  Subordination: This country continues to have the same problems **because** people keep electing the same type of unreliable politicians to office.

  Example: RJ has been a fan of poetry for years. He's just started writing his own.

  Subordination: While RJ has been a fan of poetry for years, he's just started writing his own.

JUST A MINUTE

The location of the clause beginning with the subordinator (dependent marker or connector word) to establish the subordination is flexible. Such flexibility can be used to create varied rhythmic patterns throughout a paragraph.

- **Replacement:** Replace a repeated subject or topic with relative pronouns (See Hour 4, "Elementary Sentence Components II: Pronouns," for a review of relative pronouns.) For example, you can put one sentence inside the other by using a clause starting with one of the relative pronouns listed here: **which, who, whoever, whom, that, whose.**

Example: Joanne is from Australia. She has lived there all of her life.

Relative pronoun revision: Joanne, who is from Australia, has lived there all her life.

Example: Stevie creates memorable characters. He writes horror novels.

Relative pronoun revision 1: Stevie, who creates memorable characters, writes horror novels.

Relative pronoun revision 2: Stevie, who writes horror novels, creates memorable characters.

- **Participles:** Eliminate a form of the verb **to be** (**am, is, was, were, are**) and substitute a present participle (ending in **-ing**) or a past participle (ending in **-ed, -en, -d, -n,** or **-t**) phrase. (See Hour 8 for a review of participles and Hour 9, "Phrases," for a review of phrases.)

    Example: Nicole plans to attend the banquet in her honor. She still wants to find an escort.

    With participle phrase: Nicole, *planning to attend the banquet in her honor,* still wants to find an escort.

- **Prepositions and other variations:** Turn a clause into a prepositional phrase, a phrase beginning with a preposition—**about, above, across, after, against, along, among, around, as, behind, below, beneath, beside, between, by, despite, down, during, except, for, from, in, inside, near, next to, of, off, on, out, over, past, to, under, until, up, with.** (See Hour 8 for a review of prepositions and Hour 9 for information on prepositional phrases.)

    Two sentences or main clauses: Nicole has plans to attend the banquet in her honor. She still wants to find an escort.

    Dependent clause, main clause: Because Nicole plans to attend the banquet in her honor, she still wants to find an escort.

    Prepositional phrase, main clause: After finding an escort, Nicole plans to attend the banquet in her honor.

    Subject, relative clause, predicate: Nicole, who has plans to attend the banquet in her honor, still wants to find an escort.

SENTENCE RULES

Some common rules regarding word order and sentence structure include

- Single-word subject directly in front of the verb, followed by the object or complement: **Sandy comes from Scotland.**

- All of the words that make up the subject (the subject noun or pronoun plus descriptive phrases that go with it), verb, direct object: **People who have dogs shouldn't leave their homework lying around.**

- Adverbs or adverb phrases of time in one of the following places:

    Before the subject: **Yesterday** Anna received some e-mail.

    After the object: Anna received an e-mail **yesterday.**

    Centered in the verb group or predicate: Anna has **already** received yesterday's e-mail.

- Other parts of speech that, in formal English, do not usually come between the subject and the verb or between the verb and the object, such as the adverb of frequency shown in the final preceding example: Anna has **already** received yesterday's e-mail.

Applying these few primary rules will help you avoid having word order problems in English. The examples are simple, but as you continue through this book, you'll find that the same rules usually apply to complex sentences with subordinate and coordinated clauses. (See Hour 10 for a review of clauses.)

HOUR'S UP!

1. What is an incomplete sentence usually called?
    a. dangling participle
    b. sentence fragment
    c. compound sentence
    d. complex sentence

2. What sort of sentence makes a command or request?

   a. imperative

   b. declarative

   c. subject

   d. predicate

3. What contains both a subject and a verb?

   a. independent clause

   b. subordinate clause

   c. main clause

   d. a and c

4. What is created when subjects are combined within a sentence?

   a. simple subject

   b. complex subject

   c. complete predicate

   d. compound subject

5. What type of sentence has two or more main clauses joined by a coordinating conjunction or a semicolon?

   a. independent clause

   b. compound sentence

   c. complex sentence

   d. complete sentence

6. What type of sentence error contains two complete sentences improperly joined with punctuation?

   a. complete sentence

   b. run-on sentence

   c. fused sentence

   d. b and c

7. What type of sentence has one main clause and one or more subordinate clauses?

   a. complex sentence

   b. complete sentence

   c. compound sentence

   d. simple sentence

8. What kind of sentence makes a statement?

    a. compound sentence

    b. declarative sentence

    c. imperative sentence

    d. complex sentence

9. A compound-complex sentence contains what components?

    a. two or more main clauses and one or more subordinate clauses

    b. one main clause and one or more subordinate clauses

    c. two or more main clauses

    d. one main clause and one subordinate clause

10. What is it called when similar forms of words are linked together in a sentence?

    a. onomatopoeia

    b. subject positioning

    c. parallel construction

    d. run-on sentence

ANSWERS

1. b		**6.** d	
2. a		**7.** a	
3. d		**8.** b	
4. d		**9.** b	
5. b		**10.** c	

RECAP

This Hour covered basic sentence structures. You should now understand what sentences are and how to avoid common problems in using them. Now that you know all about sentences, let's begin learning about more specific parts of grammar by moving on to nouns in the next hour.

PART II

Getting Grounded in Grammar

Hour 3   Elementary Sentence Components
             I: Nouns

Hour 4   Elementary Sentence Components
             II: Pronouns

Hour 5   Elementary Sentence Components
             III: Verbs

Hour 6   Expanding Sentences with Articles,
             Adjectives, and Adverbs

Hour 7   Reaching Agreements

Hour 8   Other Considerations

Hour 9   Phrases

Hour 10 Main and Subordinate Clauses

Hour 11 Controlling the Comma and the
             Semicolon

Hour 12 Other Forms of Punctuation

HOUR 3

Elementary Sentence Components I: Nouns

CHAPTER SUMMARY

LESSON PLAN:

In this Hour, you'll learn about nouns and their functions within a sentence.

Among the things we'll cover are

- Learning ways to determine a common noun.
- Forming possessive nouns.
- Understanding the rules for plural nouns.
- Discovering how gerunds can be used as nouns.

Nouns name stuff. It's as simple as that. The word "noun" is even a derivative of the Latin word *nomen,* which means "name." In other words, a noun is the name we give to a person, a place, or a thing. But nouns have an even broader usage; a noun can also be used to name an idea, an activity, or a quality.

Noun Examples

Category	Noun
person	girl
place	park
thing	automobile
idea	philosophy
activity	daydreaming
quality	courage

In most instances, an *article,* sometimes referred to as a *noun marker,* comes before a common noun. Articles help to define the noun from the general to the specific. (See the discussion in Hour 6, "Expanding Sentences with Articles, Adjectives, and Adverbs," about noun markers, articles, determiners, and quantifiers for more information on this topic.) For now, we'll limit our reference to the common noun markers:

a, an, the, these, those, this, that

When you want to confirm whether a word is a common noun, put the word "the" or another noun marker in front of it. If the resulting phrase makes sense, chances are the word is a noun!

COMMON NOUNS

A common noun refers to a person, place, thing, idea, or activity in general terms. A common noun isn't specific or important (as in a title), so it doesn't warrant a capital letter. Therefore, a common noun is not capitalized unless it is the first word in a sentence.

Here are some examples of common nouns:

book, author, reader, city, college

There are times when a common noun becomes part of a proper noun and is therefore capitalized. See the section on capitalization later in this hour to learn when to use "the city of New York" versus "the City of New York."

PROPER NOUNS

A proper noun is the name of a specific person, place, or thing, and it always begins with a capital letter. (An idea or activity seldom begins with a capital letter.)

Converting the common nouns used earlier to proper nouns gives us these examples:

Macmillan Teach Yourself Grammar and Style in 24 Hours

Pamela Rice Hahn

David L. Hebert

Chicago

Taylor University

Here are some general rules to help distinguish when a noun is a proper noun and requires capitalization:

1. Names and family names: **Dennis, Hensley**

2. Months, days of the week, and holiday names: **September, Thursday, Veterans Day**

3. Adjectives originating from proper nouns: **Japanese automobile, English literature, Canadian cuisine**

4. Geographic names: **Eastern Shore** (when referring to the region on the eastern side of the Chesapeake Bay), **New World** (when making a specific historical reference to the Western Hemisphere), **Western Hemisphere**

5. Names of streets, buildings, and parks: **Main Street, Empire State Building, Grand Lake State Park**

6. Titles and historic convention: **Mister Smith, Doctor Roode, Professor Hensley, the President of the United States, General Patton, God and any word describing God (He, Him, His), Heaven, Her Royal Highness Queen Elizabeth**

7. The nouns in titles of works or books: ***For Whom the Bell Tolls***

JUST A MINUTE

Conjunctions, prepositions, and articles are excluded from capitalization unless they are part of a book series name or other trademark. However, if the title begins with a conjunction, preposition, or article, remember that the first word of a title is always capitalized.

8. Names of countries and continents: **Canada, Asia**

9. Names of states, provinces, districts, counties, and townships: **Ohio, Manitoba, 2nd District, Auglaize County, Hamilton Township**

PROCEED WITH CAUTION

Don't capitalize the common noun elements of names in plural usage. The Republican **and** Democratic parties, **the lakes** Erie **and** Huron, Buckeye **and** West **streets,** and the Mississippi and Ohio **rivers** are examples of this capitalization rule.

10. Names of rivers, oceans, seas, and lakes: **Ohio River, Atlantic Ocean, Red Sea, Great Salt Lake**

11. Names of geographical formations: **the Rockies, Death Valley, Grand Canyon**

12. Familiar names: **Ivy League, Big Board**

13. The shortened form of popular names, often used as the second-reference example of such names: **the Series** (when referring to the World Series), **the Open** or **the U.S. Open** (when referring to the U.S. Open Championship), **the Street** (when referring to the Wall Street financial district)

Capitalization can sometimes be a tricky thing. For example, a reference to the City as an incorporated entity would be written as the **City of New York;** on the other hand, you would write that you plan to visit the **city** of New York on your vacation. Other examples include:

---

e.g.

Michael Freeman is a **doctor.**
One of the people on staff at the local hospital is **Doctor** Michael Freeman.

My home is near a **lake.**
My home is near **Lake** Erie.

PROCEED WITH CAUTION

 Corporate and product names don't follow specific capitalization rules. They often contain mixed upper- and lowercase letters. Corporate and product names are part of the presence or labeling the company wishes to convey and should be written as they appear in official company correspondence or documents. Some examples include **iVillage,** Microsoft **FrontPage,** and **bright.net Ohio.**

While country names are always capitalized, there isn't a reliable form of standardization when it comes to forming the adjectives and nouns used to indicate citizens of those countries. As shown in the following chart, the adjectives and nouns sometimes differ.

Nationalities

Country	Adjective	Noun
Britain	British	Brit/Briton/Britisher
China	Chinese	Chinese
Denmark	Danish	Dane
England	English	Englishman/Englishwoman
Finland	Finnish	Finn
France	French	Frenchman/Frenchwoman
Holland	Dutch	Dutchman/Dutchwoman
Iceland	Icelandic	Icelander
Ireland	Irish	Irishman/Irishwoman
Poland	Polish	Pole
Scotland	Scottish	Scot

Country	Adjective	Noun
Sweden	Swedish	Swede
United States of America	American	American
Turkey	Turkish	Turk
Wales	Welsh	Welshman/Welshwoman

Mass Nouns

Mass nouns are words that can't be identified with a number. To measure or classify them, use a unit of measurement followed by "of." Mass nouns can be isolated into these categories:

1. Food, materials, metals, and natural qualities:

    bread (loaf of bread, loaves of bread)

    wood (cord of wood)

    gold (ounce of gold)

    youth (naiveté of youth)

2. Gases, liquids, and small-particle substances:

    smoke (cloud of smoke)

    gasoline (gallon of gasoline)

    salt (teaspoon of salt)

3. Names of languages: **English, German, Yiddish**

4. Abstract nouns, many of which end in **-ness, -ance, -ence, and -ity:**

    helplessness

    dominance

    correspondence

    humidity

5. Most gerunds: **waltzing, yelling**

6. Words without a plural form: **evidence, furniture**

Three rules to keep in mind regarding mass nouns are

1. A mass noun can be quantified by an amount but not by a number.

2. A mass noun only has the singular form.

3. A mass noun can have "much" as a modifier; it cannot use "a," "an," or "one."

PLURAL NOUNS

A *plural noun* is used to indicate more than one person, place, thing, idea, or activity.

Plural Nouns

1. Add an **-s** to most nouns.

Singular	Plural
book	books
college	colleges

2. Add **-es** when the noun ends in -s, -sh, -ch, or -x.

Singular	Plural
dress	dresses
wish	wishes
church	churches
box	boxes

3. When a noun ends in the consonant -y, drop the -*y* and add **-ies.**

Singular	Plural
baby	babies
hanky	hankies

4. When a noun ends in the vowel -y, add **-s.**

Singular	Plural
boy	boys
buy	buys

5. Exceptions to 4: For colloquy, obloquy, obsequy, and soliloquy that end in -quy, change the *y* to an *i* and add **-es.**

Singular	*Plural*
colloquy	colloquies
obloquy	obloquies
obsequy	obsequies
soliloquy	soliloquies

6. In most cases, add an **s** to a word ending in -f. Some exceptions are listed below.

Singular	*Plural*
calf	calves
self	selves
wolf	wolves

7. The main word of a compound word is made plural.

Singular	*Plural*
father-in-law	fathers-in-law
football	footballs
court-martial	courts-martial
passerby	passersby
bystander	bystanders

8. Exception to 7: If the compound word doesn't contain a noun, add an **-s** to the end of the word.

Singular	*Plural*
shake-up	shake-ups
mockup	mockups

9. Exception to 7: If the compound word ends in -ful, add an **-s** to the end of the word.

Singular	*Plural*
armful	armfuls
capful	capfuls

10. More exceptions: Some nouns remain the same in plural form.

Singular	Plural
Chinese	Chinese
deer	deer

11. Even more exceptions: Some nouns, referred to as irregular nouns, change their spellings altogether when they become plural, as shown in the following examples of *irregular noun plurals*.

Singular	Plural
analysis	analyses
cactus	cacti
child	children
crisis	crises
criterion	criteria
diagnosis	diagnoses
focus	foci
foot	feet
fungus	fungi
glass	glasses
half	halves
kiss	kisses
knife	knives
leaf	leaves
life	lives
loaf	loaves
man	men
nucleus	nuclei
oasis	oases
person	people
phenomenon	phenomena
potato	potatoes
syllabus	syllabi
thesis	theses

tooth	teeth
wife	wives
woman	women

12. Add **'s** to make a number or letter plural.

Singular	Plural
9	9's
a	a's

PROCEED WITH CAUTION

When in doubt, look it up. Use the dictionary to determine the proper plural form of a noun.

Count Nouns

Every noun can be classified as *count* or *mass*. Count nouns can be quantified or counted.

1. Names of animals, insects, plants, persons, and their parts

Singular	Plural
horse	horses
cricket	crickets
daisy	daisies
lady	ladies
ankle	ankles

2. Objects with a definite shape

Singular	Plural
garage	garages
octagon	octagons
ball	balls

3. Classification words and units of measurement

Singular	Plural
clause	clauses
ounce	ounces
caret	carets

4. Abstract words

Singular	Plural
prejudice	prejudices
philosophy	philosophies
truth	truths
benefit	benefits

Three rules to keep in mind regarding count nouns are

1. A count noun can be quantified by a number.

2. A count noun has a singular and a plural form.

3. A count noun can use an article such as **a, an, one,** or **many** as a modifier.

POSSESSIVE NOUNS

A possessive noun indicates ownership or a belonging-to relationship. We specify possession by adding an apostrophe and an s ('s) or, when the noun ends in an s, an apostrophe (') at the end of the noun to show the possessor (Pam's, Dennis'). Here are the rules to keep in mind for forming a possessive noun:

1. Unless they end in **-s,** use **'s** for singular nouns.

Noun	Possessive
Taylor	Taylor's
dog	dog's

2. Use **'s** for most irregular plurals.

Noun	Possessive
children	children's
men	men's

3. Use just an **'** for singular or plural nouns ending in -s (Charles', teachers').

Noun	Possessive
Charles	Charles'
teachers	teachers'

JUST A MINUTE

If you are not sure whether the word you are using should be used in its possessive form, reverse the word order and put "of" in the middle. If it has the same meaning, you use 's.

COMPOUND NOUNS

A compound noun consists of words that function together as a single unit and that have a different meaning together than each word has on its own. The words that make up a compound noun are not always nouns.

Compound nouns can be in one temporary and three permanent formats.

1. A single word, which is known as a closed or solid compound: **football**

2. A hyphenated compound: **great-aunt**

3. Combined words that retain their own definitions but take on a new meaning when combined with other words: **stool pigeon**

4. Temporary combined words, not found in a dictionary, that are created by combining two words for a special purpose: **pseudo-art**

Note that some combinations become adjectives, such as "four-star" when used to modify the word "general" (four-star general). Others, such as "roll call," can vary according to their usage; "roll call" is a two-word compound word when used as a noun but is hyphenated as "roll-call" when used as an adjective. (See Hour 6 for more information on this usage.)

Compound Noun Examples

Word 1	Word 2	Compound Word	Part of Speech 1	Part of Speech 2
baby	sit	baby-sit	common noun	verb
back	up	backup	verb	preposition
life	cycle	lifecycle	common noun	common noun
Bible	Belt	Bible Belt	proper noun	proper noun

COLLECTIVE NOUNS

Words that name a group of people or things are known as *collective nouns:* **committee, mankind, team, accounts.**

NOUN GENDER

English nouns generally only designate gender when they relate to people. Most things are without gender and are therefore deemed *neuter* or *neutral.* They are not defined as masculine or feminine.

Noun and Pronoun Gender

Word	Gender	Pronoun
father	masculine	he
mother	feminine	she
bookcase	neuter	it

In some cases, a noun can be used as a feminine or masculine pronoun. These are sometimes referred to as generic nouns and include: **colleague, cousin, doctor, friend, partner, teacher, teenager.**

In other instances, some nouns are assigned gender:

- **Country:** Canada is north of the United States; **she** is our neighbor.
- **Possession:** That's my boat. Isn't **she** a beauty?
- **Object:** The wreck of the *Titanic* shocked the world; **she** was considered unsinkable.

GERUNDS

Adding -ing to the end of a verb forms a *gerund* when the resulting word is used as a noun.

Some Examples of Gerunds

Verb	Resulting gerund	Example in a sentence
knit	knitting	**Knitting** is her hobby.
sing	singing	**Singing** is his passion.
win	winning	**Winning** isn't everything.

Gerunds can be used as nouns as follows:

1. As the subject: *Skiing requires coordination.*

2. As a subject complement: Taylor's favorite pastime is *painting refrigerator art* for her grandmother.

3. As a noun complement and appositive: Charlie's current goal in life, *getting candy from grandma,* appeared to be within his grasp.

4. As a direct object: She tried *milking the cow.*

PROCEED WITH CAUTION

Gerunds and participles both end in -ing, but this is where the similarities end. A gerund only acts as a noun; a participle functions as a modifier.

TASK: FORM FITTING

Whenever a noun or a pronoun precedes a gerund, it usually takes the possessive form.

1. See if you know which sentence is correct.

   a. I don't like *him cheating* on the test.

   b. I don't like *his cheating* on the test.

2. Why do you think (a) or (b) is correct?

3. Sentence (a) is incorrect because, even if you don't like "him" as a person because he cheats on tests, in sentence (a) you're objecting to the cheating; therefore, you're objecting to "his cheating." That makes sentence (b) the correct one.

4. Think of three more examples of correct and incorrect possessive forms.

5. Think of three sentences in which you've used the incorrect possessive form in the past.

6. Remember to use the correct form the next time you repeat those or similar sentences.

Of course, it wouldn't be the English language if there weren't exceptions to the rule. In this situation, the exceptions are

1. If other words modify the noun preceding the gerund, use the common form of that noun, not the possessive.

   Exception: Lara was excited about Charlie, *her son,* **learning** how to say mama.

   Versus

   Rule: Lara was excited about *her son Charlie's* **learning** how to say mama.

2. If the noun preceding the gerund is abstract, collective, or plural, use the common form of that noun instead of the possessive.

   Example: She was amazed *by her grandkids* **sitting** still to listen to the entire story.

3. If using a possessive noun or pronoun creates an awkward sentence, it's better to reword the sentence. This happens most often with indefinite pronouns.

   Example: I was shocked *at anyone's* **doing** such a thing.

   Improved: I was shocked *that anyone* **would do** such a thing.

You can read more about gerund usage later in the book.

Hour's Up!

1. Which of the following nouns are capitalized?

    a. Names and family names

    b. Days of the week

    c. Geographic names

    d. a, b, and c

2. What kind of nouns can't be identified with a number?

    a. common nouns

    b. proper nouns

    c. mass nouns

    d. collective nouns

3. What kind of noun indicates ownership?

    a. mass noun

    b. proper noun

    c. compound noun

    d. possessive noun

4. What kind of noun indicates more than one person, place, thing, idea, or activity?

    a. plural noun

    b. collective noun

    c. possessive noun

    d. mass noun

5. What kind of noun can be identified with a number?

    a. mass nouns

    b. common nouns

    c. count nouns

    d. proper nouns

6. What kind of noun ends in -ing?

    a. plural noun

    b. collective noun

    c. gerund

    d. possessive noun

7. What kind of noun consists of two or more words that function together as a distinct unit?

    a. count noun

    b. collective noun

    c. mass noun

    d. compound noun

8. What kind of noun has only a singular form?

    a. common noun

    b. mass noun

    c. proper noun

    d. plural noun

9. What kind of noun is often used before a gerund?

    a. abstract noun

    b. count noun

    c. possessive noun

    d. collective noun

10. What kind of noun changes its spelling to indicate plural?

    a. irregular noun

    b. possessive noun

    c. compound noun

    d. abstract noun

QUIZ

ANSWERS

1. d		**6.** c	
2. c		**7.** d	
3. d		**8.** b	
4. a		**9.** c	
5. c		**10.** a	

RECAP

This Hour covered nouns and their usage. You should now understand what nouns are, how they are used, and how to differentiate between different forms of nouns. Now that you know all about nouns, let's move on to pronouns in the next hour.

HOUR 4

Elementary Sentence Components II: Pronouns

CHAPTER SUMMARY

LESSON PLAN:

In this Hour, you'll learn about pronouns and their functions within a sentence. You'll also learn about pronoun and noun case.

Among the things we'll cover are

- Using personal pronouns.
- Choosing the correct relative pronouns.
- Reinforcing nouns with reflexive pronouns.
- Avoiding pronoun pitfalls.

*P*ronouns are the words that take the place of nouns and noun phrases. We use pronouns to avoid repetition of the nouns in a sentence.

PERSONAL PRONOUNS

Personal pronouns show gender, number, and person (point of view).

The one doing the speaking determines the person, or point of view:

1. *First person* is the person speaking.

   I helped write this book.

2. *Second person* is the point of view of the person to whom you are speaking.

   You are reading this book.

3. *Third person* is the person or thing about whom or which you are speaking. Third person pronouns can have masculine, feminine, or neuter gender.

   He helped write the book.

   She edited the book.

   They published the book.

Remember to keep your sentences in the same person (point of view). A point of view shift is an error many people make in speech. Perhaps you've heard someone say something like, "When I drive for long distances, I find that you can stay more alert if you drink coffee." Did you notice the shift from first person to second? For the sentence to remain in the first person, it should read, "When I drive for long distances, I find that I can stay more alert if I drink coffee."

PRONOUN NUMBERS

Pronouns can indicate number but, unlike nouns, do not have an **s** or an **es** added to indicate the plural.

- Singular pronouns refer to one person, thing, or idea.

    I, me, you, he, she, it, my, your, his, her

e.g.

Kristy was surprised at **her** bridal shower.

- Plural pronouns indicate more than one person, thing, or idea.

    we, they, them, their

e.g.

Jennifer and Jason love **their** mother.

POSSESSIVE PRONOUNS

Possessive pronouns indicate possession or ownership. (See Hour 6, "Expanding Sentences with Articles, Adjectives, and Adverbs," for a review of possessive pronouns used as adjectives.)

- Short-form pronouns are those used with nouns.

    Squirt is **my** dog.

Short-Form Pronouns

Person	Singular	Plural
first	my	our
second	your	your
third	his, her, its	their
in questions	whose	whose

- Long-form pronouns replace a noun in a sentence that follows another sentence in which the noun is clearly stated.

    I love my dog. I bet you love **yours.**

In the second sentence, "yours" replaces what would otherwise be written as "your dog."

Long-Form Pronouns

Person	Singular	Plural
first	mine	our
second	yours	yours
third	his, hers, its	theirs

PROCEED WITH CAUTION

Remember that you never add an apostrophe to a possessive pronoun.

THE PRONOUN "WHO"

Who is a relative pronoun for a person.

Who hit the ball?

Use *whom* when it is not the subject. *Whom* is the form of the pronoun *who* that is used as the object of a verb or a preposition.

*For **whom** did the bell toll?*

***Whom** would you say is best for the job?*

In the latter example, most people would probably use what has become acceptable informal usage of the pronoun *who* and ask, "Who do you think is best for the job?" (Keep in mind that, although this is acceptable informal usage, it's still wrong!)

Use *whose* (the possessive form of the pronoun *who*) before a noun.

***Whose** cat is that?*

RELATIVE PRONOUNS

Relative pronouns join a subordinate clause to a main clause. The relative pronouns are **that, which, who, whom,** and **whose.**

Which and *that* are the relative pronouns for things.

> The forest, **which** is part of a national preserve, is beautiful this time of year.
>
> This is the antique oak secretary **that** I bought at an auction.

The rules to remember regarding relative pronouns are

1. In informal usage, a relative pronoun is optional when it is followed by a subject; it's required in formal usage.

e.g.

> **Formal:** This is the gift **that** I got last Christmas.
>
> **Informal:** This is the gift I got last Christmas.

2. When the relative pronoun is not followed by a subject, it must be included.

   Example: Tony is a boy **who** loves to play video games.

3. When the relative pronoun is preceded by a comma, it must be included.

   Example: Brian, **who** likes to raise chickens, is an FFA member.

4. *Whose* is the possessive relative pronoun; it cannot be omitted.

   Example: Nicole is a teenager **whose** goal is to get into a good college.

CONTRACTIONS

A pronoun is often joined with the verb that follows it to form a contraction. In such instances, an apostrophe replaces the omitted letter.

Pronoun	Verb	Contraction
I	will	I'll
it	is	it's
they	are	they're

DEMONSTRATIVE PRONOUNS

A demonstrative pronoun directs attention to its *antecedent*. (If you keep in mind that a pronoun substitutes for another noun or pronoun, it'll help you remember that an antecedent is the word or words the pronoun replaces or to which the pronoun refers.)

Imagine that you met with a friend for lunch. Perhaps somebody dropped her off at the restaurant or she walked there from her office. You're now headed out to your car so you can give her a ride home. As you near your vehicle, even if you're thinking it, chances are you wouldn't say, "The shiny new black Lexus is my car." Instead, you'd point to it and say, "That is my car." "That" is the demonstrative pronoun that replaces Lexus and its description. The car is in view. Your friend can see its appearance (and value), so the descriptive phrase isn't necessary; "that" will suffice.

- Singular demonstrative pronouns: **this, that**

    This is a great book.

- Plural demonstrative pronouns: **these, those**

    These are the times that try men's souls.

INDEFINITE PRONOUNS

Indefinite pronouns refer to nonspecific persons or things. Indefinite pronouns include **any, anybody, anyone, each, either, everyone, everything, no one, none, someone,** and **something.**

Everyone should use correct grammar.

Indefinite pronouns can also refer to unspecified amounts and quantities such as **all, any, both, each, enough, few, fewer, half, little, many, most, none,** and **several.**

Little gets done around the workplace during the holidays.

Indefinite pronouns can also indicate choice: **either, neither.**

Either could be correct.

REFLEXIVE PRONOUNS

Reflexive pronouns reflect the action back to a noun or pronoun that has just been named. Reflexive pronouns end in -self or -selves.

I made it **myself.**

- Singular reflexive pronouns: **myself, yourself, herself, himself**
- Plural reflexive pronouns: **ourselves, themselves, yourselves**

PROCEED WITH CAUTION

Never say or write hisself, themself, or theirselves. These words are not part of standard English usage and are therefore unacceptable.

Remember to use a reflexive pronoun only if it refers back to another word in the sentence.

TASK: TEST YOUR REFLEXIVES

1. Do you know which of the following sentences is correct?

   a. She did it **herself.**

   b. Jon and **myself** attended the convention.

2. Why did you choose (a) or (b)?

3. Check your answer.

> **Correct:** (a) She did it **herself.**
>
> **Incorrect:** (b) Jon and **myself** attended the convention.

Because "myself" doesn't refer back to another word, the correct pronoun in this sentence would be "I," which is appropriate as a subject pronoun.

4. Think of three ways in which you've used the incorrect pronoun in the past. Remember to use the correct one in the future.

INTENSIVE PRONOUNS

When a pronoun ending in -self or -selves directly emphasizes a noun, it is said to be an *intensive pronoun.* Intensive pronouns most often follow the noun they strengthen or emphasize.

> **The Rule:** I **myself** had to see it to believe it.
>
> **The Exception: Myself,** I'd have to see it to believe it.

INTERROGATIVE PRONOUNS

Interrogative pronouns introduce questions or noun clauses. (See Hour 10, "Main and Subordinate Clauses," for more information on noun clauses.) The interrogative pronouns are: **who, what,** and **which.**

e.g.
_____

> **What** did you make for dessert?

Interrogative pronouns are also used as determiners known as *interrogative adjectives.*

> Amy couldn't decide **which** dessert to eat first.

Another function of interrogative pronouns is to introduce noun clauses.

> Do you know **who** directed this movie?

RECIPROCAL PRONOUNS

Reciprocal pronouns represent combined ideas. They are **one another,** and **each other.**

Tiffany and Ashley help **one another** whenever they can.

RJ and I gave **each other** books as gifts.

AVOIDING PRONOUN PITFALLS

The purpose of pronouns is to eliminate redundancy in the written and spoken word. However, it's imperative that your message not get lost in the process.

TASK: AVOID AMBIGUITY

It should always be clear to what or to whom a pronoun refers. Even if you've used the identifying nouns in an earlier sentence, too many pronouns can cause confusion.

1. In the following sentence, can you accurately surmise which "her" is meant? It could be the "she" who believes he shouldn't do it or somebody else not represented in this sentence but indicated earlier.

   He told **her** that **he** planned to do **it** for **her** but **she** felt that **he** should not do **that.**

2. Rewrite the sentence to make it less ambiguous.

TASK: MAINTAIN PRONOUN AND ANTECEDENT AGREEMENT

Both a pronoun and its antecedent must be either singular or plural. Here are some examples of correct pronoun and antecedent agreement:

She drank **her** soda.

He read **his** book.

On the Internet, **anyone** can visit **his or her** favorite Web sites.

Most problems seem to occur when the singular antecedent is either an indefinite pronoun or a generic noun.

1. In which of the following sentences is the correct pronoun used?

    a. Does **anyone** want to eat **their** popcorn in the living room?

    b. Does **anyone** want to eat **his or her** popcorn in the living room?

To avoid sexist writing, people frequently mistakenly use the pronoun **their** in place of **his or her.** The correct sentence is (b).

There are three ways to rid your sentence of an incorrect plural pronoun that refers to a singular indefinite pronoun:

- Replace the plural pronoun with **he or she** or **him or her.**

  Example: When **somebody** visits a Web page, **he or she** decides if the information there is worth reading.

- Use a plural antecedent instead, making sure you also correct your verbs.

  Example: When **users** visit a Web page, **they** decide if the information there is worth reading.

- Rephrase the sentence so pronoun and antecedent disagreement doesn't exist.

  Example: When a **mother** visits a Web page, **she** decides if the information there is worth reading.

2. Write three sentences using the correct plural pronoun for the singular indefinite pronoun to which it refers.

Nonsexist writing should never be used at the expense of good grammar. Feminists object to limiting writing to all male pronouns, and males cringe at the thought of referring to them as neuter, so let's reach a compromise: When you prefer not to or are unable to rewrite a sentence that calls for a singular pronoun, in such instances, **he** or **him** can be considered *neutral.*

JUST A MINUTE

Another option is to think of your male and female pronoun usage as the seating arrangement at a child's birthday party: Alternate boy-girl-boy-girl when you use **he** and **she** or **him** and **her.**

OTHER AGREEMENT RULES

Some other rules for maintaining pronoun and antecedent agreement are

- Treat collective nouns as singular unless the meaning is clearly plural.

    Example: The **committee** completed **its** work.

    Exception: The **troop** performed **their** maneuvers.

- Compound antecedents connected by "and" usually should be treated as plural.

    Example: Jack Spratt could eat no fat and his **wife** could eat no lean, so **they** licked the platter clean.

    Exception: Old Mother Hubbard and her dog went to **her** cupboard.

- When compound antecedents are connected by **or, nor, either/or,** or **neither/nor,** the pronoun should agree with the nearest antecedent.

    Example: Neither Old Mother Hubbard nor the **dog** could find **its** bone.

    Example: Humpty Dumpty and the king's **men** each had **their** place in the nursery rhyme.

NOUN OR PRONOUN CASE

Case is how the noun or pronoun is used in relation to the other words in the sentence. These are the three cases:

1. **Subjective or nominative case**

    A noun or a pronoun is in the *subjective* or *nominative* case if it is used as

    - The subject of a sentence.

        The **dog** barked.

        She screamed.

    - A predicate noun.

        She is the **boss.**

    A predicate noun follows some form of the "be" or linking verb, and it defines or renames the subject of the sentence. Linking verbs are discussed in the next hour.

2. **Possessive case**

When a noun or a pronoun is used to show ownership, it is in the possessive case. (See Hour 3, "Elementary Sentence Components I: Nouns," for information on possessive nouns.)

Jemma liked **her** grandma's cookies.

3. **Objective case**

When a noun or a pronoun is used as a direct object, an indirect object, or the object of a preposition, it is in the objective case.

Andy gave **me** *some* **chocolate.**

SUBJECTIVE OR OBJECTIVE PRONOUN CHOICE

An easy way to remember which pronoun to use after the word "than" or "as" is to complete the sentence supplying the missing verb. (Think about the following exercise rather than saying it out loud. Repeat the correct sentence after you've reached your conclusion.)

For example, a mental rehearsal of sentences such as "You look much better in that dress than **me**," "I am a lot thinner than **her**," and "This benefited you as much as **I**" will tell you that the correct usage is "You look much better in that dress than **I** (**do**)," "I am a lot thinner than **she** (**is**)," and "This benefited you as much as (**it did**) **me**."

LAST MINUTE RULES AND REFRESHERS

1. Treat "only one of the" as singular and "one of the" as plural.

e.g.
_____

I was **only one of the** women who made **her** own dress for the party.

I was **one of the** women who made **their** own dresses for the party.

2. Remember that **everybody, anybody, anyone, each, neither, nobody, a person,** and **someone** are singular and therefore take a singular pronoun.

For **a person** to practice good grammar, **he** should abide by the rules.

3. Sometimes it can sound wrong and still be correct.

Are those Katie's books? Those are **they.**

A *subject complement* is a word that follows a linking verb and completes the meaning of the subject. Because "are" is a linking verb and the pronoun refers to the subject, it needs to be in the subjective case; therefore, "they" is the correct pronoun. See the pronoun chart for a list of subjective, possessive, and objective pronouns.

WORKSHOP: TESTING PRONOUN CHOICES

To help you "see" which is the correct pronoun to use in a compound sentence, think about the following examples.

1. When there are two pronouns or a pronoun and a noun, mentally drop one of the nouns or pronouns and test the sentence:

   Example: Taylor and **I/me** like to make pizza crusts

   Incorrect: **Me** like to make pizza crusts.

   Correct: **I** like to make pizza crusts.

   Therefore: Taylor and **I** like to make pizza crusts.

2. In formal speech or writing, use the subjective form of the pronoun after a form of the verb "to be." In informal speech or writing, use the objective form. Do you use the informal pronoun in formal speech or writing?

   Formal: It is **I.**

   Informal: It's **me.**

3. Comparison sentences usually include "than" or "as" and omit words. Mentally supply the omitted words to help you determine the correct pronoun usage.

   Example: He is smarter than **me/I.**

   Incorrect: He is smarter than **me** (*am smart*).

   Correct: He is smarter than **I** (*am smart*).

   Therefore: He is smarter than **I.**

PRONOUN CHART

Revisit pronoun functions and forms in the following chart.

Pronoun Chart

Personal Pronouns—Singular

	Subjective	Possessive	Objective
1st person	I	my, mine	me
2nd person	you	your, yours	you
3rd person	he	his	him
	she	her, hers	her
	it	its	it

Personal Pronouns—Plural

	Subjective	Possessive	Objective
1st person	we	our	ours, us
2nd person	you	your, yours	you
3rd person	they	their, theirs	them

Relative and Interrogative Pronouns

	Subjective	Possessive	Objective
	who	whose	whom
	whoever		whomever
	which		which
	that		that
	what		what

Indefinite Pronouns

	Subjective	Possessive	Objective
	everybody	everybody's	everybody

Hour's Up!

1. What kind of pronoun refers to a single person, place, or thing?

    a. plural pronoun

    b. personal pronoun

    c. indefinite pronoun

    d. singular pronoun

2. What kind of pronoun indicates ownership?

   a. relative pronoun

   b. possessive pronoun

   c. indefinite pronoun

   d. singular pronoun

3. What is formed when letters are omitted to join a pronoun with another word, such as in "you're"?

   a. fusion

   b. abstraction

   c. contraction

   d. construction

4. "This" and "that" are forms of what kind of pronoun?

   a. demonstrative pronoun

   b. indefinite pronoun

   c. personal pronoun

   d. possessive pronoun

5. What kind of pronoun refers to persons or things in a general sense?

   a. definite pronoun

   b. indefinite pronoun

   c. demonstrative pronoun

   d. personal pronoun

6. A pronoun refers to which of the following?

   a. accident

   b. precedent

   c. antecedent

   d. decedent

7. What kind of pronoun is used to introduce questions?

   a. interrogative pronoun

   b. intensive pronoun

   c. reflexive pronoun

   d. demonstrative pronoun

8. A noun or pronoun can take what case?

   a. subjective

   b. objective

   c. possessive

   d. a, b, and c

9. "Myself" and "yourself" are examples of what kind of pronoun?

   a. indefinite pronoun

   b. personal pronoun

   c. reflexive pronoun

   d. demonstrative pronoun

10. What is it called when a pronoun matches its antecedent in number?

   a. agreement

   b. ambiguity

   c. accordance

   d. assonance

ANSWERS

1. d	**6.** c
2. b	**7.** a
3. c	**8.** d
4. a	**9.** c
5. b	**10.** a

RECAP

This Hour covered pronouns. You should now understand personal pronouns, possessive pronouns, demonstrative pronouns, and relative pronouns. You have learned the usage of singular and plural pronouns and should be able to identify their proper agreement. You also learned about the case of nouns and pronouns and the difference between the subject and the object. Now that you know about nouns and pronouns, we'll cover verbs in the next hour.

HOUR 5

Elementary Sentence Components III: Verbs

CHAPTER SUMMARY

LESSON PLAN:

In this Hour, you'll learn about verbs and their function within a sentence. As you'll soon discover, verbs are there to do things.

Among the things we'll cover are

- How to understand verb tense.
- Active versus passive voice.
- Regular versus irregular verbs.
- The importance of maintaining agreement between the subject and the verb.

A *verb* describes the action in a sentence. Verbs name an action or express a state of being.

You'll recall from Hour 2, "Mastering the Basic Parts of a Sentence," that every complete sentence has two parts:

1. The subject, which conveys who or what the sentence is about.

2. The predicate, which shows what the subject does or is.

The verb is in the predicate. The verb in the predicate serves several functions:

- It informs what the subject is, did, does, was, will do, or will be doing.

- It adapts its form to show time (tense).

- It modifies its form to agree with the subject (number).

- It takes on a form to express whether the subject performs or receives the action in the sentence (voice).

- It varies its form to indicate how the speaker or writer wishes to express the sentence (mood).

SETTING THE MOOD

Mood is what shows the mindset toward the action. In English, there are three moods:

1. The *indicative mood* is used for statements and questions about actual events and things.

   David **maintains** a healthy diet.

2. The *imperative mood* is used to convey commands or to make requests.

   Shut the door. (The subject is implied in this example: (*You*) **shut** the door.)

3. The *subjunctive mood* is used in established phrases, parliamentary motions, hopes and desires, statements contrary to fact, and formal English. (See Hour 8, "Other Considerations," for additional information on the subjunctive mood.)

   If I **were** you, I would try to better understand the subjective mood.

   I move that this meeting **be** called to order.

   If that **were** true, everybody would be rich.

   Dorothy often wished she **were** back in Kansas.

The subjunctive mood has fallen out of favor in most everyday English usage. Now sentences are rephrased to eliminate the subjunctive mood. However, proper formal English requires the subjunctive mood for "that" clauses following forms of verbs such as "ask" and expressions such as "it was urged."

   David was asking that everyone **vote.**

   It was urged that all members **be** present.

UNDERSTANDING VERB TENSE

Tense is the form of the verb used to show the time of an action. Although there are only three categories of time (past, present, and future), English has other tenses to show further distinction within these categories.

Verb Tense Forms

Present Tense Forms	Past Tense Forms	Future Tense Forms
simple present	simple past	simple future
present progressive	present perfect	future perfect
	past perfect	future progressive
	past progressive	future perfect progressive
	present perfect progressive	
	past perfect progressive	

Furthermore, although all are referred to as tenses, they actually have three different divisions:

- Tense: present, past
- Aspect: perfect, progressive
- Modality

Modality describes the mood of a verb. Different levels of meaning can be expressed by using a *modal* verb. These expressed different levels of meaning result from combining a verb with an auxiliary verb. These auxiliary verbs are sometimes referred to as *modals:*

can, could, may, might, must, shall, should, will, would

Simple present, simple past, and past participle are the only tenses for which the spelling of the verb changes to reflect the tense—and such spelling changes do not occur in every instance.

As you will see, all other tenses are created using variations of the principal parts, combining them with auxiliary words to change the aspect or modality of the verb.

PRESENT TENSE

The *present tense* (sometimes referred to as the *simple present tense*) shows that an action or condition is taking place at the current time.

e.g.

I **walk** through the doorway.

Bertha **is** angry.

The present tense can also be used for statements generally regarded as true, regardless of time.

Chocolate **is** delicious.

Another form of the present tense, sometimes referred to as the *historical present,* is used to talk about things that happened in the past but are made more vivid if they are related in the present.

As you can see in this footage, the plane **flies** over the village and **drops** the bomb below.

PROGRESSIVE TENSE

The *progressive tense* (sometimes referred to as the *continuous tense*) is formed by using the helping verb "to be" combined with the present participle form of the verb. Progressive tenses are used to convey continuing or ongoing action.

PRESENT PROGRESSIVE TENSE

The *present progressive tense* describes a temporary condition or action that is currently taking place.

I **am entering** through the door.

SIMPLE PAST TENSE

Past tense shows a completed action or condition.

Charlie **unwrapped** his candy.

Charlie **was** happy.

Forms of "used to" and "would" are used with the present tense form of the verb to show an action that was repeated in the past but no longer is occurring.

Carl **used to** spend hours shopping.

We **would** spend most of our mornings sleeping late.

PRESENT PERFECT TENSE

In simple terms, the *present perfect tense* is used to convey an action or a condition that began in the past and continues on into the present.

> I **have been thinking** about entering through the door for several hours now.

Actually, there are four different instances in which it is appropriate to use the present perfect tense:

1. To repeat an endeavor in the past, the exact time of which is not important:

   > I **have rewritten** this sentence several times.

2. With the use of "for" or "since," which convey that the action began in the past and continues through to the present:

   > We **have wanted** to write a book about grammar and style **for** a long time.

3. For an action that began in the past and continues through to the present time:

   > I **have worked** on this project all day.

4. For an action or condition that occurred at an unspecified time in the past:

   > They **have sold** their house.

PAST PERFECT TENSE

The *past perfect tense* compares two actions or conditions that were completed in the past, and one occurred before the other.

> It **had never happened** to her until she became a blonde.

PAST PROGRESSIVE TENSE

The *past progressive tense* is used to portray an ongoing action in the past or one that occurred over time in the past.

> I **was reading** a novel last night.

PRESENT PERFECT PROGRESSIVE TENSE

The *present perfect progressive tense* shows an action or condition that began in the past and that continues to go on now.

I **have been reading** this novel for three days now.

PAST PERFECT PROGRESSIVE TENSE

The *past perfect progressive tense* shows an action or condition interrupted by another.

David **had been considering** changing careers for several years when he quit work to go to law school.

FUTURE TENSE

The *future tense* shows an action or a condition that will take place at a later time.

I **will go** to bed later tonight.

Kristy **is going** to redecorate her apartment.

FUTURE PERFECT TENSE

The *future perfect tense* shows a condition or an action that will be done before another one.

By the time we finish making the salad, the steaks on the grill **will be** done.

FUTURE PROGRESSIVE TENSE

The *future progressive tense* shows continuing action that will take place at a later time.

We **will be grilling** steaks again this week.

FUTURE PERFECT PROGRESSIVE TENSE

The *future perfect progressive tense* shows continuing action that takes place at another time and before another action.

By the time we eat those steaks later this week, I **will have been consuming** far too many calories.

To ensure clarity in your speech or writing, maintain the same tense throughout your sentences, paragraphs, or essays.

REGULAR VERBS

A *regular verb* is one that can be modified from the singular present tense to the plural present tense by adding

s or **es** for the present tense.

d, ed, or **t** for the past tense.

Some regular verbs require that you double the end consonant before you add the ending to create verb tenses. If the verb ends in a single, or *soft,* consonant that follows a single vowel, repeat the consonant and add the appropriate ending, as in grab, grab**bed,** grab**bing,** plan, plan**ned,** plan**ning,** and so on.

Sample Regular Verbs, Present Tense

Person	Singular	Plural
first	I work	we work
second	you work	you work
third	she works	they work
	he works	
	it works	
first	I grab	we grab
second	you grab	you grab
third	she grabs	they grab
	he grabs	
	it grabs	

Sample Regular Verbs, Past Tense

Person	Singular	Plural
first	I worked	we worked
second	you worked	you worked
third	she worked	they worked
	he worked	
	it worked	
first	I grabbed	we grabbed
	you grabbed	you grabbed
	she grabbed	they grabbed
	he grabbed	
	it grabbed	

IRREGULAR VERBS

An *irregular verb* is one for which the past tense or past participle is not formed in the conventional way of adding **d, ed,** or **t.**

The bad news is that, outside of memorizing the irregular verbs and their past and past participle tenses, there's no easy way to determine how those tenses are formed.

The good news is that the following table gives you a sampling of some irregular verbs and their past and past participle tenses.

 FYI For an extended list of irregular verbs, see the Web page prepared by the Department of Applied Linguistics & ESL, Georgia State University, at www.gsu. edu/~wwwesl/egw/verbs.htm. There is also one in *The Complete Idiot's Guide to Grammar and Style* by Laurie E. Rozakis, Ph.D. Macmillan, 1997. ISBN: 0028619560.

Sampling of Irregular Verb Forms

Base Form Present	Present (+s or +es)	Simple Past	Past Participle
awake	awakes	awoke	awoken
bear	bears	bore	born
speed	speeds	sped	sped
write	writes	wrote	written

Some irregular verbs aren't irregular because of spelling changes; they're irregular because they *don't* change their spellings. With the exception of the verb "read"—the pronunciations for which are shown in parentheses in the following table—irregular verbs don't change their pronunciations either. These verbs are pronounced the same regardless of whether they're used in the present, past, or past participle tense.

IRREGULAR VERBS WITHOUT SPELLING CHANGES

Common Irregular Verbs Without Spelling Changes

Present	Past	Past Participle
bid	bid	bid
read (reed)	read (red)	read (red)
upset	upset	upset

THE VERB "TO BE"

To call the verb "to be" an irregular verb would be an understatement. As you will see in the following table, "to be" is a highly irregular verb.

"To Be" as a Main Verb

Person	Present	Past	Future
first	am	was	will be
second	are	were	will be
third			
singular	is	was	will be
plural	are	were	will be

 FYI For a list of irregular verbs with spelling changes, see Appendix C, "Tables."

ACTION VERBS

An *action verb* is one that relates what the subject does. An example of an action verb is **bought.**

Homer **bought** Pat a diamond bracelet.

If you're uncertain as to whether the verb in a sentence is an action verb, ask yourself this question: Is the verb something an animal (*growl*), force of nature (*devastate*), person (*talk*), or thing (*drop*) could do? If it is, you have an action verb!

TRANSITIVE VERBS

An action verb can be transitive. A *transitive verb* is one that needs a direct object. (See Hour 9, "Phrases," for a review of direct objects.)

Randy **caught** *the fish.*

The fish **fell** *off the hook.*

INTRANSITIVE VERBS

An action verb also can be intransitive. An *intransitive verb* is one that does not need a direct object but can have an indirect object. (See Hour 9 for a review of indirect objects.)

Jay **tripped** on the carpet.

What **happened?**

LINKING VERBS

A *linking verb* joins the subject to the predicate. Rather than showing action, a linking verb helps the word at the end of the sentence describe or name the subject.

Keith **is** a Web page designer.

The true linking verb is some form of the verb "to be" as in

am, am being, are, can be, have been, is, was, were

Other verbs that are sometimes action verbs but can also serve as linking verbs include **appear, become, feel, grow, look, prove, remain, seem, smell, sound, stay,** and **taste.**

You can test for a linking verb by substituting **am, are,** or **is** for the verb. The sentence will still make sense if the verb replaced is a linking one.

HELPING VERBS

A *helping verb* is one that is added to another verb to add clarification to the meaning.

> The committee **will** meet at noon.

Helping verbs include any form of the verb "to be" as well as the following forms of common verbs: **can, could, do, does, did, have, has, had, may, might, must, shall, should, will,** and **would.**

One or more helping verbs can combine with a main verb to form a verb phrase. (See Hour 9 for a review of verb phrases.)

VERB VOICE: ACTIVE VERSUS PASSIVE

Voice is determined by whether the subject performs or receives the action in the sentence.

A verb is said to be in the *active voice* when the subject of the sentence is the doer of the action. The subject of the sentence performs or acts out the verb. In other words, the subject does the deed rather than having the deed done to it. Active voice uses action verbs.

A verb is in the *passive voice* when it receives the action of the sentence rather than performing that action. A *passive verb* is a form of the verb "to be" and a past participle verb.

> **Active:** Taylor **caught** the fish.
>
> **Passive:** The fish **was caught** by Taylor.

In the passive voice, the true subject of the sentence (the person or thing performing the action) is indicated by the word **by.**

The passive voice does have its time and place. Passive voice is effective

- When the doer of the action is obvious.

  > Reagan **was elected** for a second term.

- When the doer of the action is assumed or unimportant.

  > Apples **should be stored** in a cool, dry place.

- When the doer of the action is unknown.

  > The car **was stolen** from the parking garage.

- To add special emphasis to the receiver of the action.

  Almost the entire city of Xenia, Ohio, **was destroyed** by the Palm Sunday tornado.

"TO BE," "TO DO," AND "TO HAVE" AS ORDINARY VERBS

As if they don't have enough to do already, when **to be, to do,** or **to have** are used as main verbs within the sentence (instead of simply providing a grammatical function), they are treated as ordinary verbs.

- To be (to express a state of being)

  I **am** a woman.

  He **is** a professor.

  The interrogative form of the verb "to be" is created by reversing the verb and noun order.

  I **am** sleepy.

  Are you sleepy?

- To do (when referring to an effect, to finish, and so on)

  What am I going to **do** with you?

  Tiffany did **do** her homework on time.

- To have (when showing possession and when expressing an obligation or necessity)

  I **have** some antique jewelry.

  Ashley **has** her own computer.

  Kim **has** to go to work.

When the verb **to do** is used as a helping verb and combined with another verb, it forms what is sometimes referred to as the *emphatic tense.* This tense is used for emphasis, in negative statements, and in questions.

Present emphatic: Taylor **does** play hard.

Past emphatic: Janet **did** come to class yesterday.

HOUR'S UP!

1. What mood is used for statements and questions about actual events and things?

    a. indicative

    b. imperative

    c. subjective

    d. subjunctive

2. What tense is used to indicate events that are currently occurring?

    a. simple present

    b. future perfect

    c. present perfect

    d. past progressive

3. What mood is used to convey commands or make requests?

    a. subjunctive

    b. indicative

    c. objective

    d. imperative

4. What tense is used to indicate an ongoing or continuous action?

    a. future perfect

    b. present perfect

    c. simple past

    d. progressive

5. What mood is seen most often in formal usage?

    a. indicative

    b. imperative

    c. subjunctive

    d. subjective

6. What tense shows an action that hasn't yet taken place, but will take place at a later time?

   a. future

   b. future perfect

   c. future progressive

   d. future perfect progressive

7. What kind of verb does not follow traditional rules in creating past tenses?

   a. regular

   b. irregular

   c. definite

   d. illustrative

8. What tense shows an action that is interrupted by another action?

   a. simple present

   b. past

   c. past perfect progressive

   d. future perfect

9. What kind of verb requires a direct object?

   a. reflexive

   b. intransitive

   c. reflective

   d. transitive

10. What kind of verb relates what a subject is doing?

    a. reflexive

    b. intransitive

    c. action

    d. irregular

ANSWERS

1.	a	**6.**	a
2.	a	**7.**	b
3.	d	**8.**	c
4.	d	**9.**	d
5.	c	**10.**	c

RECAP

This Hour covered verbs and their usage. You should now understand what verbs are, how they are used, and how to differentiate between their different tenses. Now that you know all about verbs, let's move on to adjectives and adverbs in the next hour.

HOUR 6

Expanding Sentences with Articles, Adjectives, and Adverbs

CHAPTER SUMMARY

LESSON PLAN:

In this Hour, you'll learn how articles are used in sentences and how to "illustrate" those sentences with the use of adjectives and adverbs.

Among the things we'll cover are

- What articles are and how to use them.
- Types of adjectives and how to position them.
- Expanding sentences with the use of adjectives and adverbs.

An *article* qualifies a noun. Because of that, some grammarians classify an article as a *determiner*—a word within the sentence that determines something about the noun. To add even more confusion, some simply consider articles to be adjectives. (See the discussion later in this Hour for a review of adjectives.)

In this hour, we'll discuss articles and six other classes of determiners.

INDEFINITE ARTICLES

An *indefinite article* points out any one of a group without being specific. The two indefinite articles are

- **a**   Used before nouns that begin with a consonant.

    Barbara loves **a** parade.

- **an**   Used before nouns that begin with a vowel or a vowel sound.

    Jimmy selected **an** orange from the breakfast buffet.

THE DEFINITE ARTICLE "THE"

A *definite article* points to a specific item or person of a group or entity. There is one definite article in the English language—**the.**

e.g.

Item: Please shut **the** door.

Person: **The** man on the right is my brother.

Item, entity (country): I pledge allegiance to **the** flag of **the** United States of America.

(See Hour 3, "Elementary Sentence Components I: Nouns," for a review of why **a, an,** and **the** are sometimes referred to as *noun markers.*)

STRICTLY DEFINED

The is sometimes used as an adverb in sayings like "**the** sooner the better."

The more I eat chocolate, the more I crave it.

(See the discussion on adverbs later in this Hour.)

Although the definite article is used in front of the names of countries or entities, it is generally not used

- Before other proper nouns.
- After a possessive apostrophe.
- Before meal names.
- Before the names of languages.
- With uncountable nouns.

THE DEMONSTRATIVES

A *demonstrative article* indicates physical or psychological distance between the speaker and the object.

The Demonstratives

Singular	Plural
this	these
that	those

The position for a demonstrative within a sentence is

- Alone, if the noun is understood or implied.

    These are the times that try men's souls.

- In front of the noun.

    Implied distance, near: I am ready to buy **this** house.

    Implied distance, far: I want to look at **that** house.

THE DISTRIBUTIVES

A *distributive* shows how something is distributed, divided, or shared.

The Distributives

Distributive	Example
all	The Bill of Rights states that **all** men are created equal.
both	Have **both** reports on my desk by Monday. (indicates two)
double (used with uncountable nouns)	Lara made a **double** batch of cookies.
each	In this book, you learn something new about grammar or style in **each** hour.
either	Rick can select **either** prize.
every	John jogs **every** day.
half	I'll do **half** of the report now and the other **half** later.
neither	**Neither** option sounds good.

THE EXCLAMATIVES

An *exclamative* sets up an expression of admiration, surprise, or other strong emotion or reaction. The following are the exclamatives:

- such

    Today is **such** a lovely day.

- what

    I can't believe **what** a wonderful experience this has been.

THE NUMBERS

Numbers are expressed as a numeral (number), as a word (cardinal), or as an expression (ordinal), depending on their use in a sentence.

Numbers

Number	Cardinal	Ordinal
1	one	first
10	ten	tenth
100	one hundred	hundredth
1,000,000	one million	millionth

JUST A MINUTE

Most style authorities dictate that the numbers one through nine should be written out as words and, except for round numbers such as one hundred or one thousand, be written as numerals or numeric characters (11, 23, 65, …) thereafter.

Here are some written usage examples:

e.g.

There are **three** bases and a home plate in baseball.

A football team has **11** players on the field for each side.

David was the **fifth** person to step up to the karaoke microphone that night.

THE POSSESSIVES

As you learned in Hour 4, "Elementary Sentence Components II: Pronouns," a *possessive pronoun* refers to the possessor, not the item possessed. The adjective form is sometimes used or referred to as an article.

The Possessives

Person	Adjective	Pronoun
Singular		
first (I)	my	mine
second (you)	your	yours
third (he)	his	his
third (she)	her	hers
third (it)	it	its

Person	Adjective	Pronoun
Plural		
first (we)	our	ours
second (you)	your	yours
third (they)	their	theirs

THE QUANTIFIERS

A *quantifier* is used for amounts (quantities) that are approximate or inexact. They are

- (a) few: Tony has **a few** video games.
- (a) little: Dawn ate **a little** lunch.
- (a) lot (of): Bishop has **a lot** of paranoia.
- any: Did you have **any** trouble finding the bookstore?
- enough: Do we have **enough** milk on hand to make pudding?
- many: Hazel believes there are **many** reasons for using good grammar.
- much: Greg didn't appear to be having **much** fun.
- some: Nicole bought **some** groceries.

JUST A MINUTE

Compound words created from a quantifier combined with another word and used as adjectives have further usage distinctions. Words formed from **some** or **any** follow the usage rules. However, a word formed from **no** (**nobody, nothing, nowhere**) is used in an affirmative sentence to give it a negative sense: **Nobody** would approve the motion. There is **nothing** in this agreement to indicate otherwise. He was **nowhere** to be found.

A *graded quantifier* is one that acts as a comparative by conveying a relative position on a scale.

To signify an increase or to convey a positive meaning

many, more, or **most** is used with a plural countable noun.

more, most, or **much** is used with uncountable nouns.

e.g.

In a relationship, dishonesty causes the **most** problems.

Likewise, to show a decrease or to convey a negative meaning

few, fewer, or **fewest** is used with a countable noun.

little, less, or **least** is used with an uncountable noun.

Although **few** and **little** express a negative graded quantifier meaning, **a few** and **a little** are used to show a positive meaning. When **few** and **little** are used as adjectives, their implication is similar to the meaning of **some.**

Negative: The tax levy has **little** chance of passing.

Positive: Those suggestions should give you **a little** help.

ADJECTIVES

An *adjective* is a word that modifies or describes a noun or a pronoun. An adjective gives more distinct meaning to a noun or a pronoun by describing or limiting it.

ADJECTIVE POSITION

Adjective placement plays a role in adding meaning or distinction to the noun or pronoun it describes or modifies. An adjective can be positioned

1. Immediately before the word being modified (the most common placement).

   The **old** house is located on a **dirt** road.

2. After the word being modified.

   - To create a special compound word:

     The terms of the plea **bargain** kept the criminal from serving jail time.

   - When modified by other words:

     Elizabeth, **green** with envy, watched her competitor garner the award.

   - To add greater emphasis:

     Diamonds, **brilliant** and **glittering,** adorned her fingers and neck.

3. When used as a predicate complement.

   The diamonds looked **expensive.**

ADJECTIVE TYPES

The two general types of adjectives are

- *Descriptive adjectives,* which modify by showing a characteristic, condition, or quality.

    Jodi added a **dill** pickle to her sandwich.

    Ominous fog shrouded the landscape.

    Andy is a **creative** person.

- *Limiting adjectives,* which either indicate number or quantity or point out the person or things in some manner.

    The **first** flag of the United States of America featured **thirteen** stars.

    I'm glad you like **my** dress.

KINDS OF ADJECTIVES

The two types of adjectives can be broken down further to reveal 10 kinds of adjectives:

1. Articles: **a, an,** and **the.**

    The dress has **an** apron and **a** bow.

2. Common adjectives.

    He is a **strong** man with **muscular** forearms.

3. Compound adjectives, which are formed by more than one word.

    The **fast-food** restaurant is located on a **dead-end** street.

4. Indefinite adjectives, which describe general rather than specific qualities. These include **all, another, any, both, each, either, few, many, more, most, other, several,** and **some.**

    Some people enjoy taking on **several** jobs at the same time.

5. Nouns as adjectives.

    Alice used **cotton** batting in the **wool** quilt.

JUST A MINUTE

When more than one adjective is used to modify a noun, separate them with either a conjunction or a comma.

Taylor's eyes are **green** *and* **beautiful.**

Taylor has **green, beautiful** eyes.

6. Pronouns as adjectives.

> Alice displayed **her** quilt at the county fair.

7. Proper adjectives, which are formed from proper nouns.

> The **Japanese** tourists ate **Florida** oranges at the **Disney World** restaurant.

8. Adjectives that modify an object.

> Perfume smells **like** insecticide to someone with multiple chemical sensitivities.

9. Present and past participle verbs as adjectives.

> The **show** horse won first prize.
>
> Katie served the **chilled** wine.

10. Prepositional phrases as adjectives. (See Hour 8, "Other Considerations," for a review of prepositional phrases.)

> The dish **in the cabinet** belonged to my grandmother.

JUST A MINUTE

When a prepositional phrase is an adjective, it will answer one of these questions:

What kind?

Which one?

ADJECTIVE FORM AND FUNCTIONS

An adjective is *invariable,* which means it will not change its form based on gender or the number of the noun or pronoun it modifies.

Diana's **red** sweater has **red** buttons.

By now you've observed that adjectives serve several functions, which include

- Adding descriptive qualities.

  > Doris is a **generous** person.

- Specifying an affiliation.

  > Nathan is proud of his **Marine** uniform.

- Showing information about age.

  > Bill is a **retired** police sergeant.

- Describing color.

    Pam finally found a **blue** rose.
- Describing characteristics.

    Tony wore a **silk** shirt.
- Providing size information.

    Michelle is a **petite** woman.
- Showing measurement details.

    Michael is a **tall** man.
- Advising of nationality.

    Stevie and Phil are **English.**

ADJECTIVE ENDINGS

In some instances, nouns are made into adjectives by adding an ending, as shown in the following.

Nouns into Adjectives

Ending	Adjective
-al	Boston is a **coastal** community.
-ar	The newsletter is laid out in a **columnar** format.
-en	The couple sat at an **oaken** table.
-ish	Don exhibited **childish** behavior.
-like	The doll has **lifelike** features.
-ly	Jeeves possessed **gentlemanly** characteristics.
-ory	This is another **obligatory** example sentence.
-y	Our waiter had **dirty** fingernails.

JUST A MINUTE

Endings such as -al and -en are often dropped from the noun (actually, they're not added in the first place), and the noun itself is used as an adjective.

The couple sat at an **oak** table.

ADVERBS

An *adverb* is a word or a group of words that modifies a verb, an adjective, another adverb, or an entire clause or sentence. Before we show examples of each of these uses, let's first explain a bit more about what an adverb actually is.

There are three classes of adverbs:

- *Simple adverbs* are used as simple modifiers to convey degree, manner, number, place, or time.

How much?	Ben is **extremely** thirsty.
How?	"Grow up," he said **angrily.**
How many?	"Nah! Nah! Nah!" he shouted **repeatedly.**
Where?	The adverbs section in this chapter goes **there.**
When?	Helen called **yesterday.**

- *Interrogative adverbs* ask a question.

  When do you plan to get here?

- *Conjunctive adverbs* connect independent clauses.

  Irina struggled in her attempts to learn English; **however,** she mastered it eventually.

Common conjunctive adverbs include **accordingly, also, anyhow, besides, consequently, however, otherwise, still, then, therefore,** and **yet.**

PROCEED WITH CAUTION

Remember that a semicolon goes before the conjunctive adverb to separate the two clauses. (See Hour 10, "Main and Subordinate Clauses," for a review of clauses and Hour 11, "Controlling the Comma and the Semicolon," for a review of the semicolon.)

ADVERB POSITION

Adverbs don't like to stay in one place. They're transient little critters that can move to just about anywhere they like in a sentence. Most people who've read or spoken English for any length of time are familiar with words that end in **-ly** and often immediately follow a verb.

Kerry listened **impatiently.**

It's easy to find the adverbs in this example. "Impatiently" tells us the manner in which Kerry "listened." Adverbs can show up in other locations within a sentence, too. Some examples are

Before the sentence itself:

Luckily, Diana had her four-leaf clover with her at the gambling table.

As a phrase at the end of a sentence:

Sylvia decided **to take out the garbage.**

Before the verb:

Hector **carefully** glued the handle back on the broken cup.

Although adverbs can be positioned almost anywhere within a sentence, keep in mind that their position can and does change their meanings. For example, **only is** has a different meaning than **is only.**

Keep These Straight

Adjective	Adverb
easy	easily
good	well
most	almost

Always use **well** as an adverb and **good** as an adjective.

David is a **good** singer.

He sang that song really **well.**

ADJECTIVE AND ADVERB COMPARISONS

In grammar, a *comparison* is used to show a greater degree of a characteristic or quality. Adjectives and adverbs have three comparative forms. They are

1. **Positive**   The original word form.
2. **Comparative**   Usually used to compare two things or people.
3. **Superlative**   Used to compare more than two.

FORMING THE COMPARATIVE AND SUPERLATIVE

In most cases, you form an adverb by adding **-ly** to an adjective. If that adjective ends in *y,* you drop the *y* and add **-ily.**

Forming Adverbs from Adjectives

Adjective	Adverb
glad	gladly
noisy	noisily

For regular adjectives and adverbs, you form the comparative degree by adding **-er** to the adjective. To form the superlative, add **-est.**

Forming Regular Degree Comparisons

Positive	Comparative	Superlative
near	nearer	nearest
weird	weirder	weirdest

If the word ends in a silent *e*, drop that *e* and add **-er** or **-est**

close	closer	closest
large	larger	largest

If the word ends in a consonant that follows a single vowel, repeat the consonant and add **-er** or **-est**

big	bigger	biggest
thin	thinner	thinnest

Irregular Adjective Degree Comparisons

Positive	Comparative	Superlative
bad	worse	worst
far	farther	farthest
	further	furthest
good	better	best
little	less	least
much	more	most

Irregular Adverbs

Positive	Comparative	Superlative
badly	worse	worst
far	farther	farthest
	further	furthest
little	less	least
much	more	most
well	better	best

There are times when **more** or **most** is used to add greater emphasis to the degree.

Emphasis on crazy:

No one is **crazier** than Robin.

Emphasis on the degree:

No one is **more** crazy than Robin.

Emphasis on crazy:

Robin is the **craziest** person I know.

Emphasis on the degree:

Robin is the **most** crazy person I know.

On the other hand, some words—including almost all words with three or more syllables—form their comparisons by the addition of **more** and **most.**

Other Comparisons

Positive	Comparative	Superlative
beautiful	more beautiful	most beautiful
frustrating	more frustrating	most frustrating
satisfied	more satisfied	most satisfied

When using comparisons in a sentence, here are some rules to remember:

- **the** goes before the superlative

  That is **the** best book I've ever read.

- **than** goes after the comparative

  It is better **than** anything else I've ever read.

- **as** + comparative + **as**

    You are **as** young **as** you feel.

- **not** + **as** + comparative + **as** to show a difference

    That album **is not as** good **as** her others.

- **as** + **many** + **as** to show comparisons of quantity with countable nouns

    Tam doesn't have **as many** books **as** I.

- **as** + **much** + **as** to show comparisons of quantity

    I don't have **as much** money **as** Bill Gates.

- **fewer** + **than** to show comparisons of quantity

    Our neighborhood has **fewer** barking dogs **than** some do.

- **less** + **than** to show comparisons of quantity

    In 2001, there will be **less than** a thousand years until the next millennium.

- **more** + **than** to show comparisons of quantity

    That leaves **more than** enough time for programmers to mess up the next generation of computers.

In formal English, words like "dead," "impossible," and "unique" are only used with their original meanings; therefore, they do not vary in degree.

In informal English, "dead" is used to describe something that's dull, "impossible" is used to portray something that's really only difficult, and "unique" is used to describe something that's rare. When such words are informally given these broader meanings, they are also compared.

HOUR'S UP!

1. What kind of article points to a group or object in general, without being specific?

    a. definite article

    b. indefinite article

    c. demonstrative article

    d. distributive article

2. What modifies a noun or a pronoun, clarifying the meaning?

   a. article

   b. verb

   c. gerund

   d. adjective

3. What kind of article points to a specific item or group?

   a. indefinite article

   b. demonstrative article

   c. distributive article

   d. definite article

4. True or False: Some nouns can be turned into adjectives by modifying the ending of the noun.

   a. True

   b. False

5. "All," "both," "either," and "half" are examples of what kind of article?

   a. definite article

   b. indefinite article

   c. distributive article

   d. demonstrative article

6. What kind of adjective does not change its form to agree with a noun or pronoun?

   a. demonstrative adjective

   b. descriptive adjective

   c. invariable adjective

   d. limiting adjective

7. What kind of adjective helps to indicate number or quantity?

   a. demonstrative adjective

   b. invariable adjective

   c. limiting adjective

   d. descriptive adjective

Quiz

8. "One," "ten," and "thirty" are examples of what kind of article?

   a. ordinal

   b. cardinal

   c. demonstrative

   d. definite

9. "Nearer," "closer," and "bigger" are examples of what kind of comparison?

   a. positive

   b. superlative

   c. comparative

10. "Weirdest," "largest," and "thinnest" are examples of what form of comparison?

   a. superlative

   b. positive

   c. comparative

ANSWERS

1. b	**6.** c
2. d	**7.** c
3. d	**8.** a
4. b	**9.** c
5. c	**10.** a

RECAP

This Hour covered adjectives and adverbs. You should now understand what adjectives and adverbs are, how they are used, and how to use them effectively in a sentence. Now that you know all about articles, adjectives, and adverbs, let's move on to "agreements" in the next hour.

HOUR 7
Reaching Agreements

CHAPTER SUMMARY

LESSON PLAN:

In this Hour, you'll learn how to maintain agreement between pronouns, subjects, and verbs. You'll learn to watch for word forms that can create ambiguous or confusing sentences.

Among the things we'll cover are

- Pronoun and antecedent agreements.
- Unclear pronoun reference.
- Subject and verb agreement.
- Adverb agreement.

Because pronouns can be used for so many different things, there can sometimes be ambiguity in their usage. You've probably seen sentences in which you know a pronoun is supposed to refer to another noun, but you can't tell which one. (Refer to Hour 3, "Elementary Sentence Components I: Nouns," for more information on pronoun and antecedent agreement.)

When you use pronouns, you have to make sure others can easily understand the meaning of your sentence. To achieve this, you must pay particular attention to pronouns and the words they are replacing. Pronouns must agree with their antecedents. Simply stated, *agreement* means that the pronoun and antecedent must match in number. For the most part, the correct choice will be obvious. Some pronouns, however, may be tricky.

PLURAL PRONOUN WITH A COMPOUND ANTECEDENT

When pronouns are used in place of two or more nouns, the pronoun must match the antecedent. In general, whenever two or more nouns are joined by **and,** they will take a plural pronoun.

e.g.

When Jack and Jill went up the hill, **they** took a pail with **them.**

In this sentence, "they" and "them" refer to Jack and Jill together. Jack and Jill together equal a plural antecedent; therefore, because it isn't proper to use "his and her" with a plural antecedent, plural pronouns were used in this sentence. "His or her" is used only when the antecedent is singular.

INDEFINITE PRONOUN AGREEMENT

Some singular indefinite pronouns cause difficulty for many people. They are singular even though they can appear, at first glance, to be plural.

Singular Indefinite Pronouns

anyone	If **anyone** objects, he or she can do the work.
anybody	Has **anybody** seen my other shoe?
each	**Each** is expected to attend.
everyone	Is **everyone** here?
everybody	**Everybody** is encouraged to attend.
someone	**Someone** should make a decision here.
somebody	What are the chances that **somebody** is reading this sentence?
no one	**No one** is expected to object.
nobody	It's a good day when **nobody** proves us wrong.

These pronouns all refer to a single antecedent.

Anyone can write a proper sentence once **he** or **she** learns the rules.

Here, "anyone" is singular. The speaker is addressing a group but is advising the individual members of the group that they may choose to learn the rules.

e.g.

Someone left **his or her** project in the copier.

In this example, "someone" is a specific individual. "Their" would be inappropriate in this sentence because it's a plural possessive pronoun; it was not a group of people who left the project in the copier.

Even though "everyone" and "everybody" appear to be plural (because of the "every"), the "one" and "body" are the active parts of the pronouns and are singular.

e.g.

> **Everybody** knows what **his or her** plans are for the day.
>
> **Everyone** should bring **his or her** umbrella.

Although it can be tempting to use a plural pronoun in cases like this, it is technically incorrect and should not be done. It can also cause ambiguity, as in this example:

> Either **Tara** or **Jane** will let you stay at **their** place.

Do Tara and Jane live together but only one needs to give permission? Do Tara and Jane each have separate places? From the example sentence, you cannot tell anything with much certainty; there are just too many possibilities in this sentence.

When faced with such ambiguities, rearrange your sentence until the meaning is clear:

> Either **Tara** will let you stay at **her** place, or **Jane** will let you stay at **hers**.

> Either **Tara** will let you stay at **her** place, or you might be able to stay at **Jane's.** (place is implied)

> Either **Tara** will let you stay at **her** place, or **Jane** might let you stay with **her.**

See the following section, "Avoiding Unclear Pronoun Reference," for additional information on proper pronoun usage.

To add to the confusion, some indefinite pronouns can be singular or plural.

Dual Duty Indefinite Pronouns

Pronoun	Singular and Plural Usage
all	Singular example: **All** of the report must be done by Monday. (one report)
	Plural example: **All** (implied: **members**) attended the meeting.
any	Singular example: Is there **any** turkey left? (single serving from a single roasted bird implied)
	Plural example: Are **any** of the cookies ready?

continues

Dual Duty Indefinite Pronouns (continued)

Pronoun	Singular and Plural Usage
some	Singular example: **Some** is left. (single serving implied)
	Plural example: **Some** of the cookies are ready.
most	Singular example: **Most** chocolate is sweet.
	Plural example: **Most** of us like chocolate.
more	Singular example: **More** sugar is needed.
	Plural example: **More** people are coming.
none	Singular example: **None** of the cars is a standard. (model is implied)
	Plural example: **None** of us have enjoyed this movie.

The usage of these pronouns is derived from the context of the sentence.

AVOIDING UNCLEAR PRONOUN REFERENCE

Pronouns make things easier, but only when you can tell what they mean. Unclear pronouns can confuse your listener or reader. If someone has to stop to figure out what you are saying, you run the risk of losing your audience entirely.

MORE THAN ONE POSSIBLE ANTECEDENT

The antecedent should be obvious when pronouns are used. Watch your pronoun usage to make sure you are not becoming ambiguous.

e.g.

When Dick was at Robert's, **he** spilled **his** drink.

Who spilled whose drink? Did Dick spill Robert's drink or vice-versa? Or did one of them spill his own?

You can avoid this ambiguity by rearranging your sentence.

e.g.

Dick spilled **his** drink when **he** was at Robert's.

Now "his" and "he" obviously refer to Dick.

To avoid ambiguity, you may need to use a noun instead of a pronoun.

e.g.
_____

When Dick was at Robert's, he spilled **Robert's** drink.

SUBJECT AND VERB AGREEMENT

Just as pronouns and their antecedents must agree, the subject and verb of a sentence must match in number and person. (Refer to Hour 3 for more information on subjects and Hour 5, "Elementary Sentence Components III: Verbs," for a review of verbs.)

I **am going** to a movie.

She **is** reading a book.

You **are** very smart.

With plural subjects, the verb is used in the plural form:

We **want** cake.

They **write** well.

PROCEED WITH CAUTION
_____

Never use "they" as a singular subject. If you are referring to an individual whose gender is not known, "he or she" is the correct choice.

He or she writes well.

COMPOUND SUBJECTS

When two or more subjects are joined by a conjunction (such as "and"), a plural verb is used because the subjects are considered to be acting together:

Dick and Jane **were** here.

Red, yellow, and green **are** my most favorite colors.

Note, however, that the "and" is linking the subjects together. If "and" is used as a conjunction to join clauses or objects, the verb still agrees with the subject:

Laurie **is** smart, pretty, and fun.

Daniel **is buying** chips, chocolate bars, and drinks for the party.

Other words can also be used to form compound subjects. However, their context will determine whether a singular or plural verb is necessary. Here are some examples:

- as well as

  The editor, *as well as* the author, *was* instrumental in this project.

  Here, "the editor" is the subject of the sentence. "As well as" modifies the subject, which remains singular.

- together with

  The butter, *together with* the sugar, **is** a necessary ingredient.

  In this example, the only thing being combined "together with" the sugar is the butter, so the verb is singular.

- along with

  My net **is packed** *along with* my other fishing gear.

  In this example, "net" is singular and "my other fishing gear" is not integral, so the singular is correct.

- in addition to

  The entertainment section, *in addition to* the sports section, **is** interesting.

  Here, the sports section is being considered separately from the entertainment section, which receives the emphasis. It uses a singular verb.

COLLECTIVE NOUNS

Collective subjects can cause confusion for many people. *Collective nouns* refer to a group, so they appear to be plural. Because they refer to the group as a unit, however, they are usually singular:

The **jury** is deliberating.

The **audience** is applauding.

To use a plural verb with a collective noun, insert "members of" before the noun. This creates a plural subject because you are referring to individuals within the group. The verb is then plural. Likewise, any pronouns relating to the subject would also be plural.

The **members** of the jury *are deliberating.*

The **members** of the audience *are applauding.*

CONFUSING NOUNS

Some nouns are misleading when used with verbs. Nouns that end in **-ics** are usually singular because they refer to a specific idea:

Physics *is* difficult.

Mathematics *is* my favorite subject.

Linguistics *is* interesting.

In these cases, "the study of" is implied as the actual subject:

(The study of) physics *is* difficult.

(The study of) linguistics *is* interesting.

Other *-ics* nouns can be considered plural, depending on the context of the sentence. Compare the following examples:

Aerobics *are* good for you.

Aerobic exercises *are* good for you.

"Aerobics" is used to replace "aerobic exercises" and requires a plural verb.

When using *-ics* nouns, look to see which words are implied to determine the proper verb agreement.

QUANTITY EXPRESSIONS

Some plural nouns are considered singular because the noun is considered to be a collective unit:

Four quarts *is* enough.

Although "four quarts" is plural, it is being considered together as a unit. If the subject is considered to be individual units, however, the plural is used:

Four quarts *have been poured* out of the pitcher.

AVERTING WORD PATTERN DIFFICULTIES

The verb always agrees with the subject. When other phrases appear between the subject and verb, be careful not to choose the wrong agreement:

One of those guys **is** my uncle.

The pronoun "one" is the subject; "of those guys" modifies it. The singular is the correct choice.

Every **employee,** including Danielle and Andre, **has** a key.

"Employee" is the subject. "Danielle and Andre" are used to modify the sentence and do not affect the verb.

When you change word order to pose a question, be careful to maintain your agreement:

Is anyone watching the *children?*

"Anyone" is the subject, which makes "is" the proper verb. Therefore, although "children" is plural, it doesn't affect the verb.

Some nouns are used to limit the discussion to a specific group. When these are used, a singular verb is correct:

A **portion** *of the proceeds* **goes** to charity.

A **series** *of pamphlets* **is** available.

One *type of noun* **is** a gerund.

"A portion," "a series," and "one type" are the subjects and are singular. Therefore, the singular choice of the verb is correct.

AGREEMENT OF ADVERBS

When adverbs are used, they must also agree with the rest of the sentence. The proper form must be used.

As illustrated in Hour 6, "Expanding Sentences with Articles, Adjectives, and Adverbs," adverbs show how, where, or when something happened by modifying nouns, prepositions, verbs, or other adverbs. Adjectives can only modify nouns and cannot be used to modify other parts of the sentence.

When an adverb is used to indicate *how* something is done, certain problems can arise. Here are the answers to some common questions about using adverbs.

Q&A

Q. What's the distinction between "well" and "good"?

A. "Good" is an adjective and can only modify a noun: You make **good** cookies. Here, "good" modifies cookies. It shows that the cookies taste good. "Well" is an adverb: You make cookies **well.** In this example, "well" explains *how* the cookies are made. "Well" modifies the verb. When discussing health, "well" is the appropriate choice: She isn't feeling **well.**

Q. How can you be sure you're using the appropriate ending for an adverb and not creating confusion?

A. Most adverbs end in -*ly.* If a word is used as an adverb, it should have the appropriate ending: She writes **moderately** fast. Here, "moderately" shows how fast she writes. "Moderate" is an adjective and should only modify a noun: She writes at a **moderate** pace.

Q. Aren't there exceptions?

A. Yes. When certain verbs are used, a different test is needed. Asking "how" will not answer the question. You must look at the sentence to see how the verb is used:

- **to feel:** "I feel **terrible.**"
  "Terrible" is an adjective and indicates that the subject has that quality. An adverb brings a different meaning to the sentence: "I feel **terribly.**" Here, the speaker is referring to his or her abilities to reach out and feel something (with his or her fingers). Using the wrong form changes the meaning of the sentence.

- **to look:** "The cake looks **delicious.**"
  "Delicious" is an adjective and modifies "cake." Using an adverb in this example would imply that cake can have the ability to see. Therefore, only an adjective can be used.

- **to smell:** "The dog smells **bad.**"

  "Bad" is an adjective describing the odor of the dog. Again, an adverb means something different: "The dog smells **badly.**" "Badly" is an adverb and describes how the dog performs the act of smelling. In other words, the dog can't track, so chances are it wouldn't be a part of a police department K-9 unit.

- **to taste:** "This chicken tastes **good.**"

  "Good" is an adjective describing the taste of the chicken. Using an adverb brings an entirely different meaning: "This chicken tastes **well.**" This example infers that the chicken has a good ability to taste other things.

At times you will want to use adverbs with these nouns, but only when trying to achieve a desired result. Remembering the absurd results of using adverbs with these verbs will help you decide which is proper to use in a sentence.

Q. **How can you tell which ending to use in a comparison?**

A. When an adverb is used in a comparison, the proper form should be used: "He walked **more slowly** than she did." Although it can be tempting to say "slower," remember that "slower" is a comparative adjective. More slowly is the appropriate adverb.

HOUR'S UP!

1. True or False: "Everyone," "everybody," and "somebody" take plural verbs.

   a. True

   b. False

2. What nouns are singular, but are often misinterpreted as plural?

   a. compound nouns

   b. collective nouns

   c. plural nouns

   d. abstract nouns

3. Fill in the appropriate verb choice: Two gallons ——— been added to the tank.

    a. has

    b. have

    c. should

    d. must

4. Singular or Plural: Jury

    a. singular

    b. plural

5. Fill in the appropriate verb choice: Economics ——— interesting.

    a. be

    b. are

    c. is

6. Fill in the appropriate subject choice: —- was happy with the purchase.

    a. Sara and I

    b. They

    c. Bruce and Brian

    d. I

7. Singular or Plural: Gymnastics

    a. singular

    b. plural

8. Fill in the appropriate verb choice: I ——— for a walk.

    a. going

    b. is going

    c. are going

    d. am going

9. Fill in the appropriate subject choice: ——— were late for the movie.

    a. I

    b. She

    c. They

    d. He

Quiz

10. Fill in the appropriate verb choice: Matt and I ——— there last night.

    a. was

    b. were

    c. won't

    d. wasn't

ANSWERS

1. b		**6.** d	
2. b		**7.** b	
3. b		**8.** d	
4. a		**9.** c	
5. c		**10.** b	

RECAP

This Hour covered agreement of pronouns, subjects, adverbs, and verbs. You should now understand how to maintain these agreements in your use of written and spoken English. Now that you know all about form agreements, let's move on to special grammar constructions in the next hour.

HOUR 8
Other Considerations

LESSON PLAN:

In this Hour, you'll learn about some other parts of grammar that can enrich your use of the English language. You'll also learn how to avoid the things that could cause difficulty.

Among the things we'll cover are

- Defining and using prepositions.
- Learning about contractions and conjunctions.
- Using idioms and avoiding clichés.
- Understanding similes and metaphors.

Prepositions are used in the English language to show the *object of the preposition*—a word's relationship to other words in a sentence. By definition, a preposition is placed before a word ("prepositioned") to indicate the word's meaning within the context of the sentence.

There are many prepositions in the English language, and they can be used with either verbs or nouns. Whenever a preposition is used, it must be followed by another word. An exception to this rule will be covered later in this Hour in the section "Phrasal Verbs."

Commonly Used Prepositions

about	above	across	after	against	around
at	before	behind	below	beneath	beside
besides	between	beyond	by	down	during
except	for	from	in	inside	into
like	near	of	off	on	out
outside	over	since	through	throughout	till
to	toward	under	up	upon	with
without					

PREPOSITIONAL PHRASES

Whenever a preposition and a noun are used together, they create a *prepositional phrase* that modifies the sentence. A prepositional phrase is used to indicate the function of the noun, as in the following examples:

Dick gave the book *to Jane.*

Here, the preposition "to" indicates that Jane is receiving "the book" (which is the direct object of the sentence).

I like to ride my bicycle *in the evening.*

In this example, "in the evening" modifies the independent clause ("I like to ride my bicycle").

Prepositions can also be combined with other words to create *compound prepositional phrases* that have a new and independent meaning, much like the compound nouns covered in Hour 3, "Elementary Sentence Components I: Nouns." Here are some examples:

Compound Prepositional Phrases

according to	because of	by way of
in addition to	in front of	in place of
in regard to	in spite of	instead of
on account of	out of	

PHRASAL VERBS

A *phrasal verb* is created when a verb and a preposition are combined. In such cases, the preposition becomes part of a new and combined verb that carries a new meaning. Since the verb is complete, the preposition does not require a word after it.

Phrasal verbs are not often seen in formal usage but are plentiful in general usage. Here are some examples of phrasal verbs:

> When will you *grow* **up?**
>
> I'm going **out.**

INFINITIVES

When a verb is in its infinitive state, it has no subject or object. It is used to define the action of the verb without tying it to a specific person. It is a verb acting without a subject. The infinitive is the verb in its purest form.

Placing "to" in front of the root form of the verb creates the infinitive, as shown in these examples:

- to draw
- to sing
- to be
- to do

When used in a sentence, the infinitive of a verb is called a *present infinitive.*

> I want **to go** to the store.
>
> I wish I could learn **to draw.**

An infinitive can also be used in the past tense as a *perfect infinitive.*

> I wanted **to have gone** to the store.

An infinitive should be treated as a single word with a single meaning.

PROCEED WITH CAUTION

In formal writing, the infinitive should never be *split*—modifiers should not be placed between the verb and the preposition. In speech and informal writing, however, this rule is not strictly observed.

Some verbs do not have an infinitive form:

- can
- may
- must
- shall
- should

To refer to an infinitive in such cases, an alternate choice must be used such as "to be able to (do)" for "can."

CONTRACTIONS

As seen in Hour 4, "Elementary Sentence Components II: Pronouns," contractions are formed when two words are joined into one to make it easier to say certain phrases. When written, contractions use an apostrophe to indicate the missing letters. Here are some common contractions:

Common Contractions

First Word	Second Word	Contraction
I	will	I'll
will	not	won't
it	is	it's
they	had	they'd
would	have	would've
would	not	wouldn't
can	not	can't
they	are	they're

When writing contractions, pay particular attention to the meaning of your sentence to ensure that you are using the proper form. Consider the following examples:

If **you're** going to the store, get me some milk.

"You're" is a conjunction of "you" and "are." "Your" is a possessive personal pronoun and would be incorrect.

The neighbors want me to watch **their** dog.

"Their" is a personal pronoun. "They're" is a conjunction of "they" and "are" and would be incorrect.

Contractions are prevalent in speech and informal writing. In formal writing, however, contractions should be used sparingly and only when necessary.

Conjunctions

Conjunctions are used to join parts of a sentence together. A *coordinating conjunction* creates a relationship between two or more parts. The most common coordinating conjunctions are:

- and
- but
- for
- nor
- or
- yet

e.g.

I drove to the store **and** bought milk.

It snowed, **but** the snow has melted.

Because a conjunction joins parts of a sentence together, a coordinating conjunction should never be used to start or end a sentence.

Some conjunctions are used only with subordinate clauses. These are known as *subordinating conjunctions*. Here are the most common:

Common Subordinating Conjunctions

after	although	as	as if
as long as	as though	because	before
even if	even though	if	if only
in order that	now that	once	rather than
since	so that	than	that
though	till	unless	until
when	whenever	where	whereas
wherever	while		

A subordinating conjunction always precedes its subordinate clause. Unlike a coordinating conjunction, it can be used to begin a sentence.

e.g.

Whenever I open the fridge, the light goes on.

Now that I'm older, I feel wiser.

Although I can't get there very often, I like to go to the stadium.

Note that the subordinate clause can also go after the independent clause:

e.g.

The light goes on **whenever** I open the refrigerator.

I feel wiser **now** that I'm older.

I like to go to the stadium, **although** I don't go often.

Another common form of conjunction is the *correlative conjunction*. These conjunctions are always used together to indicate the relationship between the words they join. Here are some of the most common:

- as … as
- both … and
- either … or
- neither … nor
- not … but
- not only … but also
- whether … or

Although some of these conjunctions can stand on their own, when used in a correlative sense, both words must be present:

Either you want to go **or** you don't.

Mike does not know **whether** it's right **or** wrong.

FAULTY PARALLELISM

Many people accidentally create unbalanced sentences when using conjunctions and prepositions. *Parallelism* simply means that similar ideas are expressed in the same grammatical fashion. Parallelism becomes faulty when different grammatical constructions are used.

When using more than one noun with a preposition, the nouns can be expressed in a *series*. A series is a list of the nouns followed by a proper conjunction:

I went **to** the store, the post office, and the doctor's office.

Note that the preposition does not have to be repeated after its first appearance. However, if the preposition is repeated, it must appear before all nouns:

I went **to** Fred's, **to** Anna's, and **to** Phil's.

Faulty parallelism will often bring bizarre results. Consider the following:

I went **to** Fred's, Anna's, and Phil's.

Here, the sentence is unclear. Do Fred, Phil, and Anna live together? Or did the subject of the sentence go to three separate houses? The preceding example, with the prepositions repeated before the nouns, doesn't leave the reader wondering about the intent of the sentence.

Watch your parallelism when you use conjunctions in a series. The form of each noun must agree with the others:

A blue, red, green, or yellow marker will do.

In this example, the "a" at the beginning of the sentence modifies "blue," "red," "green," and "yellow."

The blue, red, green, or **a** yellow marker will do.

In this sentence, "the" should modify the nouns that follow it. The "a" before "yellow" creates faulty parallelism.

Parallelism is used to make things easier to understand. When used incorrectly, parallelism can create confusion or ambiguity. Be careful not to lose your reader with faulty parallelism.

PARTICIPLES

A *participle* is a verbal phrase that acts as an adjective. A participle, like a gerund, always ends in **-ing,** but it is used to modify other nouns.

When using participles, make sure the noun being modified is easily identifiable. A *dangling participle* exists when a participle could apply to more than one noun:

Walking by the theater, I saw Jim.

In this example, we don't know whether the subject ("I") or Jim was walking by the theater. Dangling participles can usually be fixed by bringing them closer to the noun or by modifying the sentence.

e.g.
_____

I saw Jim **walking** by the theater.

I saw Jim when I was **walking** by the theater.

I was **walking** by the theater when I saw Jim.

METAPHORS   IMPLIED COMPARISON

Metaphors are descriptions that give a quality to a noun but aren't literal definitions. At first glance, metaphors really don't make that much sense. The meaning is abstract.

Metaphors can be simple, as in the phrase "nerves of steel." Nerves are not tangible things that can be seen or felt. However, when "steel" is used to describe them, you understand that these nerves are strong, perhaps even unbendable. "Steel" gives "nerves" its strong qualities, but it would be absurd to think that the nerves are made of metal.

"An icy glare" doesn't cool someone off in the summer. It is intended to be cold and critical. The metaphor gives the glare the qualities of ice. It doesn't try to say that the glare is ice.

Metaphors are always implied; they are never stated directly. When you are using one, you are implying that the object has those qualities.

SIMILE *DIRECT COMPARISON.*

A simile is similar to a metaphor but uses "like" or "as" to compare ideas directly. A simile tends to be more concrete in meaning than a metaphor, but it can also be used for abstract ideas.

e.g.

> He's as *dumb **as** a post.*
> Her eyes *shone **like** diamonds.*

Unlike metaphors, similes are stated as direct comparisons.

IDIOMS

An *idiom* is any word or phrase that has a meaning specific to a particular community. An idiom usually has a specific meaning within a social, geographic, or ethnic group, but that meaning may not be understood in other areas.

JUST A MINUTE

Over time, idioms often become standard usage. Before the television remote was invented, "surfing" could only be done in the ocean. Now surfing can also be done on computer.

Before the telephone was introduced, "giving someone a ring" carried an entirely different meaning. Since the telephone gained popularity, however, most people will understand that you are calling someone on the phone. Computer users will understand what a "click" is; someone who has never used a computer mouse may not.

Depending on your audience, you may need to avoid idiomatic expressions. If you're addressing a specific group that will understand the idiomatic expression you're using, it is acceptable (if not preferable) to use the words everyone will understand. If you're unsure of your audience, play it safe and use words that are easily understood.

COLLOCATION

Some words have many different meanings. When the meaning of a word must be derived from its context, it is known as *collocation*.

STRICTLY DEFINED

Collocation is the process of discerning which of several meanings a word may have in a particular sentence by referring to the context in which it is used.

For example, the word "bar" can be used in place of "pub" or "tavern" when discussing a drinking establishment. It can also be used to describe a bar of soap, a sandbar, and a steel rod.

When using words that have multiple meanings, make sure what you mean is obvious to the reader or listener.

CLICHÉS

A *cliché* is any expression that is trite or overused. The preceding simile examples are clichés; they are considered old and unoriginal.

Many clichés are similes or metaphors that have become commonplace; however, any expression can be a cliché. Here are some examples:

It goes without saying.

In the nick of time

What's good for the goose is good for the gander.

Try to watch for clichés when you communicate. Clichés detract from your ideas. When you come up with an original and fresh idea, your words carry more importance if you don't use old, tired ones.

SUBJUNCTIVES

As seen in Hour 5, "Elementary Sentence Components III: Verbs," in addition to the imperative and the indicative, verbs can be in the *subjunctive* mood. It usually is used only in formal writing; however, if you're using the subjunctive, you must ensure that you are using the proper form. (Refer to Hour 5 for additional information regarding the subjunctive mood.)

The subjunctive mood usually takes the *plural* form of the verb, even with a singular subject. The subjunctive is used to indicate things that haven't happened or may not happen. You can think of it as the *wish mood*.

e.g.

> I wish I **were** home.
>
> **If only** I had more money!

There are instances in which the subjunctive mood doesn't always take the plural form of the verb. For example, you may wish to refer to a condition that doesn't apply to anyone directly but applies to everyone indirectly, such as in these examples:

> He insisted that patrons **be** over 21.
>
> She asked that we **be** quiet.

In such cases, the infinitive of the verb is used without the preposition. "We are quiet" is correct in the indicative mood; in the subjunctive, the preceding example is correct.

The subjunctive mood is used only to express a conditional idea; however, it is not necessary to use the subjunctive for all conditionals. If your sentence contains "as if" or "as though," it will almost always use the subjunctive mood. When a verb of general demand or instruction is followed by "that," it uses the verb root.

HOUR'S UP!

1. What verb form appears in a sentence without a subject or object?

   a. indicative

   b. subjunctive

   c. imperative

   d. infinitive

2. What is the best description of *it's*?

   a. third person possessive

   b. third person plural

   c. contraction of it and is

   d. plural direct object

3. What forms can an infinitive take?

   a. present infinitive

   b. past infinitive

   c. future infinitive

   d. a & b

4. Choose the correct form: The managers are coming in for —— monthly meeting.

   a. it's

   b. they're

   c. there

   d. their

5. *After*, *although*, *since*, and *than* are examples of what kind of conjunctions?

   a. subjunctive

   b. subordinating

   c. subjective

   d. supplementary

6. What verb form is used as an adjective?

    a. imperative

    b. participle

    c. infinitive

    d. gerund

7. What uses an abstract description to imply that a noun has certain qualities?

    a. colloquialism

    b. simile

    c. metaphor

    d. cliché

8. What is a word or phrase that has meaning only to a certain community, whether geographic or social?

    a. colloquialism

    b. ideology

    c. idiom

    d. metaphor

9. Choose the most appropriate verb form: I wish I —— rich.

    a. had been

    b. were

    c. was

    d. will be

10. What is it called when the meaning of a word must be determined from the context in which it is used?

    a. syncopation

    b. collocation

    c. alliteration

    d. conjugation

Answers

1. d		**6.** a	
2. c		**7.** c	
3. d		**8.** c	
4. d		**9.** a	
5. b		**10.** b	

Recap

This Hour covered special grammar rules that need to be observed. You should now understand prepositions, phrasal verbs, contractions, conjunctions, similes, and metaphors. Now that you know all about special grammar rules, let's move on to phrases in the next hour.

HOUR 9
Phrases

LESSON PLAN:

In this Hour, you'll learn about phrases and how they are used in sentences. You'll learn the various forms of phrases and how they are combined to perform different grammatical functions.

Among the things we'll cover are

- Creating noun phrases.
- Using verbs to construct verbal phrases.
- Forming sentences with phrases as objects.
- Using phrases and auxiliary verbs.

In Hour 8, "Other Considerations," you were introduced to prepositional phrases. A *phrase* is simply any collection of words that carries a meaning but contains no subject or verb. Some phrases can act as subjects; some can modify the verb or the entire sentence.

Phrases can appear within other phrases, but they are then considered part of a larger phrase. For example, a prepositional phrase can appear in a noun phrase as a modifier; it is still a prepositional phrase, but it is now a part of a noun phrase.

Phrases are described by their function in a sentence. The big thing that sets phrases apart from other parts of a sentence is that they lack a verb.

NOUN PHRASES

A *noun phrase* is created whenever words are added to nouns:

Noun Phrases

a coloring **book**	a green and yellow **basket**
the white **house**	English **grammar**
a personal **computer**	five or six **times**
only seven more **days**	an itsy-bitsy teeny-weenie yellow polka-dot **bikini**

In the preceding examples, the nouns are in bold; the additional words are used as modifiers.

Noun phrases are often combined with other words to create other phrases that perform a specific grammatical function within a sentence.

ADJECTIVE PHRASES

An *adjective phrase* consists of a noun and a modifier. It is considered an adjective phrase because, as a unit, it modifies other words in a sentence.

e.g.

The stockbroker, **feeling lucky,** sold the stock.

"Feeling lucky" is an adjective phrase because it modifies "stockbroker."

Adjective phrases appear closest to the noun or phrase they modify, as in the following examples:

The fisherman watched the water **rippling on the lake.**

"Rippling on the lake" is an adjective phrase modifying "water."

The dancer, **smiling brightly to the crowd,** took her bow.

"Smiling brightly" is an adjective phrase. "To the crowd" is a prepositional phrase used within it.

My uncle, **being as blind as a bat,** is a danger on the road.

In this example, "being as blind as a bat" includes both a prepositional phrase and a participial phrase. Adjective phrases often include participial phrases, which are covered later in this hour.

ABSOLUTE PHRASES

When noun phrases are combined with participles, they are known as *absolute phrases* because their meanings can stand on their own.

e.g.

Her eyes glistening in the dark, she looked out over the water.

"Her eyes glistening in the dark" is an absolute phrase because it doesn't actually require anything else to complete its meaning. It is an adjective phrase that acts as an absolute phrase within the sentence.

e.g.

He pressed his head against the wall, **listening carefully to the conversation.**

"Listening carefully to the conversation" is an adjective phrase that modifies the entire sentence and is absolute.

e.g.

Winning the lottery, Homer fulfilled a life-long dream.

Since an absolute phrase modifies the entire sentence, it can usually go anywhere within it.

JUST A MINUTE

An absolute phrase is sometimes known as a *nominative phrase* because it can contain a subject ("her eyes" in the first example).

APPOSITIVE PHRASES

Noun phrases can also exist as an *appositive phrase* when no verb separates two nouns that mean the same thing.

Tony, **a very good speaker,** presented the report.

Here, "Tony" is the subject. "A very good speaker" is considered to be in apposition—the words are completing the exact same function as the subject within the sentence.

Appositive phrases and nouns are considered to be *parenthetical* because they can stand on their own in a sentence (and could be separated from the rest of the sentence using parentheses). Instead of using parentheses, however, appositive phrases are separated from the noun with a comma. (See Hour 11, "Controlling the Comma and the Semicolon," for a review of the other rules concerning comma use with phrases.)

You can test for an appositive phrase by trying the nouns alone with the verb:

Tony presented the report.

A very good speaker presented the report.

Because both sentences make sense, "a very good speaker" is an appositive phrase.

Artemis, **purring contentedly,** rolled around on the couch.

"Artemis rolled around on the couch" works, but "purring contentedly" does not. Therefore, it is an adjective phrase and not an appositive one.

Appositive phrases can be longer, incorporating other phrase forms:

My uncle, **a minister in the Episcopalian Church,** wrote a sermon about love.

In this example, "in the Episcopalian Church" is a prepositional phrase; it's combined with "a minister" to form the appositive phrase.

Lara, **a nurse in the hospital down the street,** received a commendation for her work.

This example has two prepositional phrases within it—"in the hospital" and "down the street."

Appositive phrases can also be used in the objective case at the end of a sentence.

I gave the paper to Michael, **a lawyer.**

Here, "a lawyer" is an appositive phrase used as an indirect object. Objects will be discussed later in this Hour.

Be careful not to separate other phrases within the appositive phrase, such as prepositional phrases. Commas separate the appositive phrase from the rest of the sentence but not individual phrases within the appositive phrase. (See Hour 11 for a review of the comma.)

Sometimes, an appositive phrase can be used as an adjective phrase instead. Consider the following examples:

Jim, **my uncle,** drives a Ferrari.

In this sentence, "my uncle" is an appositive phrase.

My uncle Jim drives a Ferrari.

Here, "my uncle" is an adjectival phrase modifying "Jim." It is not separated by commas because it is not used in the appositive, even though either could pass the appositive test.

PROCEED WITH CAUTION

Remember not to use a comma with an adjective phrase. When an adjective phrase appears before a proper noun, it's not an appositive phrase; a phrase is only appositive when it is duplicating the noun.

See Hour 11 for information on commas and other forms of punctuation.

VOCATIVE PHRASES

A *vocative phrase* appears at the beginning of a sentence, indicating someone being addressed. It is used for emphasis, calling attention to the subject or object of a sentence:

Peter, please bring me the phone book.

Here, "Peter" is used for emphasis. The rest of the sentence is an imperative order, asking him to bring the book.

Professor, could you mark my exam early?

"You" is the subject. "Professor" is a vocative phrase emphasizing the subject.

Other words can be used in the vocative, too. Nicknames or pet names are often seen:

Honey, I love you.

"Honey" is a vocative phrase for the direct object "you."

Animals can appear in the vocative, too:

Fido, get in the house!

Secretariat, you must win this race!

If the word or phrase serves only to call attention to someone in a sentence, either as subject or object, it's a vocative phrase. Phrases used with objects will be covered later in this Hour.

Vocative phrases are always separated from the rest of the sentence by a comma.

VERBAL PHRASES

Phrases that use verb forms are known as *verbal phrases*. They don't actually use a verb; they use a gerund, a participle, or an infinitive to indicate the action of the verb.

When phrases are combined with actual verbs, they become clauses; this will be covered in Hour 10, "Main and Subordinate Clauses."

GERUND PHRASES

A *gerund phrase* is any phrase that uses a gerund:

Writing e-mail is a tedious process.

"Writing e-mail" describes the process of writing e-mail and uses the phrase as the subject. Since it is acting as a noun, it is a gerund phrase.

Tearing up the ticket was a nice thing for the cop to do.

This sentence refers to the act of "tearing up the ticket" and uses it as the subject. Therefore, it is also a gerund phrase.

JUST A MINUTE

Remember that a gerund is a noun, so a gerund phrase can only function as a noun. It can appear as the subject or the object in a sentence.

If a phrase is being used as an adjective, it is most likely a participle and not a gerund. Participial phrases will be covered in the next section.

Refer to Hour 3, "Elementary Sentence Components I: Nouns," for additional information on gerunds. Gerunds and participial phrases will also be discussed later in this hour in the "Direct Objects" section.

PARTICIPIAL PHRASES

A *participial phrase* uses a participle and always acts as an adjective:

The cop, **tearing up the ticket,** walked back to his car.

In this example, "tearing up the ticket" is no longer a gerund because it is describing what the cop is doing. It is acting as a participle.

Seven people, **standing in the lobby,** saw the man propose to his fiancée.

"Standing in the lobby" is a participial phrase.

Participial phrases can appear in absolute phrases:

Her eyes **glistening in the dark,** she looked out over the water.

The first part of the sentence is an absolute phrase, but "glistening in the dark" is a participial phrase modifying "her eyes."

Many adjective phrases are also participial phrases. However, an adjective phrase doesn't always contain a participle.

INFINITIVE PHRASES

An *infinitive phrase* uses an infinitive. Infinitive phrases appear to have a verb, but the verb doesn't actually have a subject.

e.g.

Richard wanted **to go to the movies.**

"Wanted" is the verb in this sentence; "to go to the movies" is an infinitive phrase completing the action of the verb.

e.g.

To take the bus, Sarah would have to walk four miles.

Even though it appears at the beginning of a sentence and looks like a prepositional phrase, it's actually an infinitive phrase.

e.g.

I am reading this book **to learn grammar.**

Here, "to learn grammar" is an infinitive phrase used as the indirect object, but it's not a true prepositional phrase because it leaves out the preposition.

e.g.

I am reading this book [in order] to learn grammar.

It still has a preposition, but it's part of the infinitive.

PROCEED WITH CAUTION

Infinitive phrases contain the preposition **to,** but they are not prepositional phrases. Refer to Hour 8 for a discussion on prepositional phrases and for additional information on infinitives.

PHRASES AND CASES

Phrases are often used in sentences as objects of verbs; they appear in the objective case as either direct objects or indirect objects. (Refer to Hour 4, "Elementary Sentence Components II: Pronouns," for more information on noun cases.)

THE SUBJECTIVE CASE

When a phrase is used as the subject of a sentence, it is used in the subjective case. (See Hour 12, "Other Forms of Punctuation," for a review of the subjective case.)

Playing baseball is a fun pastime.

"Playing baseball" is a gerund phrase being used as the subject in the subjective case.

Most phrases will not change form when moving from the subjective to the objective case.

JUST A MINUTE

Remember that nouns and pronouns can be used in the subjective or objective case, depending on the usage in the sentence.

Refer to Hour 4 for information on noun cases.

DIRECT OBJECTS

When a phrase receives the action of a verb, it is acting as the direct object of the verb. The direct object usually follows the verb in a sentence:

I picked up the second **book** in the series.

Here, "the second book" is an adjectival phrase and "in the series" is a prepositional phrase. Together they make up an adjective phrase modifying "book," which is the direct object of the sentence. "Second" and "in the series" merely qualify it.

I wrote a long and rambling **e-mail.**

"E-mail" is the direct object. "A long and rambling" is an adjective phrase modifying the direct object; the phrase includes both a regular adjective and a participle.

I picked a pretty **rose.**

"Pretty" is an adjective modifying "rose," which is the direct object.

An **-ing** word used as a direct object is usually a gerund:

I hate **writing.**

"Writing" is a gerund in this sentence because it is used as a noun.

I took **studying** seriously.

"Seriously" is an adverb that modifies "took." "Studying" is the direct object and is a gerund.

Lee liked **looking** at the **painting.**

This example includes two gerunds. "Looking" is the direct object of the sentence. "Painting" is also a gerund, used in a prepositional phrase as the indirect object. Indirect objects will be covered in the next section.

Not all words ending in -ing will be used as a gerund. A participial phrase can be used as an adjective modifying a direct object:

Bill grabbed **the fluttering pages.**

"Pages" is the direct object; "fluttering" is the participle modifying "pages." This makes "the fluttering pages" a participial phrase being used as the direct object. If "fluttering" were not modifying anything, it would be a gerund:

Despite the wind, Bill stopped the **fluttering** and straightened the pages.

Refer to Hour 4 for information on the objective case and direct objects.

INDIRECT OBJECTS

Indirect objects are indirectly affected by the verb and are almost always prepositional phrases. An indirect object shows how things are affected within the sentence, even though it doesn't receive the direct action of the verb.

Tammy gave the book **to Jane.**

"The book" is the direct object of the sentence because it is the thing being given. "To Jane" indicates that Jane is receiving the book as the indirect object.

I wrote a long and rambling e-mail to **my aunt in Ohio.**

This indirect object ("my aunt in Ohio") is in a prepositional phrase that includes another prepositional phrase ("in Ohio").

I picked a pretty rose **from the garden.**

"From the garden" is being indirectly affected by the verb because the rose (the direct object) is being picked from it.

A prepositional phrase is often a clue that the phrase is acting as an indirect object. However, an indirect object can sometimes hide in the sentence, losing the preposition, and can appear to be a direct object:

Tammy gave **Jane** the book.

I wrote **my aunt** in Ohio a long e-mail.

"Jane" and "my aunt" are still the indirect objects of these sentences, but they are no longer prepositional phrases.

Any phrase can appear as an indirect object, depending on the word order; however, an indirect object can always be rewritten as a prepositional phrase.

Word order won't always tell you the case of a phrase. However, an indirect object can always be tested. If it can be reworded as a prepositional phrase and if it complements the verb, it's probably the indirect object.

Refer to Hour 4 for information on the objective case and indirect objects.

OBJECT COMPLEMENTS

A linking verb doesn't have a direct or indirect object, but it still takes an object to complete its meaning. Phrases are often used as object complements:

Cynthia appears **to be happy.**

Here, an infinitive phrase is used to complement the linking verb "to appear."

Billy grew **four inches taller.**

"Four inches taller" is an adjective phrase complementing the verb "to grow."

Remaining under the tree, I waited for the rain to stop.

"Remaining under the tree" is an adjective phrase using a participial phrase.

Fortunately, it became **as clear as day.**

Here, "as clear as day" is a prepositional phrase acting as an adjective phrase.

Refer to Hour 4 for additional information on complements and Hour 5 for additional information on linking verbs; see Hour 10 for information on phrases used in noun clauses.

A linking verb always uses an object complement to complete it. Refer to Hour 5, "Elementary Sentence Components III: Verbs," for a list of linking verbs.

AUXILIARY VERBS

Pay special attention to auxiliary verbs that can act independently. Here are the ones to watch:

- To be
- To do
- To have

When one of these verbs is used in its distinct form, it requires an object:

Lisa will be the prettiest person there.

"The prettiest person" is an adjectival phrase modifying "there," the direct object.

Frank did the fourth exam question perfectly.

"Perfectly" is an adverb modifying "did." "The fourth exam question" is an adjectival phrase acting as the direct object.

Josh has a winning smile.

"A winning smile" is an adjectival phrase using a participle. "Smile" is the direct object.

These verbs can also be used as an auxiliary verb to aid another verb:

I have to go to the store.

The infinitive phrase "to go to the store" modifies "have" and includes the prepositional phrase "to the store" as an indirect object.

I did go to the store.

Here, "did" is acting as an auxiliary verb to the verb "to go," showing the past tense. "To the store" is the indirect object of the sentence.

I am going crazy.

"Am" is using "going crazy" as a participial phrase to modify the subject. In this example, it is not used as an auxiliary verb.

HOUR'S UP!

1. What kind of phrase is created when words are added to nouns?

    a. adjective phrase

    b. noun phrase

    c. appositive phrase

    d. absolute phrase

2. Which phrases include forms of verbs?

    a. gerund, participial, and infinitive

    b. appositive, prepositional, and gerund

    c. gerund, infinitive, and prepositional

    d. participial, noun, and appositive

3. What kind of phrase uses a participle, and always acts as an adjective?

    a. gerund phrase

    b. vocative phrase

    c. participial phrase

    d. verbal phrase

4. What kind of phrase consists of a noun and a modifier?

    a. noun phrase

    b. absolute phrase

    c. appositive phrase

    d. adjective phrase

5. When a phrase performs the action of a verb, it is said to be in which of the following cases?

    a. appositive

    b. subjective

    c. objective

    d. adjective

6. What kind of phrase often appears as an indirect object?

   a. gerund phrase

   b. prepositional phrase

   c. infinitive phrase

   d. participial phrase

7. What kind of phrase contains a participle and whose meaning can stand on its own, without requiring other phrases or clauses?

   a. vocative phrase

   b. gerund phrase

   c. absolute phrase

   d. appositive phrase

8. What kind of verb doesn't require an object, but instead takes an object complement?

   a. auxiliary

   b. irregular

   c. reflexive

   d. transitive

9. What case shows the object being directly affected by the action of the verb?

   a. vocative

   b. direct object

   c. subjective

   d. indirect object

10. What phrase appears at the beginning of a sentence to call attention to the person being addressed?

   a. vocative phrase

   b. participial phrase

   c. verbal phrase

   d. absolute phrase

Answers

1. b		**6.** b	
2. a		**7.** c	
3. c		**8.** a	
4. d		**9.** b	
5. b		**10.** a	

Recap

This Hour covered phrases and their different uses. It also covered phrases used as objects of verbs. You should now understand how phrases are formed and where they can be used in a sentence. Now that you know all about phrases, let's move on to clauses in the next hour.

Main and Subordinate Clauses

Chapter Summary

LESSON PLAN:

In this Hour, you'll learn about clauses and how they are combined with phrases to create sentences.

Among the things we'll cover are

- Defining and using main clauses.
- Forming and placing subordinate clauses.
- Using noun clauses that function as nouns.
- Learning about adjective and adverbial clauses.

A *clause* is similar to a phrase in that it is a collection of words that bring meaning to a sentence. However, unlike a phrase, a clause includes a verb and a subject.

A *main clause* consists of a subject and a predicate. (Refer to Hour 2, "Mastering the Basic Parts of a Sentence," for more information on predicates.) It has a subject, a verb, and the words that go along with the verb.

e.g.

Kevin dried the dishes.

"Kevin" is the subject; the rest of the sentence is the predicate, consisting of the verb and the direct object. Combined, they make a main clause, which stands as a complete sentence.

e.g.

Trevor is taking the bus home.

This example has "Trevor" as the subject. The rest of the sentence is the predicate including the direct object ("the bus") and the indirect object ("home"). Together, they form a main clause.

COMPOUND SENTENCES

A main clause is really nothing more than a basic sentence. In the last hour, you learned that an absolute phrase doesn't require anything else within the sentence because it modifies the entire sentence. A main clause doesn't need anything else either; however, sometimes main clauses are combined to form a *compound sentence*.

Erin is in high school now, but next year she will be at the university.

Each main clause can stand alone as a complete sentence:

Erin is in high school now.

Next year she will be at the university.

Each clause holds the same rank in a compound sentence, which means that one part isn't more important than any other. The clauses in a compound sentence are often referred to as *coordinate* because they're of equal importance.

COORDINATING CONJUNCTIONS

Compound sentences are often formed using coordinating conjunctions. The example for compound sentences used "but" to join the two clauses, but any coordinating conjunction can be used.

e.g.

Marlene is a single parent, **yet** she works full-time.

Conjunctions are not required to create compound sentences, however; semicolons can also be used. (Refer to Hour 8, "Other Considerations," for additional information on conjunctions.)

e.g.

The last sentence in the preceding paragraph uses a semicolon; no coordinating conjunction is required.

In case you didn't notice, the example also uses a semicolon instead of a coordinating conjunction.

CONJUNCTIVE ADVERBS

In Hour 6, "Expanding Sentences with Articles, Adjectives, and Adverbs," you learned about conjunctive adverbs. When conjunctive adverbs are used to join main clauses in a compound sentence, they are used as modifiers instead of simple linking words. Since conjunctive adverbs don't link the way coordinating adjectives do, they are separated using a semicolon.

Ivan replaced all four tires on his car a month ago; **nevertheless,** he still ended up with a flat tire last week.

Craig scored low on his final exam; **consequently,** he probably won't pass the course.

Bruce gets paid on Friday; **therefore,** he can give you a payment next week.

SUBORDINATE CLAUSES

A *subordinate clause* has both a verb and a subject, just as a main clause does, but it is not a complete statement. To complete its meaning, it must be linked to a main clause.

STRICTLY DEFINED

Subordinate clauses are often called *dependent clauses* because they depend on a main clause to exist in a complex or compound-complex sentence.

COMPLEX SENTENCES

Main clauses can also be combined with subordinate clauses to form *complex sentences.* A complex sentence is any sentence that has both a main clause and a subordinate clause.

e.g.

Rebecca can't go to the show **because it is sold out.**

The subordinate clause is bolded in the example. The subordinate clause cannot stand alone—"because it is sold out" is not a complete sentence, even though it has a subject and a verb. It is an incomplete thought that relies on the main clause (the rest of the sentence).

e.g.
> Ellen bought two roses from the woman **who was selling them on the corner.**

Note that subordinate clauses are very similar to phrases. The above example could also use an adverbial phrase:

e.g.
> Ellen bought two roses from the woman **selling them on the corner.**

Since this portion of the sentence uses a participle instead of a verb, it is not a subordinate clause.

Refer to Hour 9, "Phrases," for information on participles used in phrases.

COMPOUND-COMPLEX SENTENCES

When a sentence exists with two or more main clauses and at least one subordinate clause, it is known as a *compound-complex sentence.*

> It doesn't take long to mow the lawn, but you cannot do it **while it's raining.**

"While it's raining" is the subordinate clause. There are also two main clauses in this compound-complex sentence, separated by the coordinating conjunction "but."

Subordinate clauses can be broken into three forms—noun clauses, adjective clauses, and adverbial clauses.

NOUN CLAUSES

Noun clauses are clauses that function as nouns and can be used as subjects, objects, or complements. They are usually introduced using "that."

> The fact **that John went to university** helped him land his job.

> Angela knew **that she was going to win.**

Other words can also be used to introduce noun clauses:

Noun Clause Introductory Words

what	whatever	when	where
whether	who	whoever	why

e.g.

Tracy doesn't know **what** David is trying to say.

Martha can do **whatever** she likes.

The man **who** bought my pony is coming to get it today.

You can buy it from **whoever** is working at the desk.

In the last example, even though the noun clause follows the preposition, "whoever" is the subject of the clause and is used in the subjective case. "Whomever" is in the objective form and would be incorrect.

PROCEED WITH CAUTION

Remember that "whomever" is the objective form of "whoever." When "whoever" is used as the subject of a subordinate noun clause, it stays in the subjective case, even if it is used as an object after a preposition.

Refer to Hour 3, "Elementary Sentence Components I: Nouns," for more information on choosing between who and whom.

Noun Clauses Used as Subjects

Noun clauses can be used as subjects of main clauses:

Where Patrick lives now is anybody's guess.

What Sarah wants is a red corvette.

When the noun clause begins with "that" or "whether," however, the sentence is usually reworded for clarity.

That Judy won is a great relief.

It's a great relief **that Judy won.**

Noun clauses can also appear as appositives:

The fact **that Judy won** is a great relief.

Note that, when clauses are used as appositives, they are not separated with commas. (See Hour 11, "Controlling the Comma and the Semicolon," for a review of comma usage.)

NOUN CLAUSES USED AS DIRECT OBJECTS

Noun clauses are commonly used as the objects of verbs in the English language, following the verb to complete the sentence.

e.g.

Diana said **that she liked her job.**

The columnist reported **that the economy is improving.**

Everyone wonders **what the future will be like.**

Refer to Hour 8 for additional information on direct objects.

NOUN CLAUSES USED AS INDIRECT OBJECTS

Noun clauses can also be used as indirect objects of verbs, usually following a preposition.

e.g.

Regis Philbin is a hero to many people **who want to be millionaires.**

This color is perfect for **what you're planning to do.**

Refer to Hour 8 for additional information on indirect objects.

NOUN CLAUSES USED AS OBJECT COMPLEMENTS

When noun clauses are used as complements, the language can appear stilted. Most often, sentences are reworded to avoid this.

e.g.

The winner is whoever has the most votes.

Whoever has the most votes is the winner.

Money is why most people work.

Most people work in order to get money.

The last example removes the complement completely and replaces it with a prepositional phrase.

There is no absolute rule to rewording a noun phrase used as an object complement. If the language sounds stilted, you can modify the sentence so it sounds better.

ADJECTIVE CLAUSES

When a clause is used to modify a noun or a pronoun, it is an *adjective clause.* Adjective clauses are usually introduced using the relative pronouns "that," "who," and "which." (Refer to Hour 4, "Elementary Sentence Components II: Pronouns," for additional information on relative pronouns.)

Adjective clauses can modify subjects, objects, or complements.

ADJECTIVE CLAUSES AS SUBJECTS

Adjective clauses are often used to follow the subject of a sentence, making the subject more specific.

Speakers **who give interesting lectures** are usually more effective.

"Who" is the subject of the adjective clause. It modifies "speakers."

Many shows **that you see on television** are filmed in Hollywood.

"That" is the subject of the adjective clause; it modifies "many shows."

The newspaper **for which he wrote** stopped publishing last year.

"Which" is the subject of the clause. It is used as the object of the preposition "for" and modifies "newspaper."

ADJECTIVE CLAUSES AS OBJECTS

Adjective clauses can also appear as the direct or indirect object of verbs.

Sharon found a dog that had been lost by its owners.

"Dog" is the direct object of the sentence, and the adjective clause modifies it.

Laurie found a hairdresser **who used organic products.**

The adjective phrase modifies "hairdresser," which is the direct object of the sentence.

Albert received a thank-you card from the person **whom he hired last week.**

Note that "he" is actually the subject of this adjective clause; "whom" is the appropriate choice because "the person" is the direct object of the clause.

TASK: AGREE TO AGREE

Because a clause has a subject and a verb, relative pronouns must agree within it. The proper case must be used no matter how the clause is used in a sentence.

To see whether your clause is using the proper case of pronoun …

1. Take it out of the sentence. If it works on its own, it's accurate.
2. If it still needs something else from the other sentence to make sense, you probably have chosen the wrong case.
3. Refer to Hour 3 for more information on relative pronouns.
4. Rewrite the sentence and repeat step 1.

ADJECTIVE CLAUSES AS COMPLEMENTS

Adjective clauses can also be used as the complements of linking verbs.

e.g.

Alex felt **that Henry wasn't pulling his own weight.**

It became apparent **that there was more work than Derek thought.**

Refer to Hour 4 for additional information on complements; Hour 5, "Elementary Sentence Components III: Verbs," for additional information on linking verbs; and Hour 9 for information on adjective phrases used as complements.

RESTRICTIVE CLAUSES

When a clause is required in a sentence, it is known as a *restrictive clause* or *restrictive modifier* because it limits the meaning of the sentence. It makes the sentence refer to something specific, and the sentence doesn't mean the same thing without it. It's restrictive because it can't be removed without changing the meaning of the sentence.

Bob interviewed the man **who gave the demonstration.**

"Who gave the demonstration" is a restrictive clause because the sentence does not carry the same meaning without it. If the clause is not included, the sentence is ambiguous because the man is not known. The restrictive clause identifies the man, making the sentence refer to something specific.

The woman **who won the boat in the contest** let me drive it.

Without the restrictive clause, the sentence means no more than "a woman let me drive her boat." The restrictive clause identifies the woman, telling us that she won the boat in a contest. The meaning of the sentence depends on the clause.

Jeremy lives on the street **where the accident happened.**

The restrictive clause identifies and limits the street. Without it, an entirely different sentence emerges:

Jeremy lives on the street.

You can see how integral a relative clause can be to the intended meaning of a sentence.

Refer to Hour 4 for additional information on modifiers.

ADVERBIAL CLAUSES

An *adverbial clause* is a subordinate clause that modifies a verb, adverb, adjective, or entire main clause. Adverbial clauses are joined to the main clause using subordinators.

SUBORDINATORS

Subordinators are words that introduce subordinate clauses. They are often used to introduce adjective clauses.

The following are some of the many subordinators in the English language:

Examples of Subordinators

after	although	as	as if
as long as	as soon as	as though	because
before	even if	even though	except if
in order that	provided that	since	so … as
so that	than	that	till
though	unless	until	when
whenever	where	wherever	whether
while			

Subordinators are used to express an idea about the main clause, calling attention to it in a particular area. Subordinators can be used to indicate:

1. **Cause:** Stephanie told Laurie to hurry, **as they were going to be late.**

   The adverbial clause shows the reason behind the action in the sentence.

e.g.

Kay's boss loves her **because she is a dedicated worker.**

2. **Comparison:** David stayed later **than Jessica did.**

   Here, the adverbial clause provides a comparison between David and Jessica.

e.g.

The parking lot is bigger **than the building.**

3. **Concession:** Eric will finish the project on time **although he is very busy.**

   Despite the fact that Eric is busy, he will finish the project. The adverbial clause is used to show that something is happening in spite of something else.

e.g.

John would like to buy that painting **even though it costs a lot of money.**

4. **Condition:** Thomas will drive **provided that you pay for the gas.**

   The adverbial clause illustrates a condition for the main clause. The action described in the main clause cannot happen without the action described in the adverbial clause.

e.g.

Lynn wants to go **unless she is doing something else.**

5. **Degree:** The parking lot is not **as big as it used to be.**

   The adverbial clause defines the extent of the main clause, establishing its degree.

6. **Manner:** Brenda acts **as if she were famous.**

   The adverbial clause shows the fashion in which Brenda acts.

7. **Place:** The sale items should be placed **where they'll be seen.**

   Here, the adverbial clause defines where items should be placed—not in a specific fashion but in a general one.

e.g.

You can put that **wherever you like.**

   An adverbial clause can also be used to indicate a specific place: The house **where I grew up** was torn down last week.

8. **Purpose:** Luanne writes every day **so that she'll finish her novel.**

   The adverbial clause shows the reason Luanne is writing every day.

e.g.

Kids are good at Christmas **so that Santa will bring them presents.**

9. **Result:** The review was **so good that I finally decided to see the show**.

   The adverbial clause shows what happened because of the main clause.

e.g.

Amy hurried **so that the others wouldn't be late.**

JUST A MINUTE

The categories defined here are not exclusive. Some word constructions may convey more than one of the objective meanings in the list. Note how similar the "Cause" and "Result" categories seem.

The categories are included to show you the ways in which subordinators can be used.

10. **Time:** Ted bought a newspaper **while he waited for the bus.**

The adverbial clause adds an element of time to the main clause.

e.g.

I always drink coffee **whenever I go out.**

Adverbial clauses can also go at the beginning of a sentence. When placed there, they are separated from the main clause using commas:

e.g.

Whenever I begin with an adverbial clause, I follow it with a comma.

I don't use a comma **if I don't begin with an adverbial clause.**

See Hour 11 for information on commas and other forms of punctuation. Refer to Hour 6 for additional information on adverbs.

Q&A

Q. Why are there clauses?

A. Clauses help us convey ideas. They allow us to define the components of a sentence, adding depth and meaning. Clauses are what make the sentence interesting.

Q. Why can't a subordinate clause stand alone?

A. A subordinate clause is a group of words that doesn't carry the meaning of a full sentence. It requires something else to complete its meaning. "The man who bought that car" is a subordinate clause. It has a verb, but that verb is within the clause "who bought that car." "The man" needs to be the subject of a main clause for the subordinate clause to mean anything: "The man who bought that car is paying for it today."

Q. When do you use subordinators?

A. Subordinators are used when you want to add an adverb to a main clause. Subordinators help convey a certain meaning about a clause such as time, place, or reason. Subordinators add to the main clause by modifying it and indicating the circumstances surrounding the main clause. Subordinators allow us to create grammatically correct sentences that use fewer words than otherwise might be required if only main clauses had to be used.

HOUR'S UP!

1. What kind of clause contains a subject and predicate?

    a. subordinate clause

    b. main clause

    c. noun clause

    d. restrictive clause

2. What kind of clause can modify a verb, adverb, adjective, or main clause?

    a. subordinate clause

    b. adjective clause

    c. adverbial clause

    d. absolute clause

3. What kind of clause can modify the subject, object, or complement?

    a. restrictive clause

    b. subordinate clause

    c. adverbial clause

    d. adjective clause

4. What kind of clause contains both a subject and verb, but is not a complete statement?

    a. adjective clause

    b. subordinate clause

    c. noun clause

    d. main clause

5. What kind of clause is sometimes known as an independent clause?

   a. main clause

   b. adjective clause

   c. restrictive clause

   d. subordinate clause

6. What kind of sentence has more than one main clause, but no subordinate clause?

   a. descriptive

   b. complex

   c. compound

   d. complete

7. What kind of clause is required to complete the meaning of a sentence?

   a. restrictive

   b. adjective

   c. main

   d. noun

8. What kind of clause is sometimes known as a dependent clause?

   a. main clause

   b. subordinate clause

   c. adjective clause

   d. restrictive clause

9. What kind of sentence has a main clause and one or more subordinate clauses?

   a. complex

   b. compound

   c. absolute

   d. imperative

10. What kind of clause can appear as a subject, object, or complement?

   a. main clause

   b. restrictive clause

   c. noun clause

   d. subordinate clause

QUIZ

ANSWERS

1.	b	**6.**	c
2.	c	**7.**	a
3.	d	**8.**	b
4.	b	**9.**	a
5.	a	**10.**	c

RECAP

This Hour covered clauses and how they are used to build sentences. You should now understand how they can be used to add meaning in a sentence. Now that you know all about clauses, let's move on to punctuation in the next hour.

HOUR 11

Controlling the Comma and the Semicolon

CHAPTER SUMMARY

LESSON PLAN:

In this Hour, you'll learn how to use the comma and the semi-colon.

Among the things we'll cover are

- How to use the comma to punctuate your sentences properly.
- How commas are used with geographical names and addresses.
- The rules for comma and semicolon usage.
- When it's okay to forego the comma.

The *comma* is the form of punctuation used to indicate a slight separation of information or a slight pause in speech. Its purpose is to add clarity to a passage of text.

SIMPLE SENTENCE DIVISIONS

A comma is used to indicate simple breaks in the information in a sentence:

- To separate the statement from a question

e.g.

Tam plans to **attend,** doesn't she?

- To separate contrasting parts in a sentence

e.g.

These are my **tickets,** not yours.

- To separate introductory words such as "now," "well," or "yes" when they appear at the beginning of a sentence

e.g.

Now, let's hear your side of the story.

PHRASES THAT END A SENTENCE

A comma also is used to set off phrases at the end of a sentence that refer back to the beginning or middle of the sentence. For this rule to apply, such phrases must be modifiers that can be placed anywhere in the sentence without changing the meaning or causing confusion.

Joyce smiled at **Doug,** who was flirting mercilessly.

Refer to Hour 10, "Main and Subordinate Clauses," for information on modifying clauses.

BETWEEN TWO MAIN CLAUSES

When two main clauses and a coordinating conjunction (**and, but, for, nor, or, yet**) appear within a sentence, the rules for comma usage are as follows:

- A comma is optional when separating two sentences joined by a coordinating conjunction in informal usage.

e.g.

Formal: Brian takes after his **father, but** he resembles his mother, too.

Informal: Brian takes after his **father but** he resembles his mother, too.

Because the comma is expected in formal usage, it is best to use it:

Paula wrote the **introduction,** and Donald did the index.

- Use the comma to separate two sentences when it helps to avoid confusion.

e.g.

When it comes to ice cream flavors, Cindy likes coffee and **chocolate,** and strawberry is Zachary's first choice.

JUST A MINUTE

If a subject only appears once in the sentence, do not use a comma.

Kay posed the question twice and still did not receive an answer.

A subject does not appear after the "and," so no comma is used.

After Introductory Subordinate Clauses

When a subordinate clause appears at the beginning of a sentence, use a comma after that clause.

e.g.

When a subordinate clause appears at the beginning of a **sentence, use** a comma after that clause.

e.g.

Do not use a comma when the subordinate clause appears at the end of the sentence.

Refer to Hour 10 for more information on subordinate clauses.

Here are some common words that begin an introductory clause that should be followed by a comma:

after

although

as

because

if

since

when

while

(Refer to Hour 10 for a review of introductory clauses.)

These common introductory phrase types should be followed by a comma:

Absolute phrases

Infinitive phrases

Nonessential appositive phrases

Participial phrases

(Long) prepositional phrases

(Refer to Hour 9, "Phrases," for a review of phrases.)

SEPARATING A WEAK CLAUSE

When a sentence starts with a weak clause, use a comma after it.

e.g.

If you can't get the work done in **time, please** let me know now.

Do not use a comma when the sentence starts with a strong clause followed by a weak clause.

e.g.

Let me know today if you are not sure you can complete the work on time.

Refer to Hour 10 for a review of clauses.

AFTER INTRODUCTORY WORDS AND PHRASES

When phrases of more than three words begin a sentence, use a comma after the phrase.

To finish on deadline, you must budget your time wisely.

On September 30, this offer will expire.

JUST A MINUTE

In formal writing, do not add letters to indicate date pronunciation (-th, -rd, -st, and so on).

Regardless of religious beliefs, on December 25, most people celebrate Christmas.

In informal writing, a comma after the date is optional.

THE SERIAL COMMA

To avoid confusion, use commas to separate a series of words or word groups when there are three or more in the series.

e.g.

This candy is to be divided among my daughter, granddaughter, grandson, niece, and nephew.

Use of the *serial comma* (the last comma in the series used before the conjunction—"and" in our example) eliminates any ambiguity; otherwise, it could appear that the daughter, granddaughter, and grandson each get a share, and the other portion goes to the niece and nephew to divide. When it comes to important things like candy, don't mess around! Those receiving it will expect equal shares (five portions, not four), so the sentence needs to reflect that.

JUST A MINUTE

 Remember that if commas are used within the series, use a semicolon to separate them within the sentence:

Fawn Corporation has offices in Podunk Junction, Ohio; Pensacola, Florida; and Winnipeg, Manitoba.

SEPARATING COORDINATE ADJECTIVES BEFORE A NOUN

A comma is used to separate two coordinate adjectives when the word **and** could be inserted between them.

> Charlie is a *happy, rambunctious* child.
> (Charlie is a *happy **and** rambunctious* child.)

If the word "and" isn't appropriate, neither is the comma. If saying "adjective one *and* adjective two" changes the meaning, do not use a comma.

Another way to decide whether the two adjectives are coordinate ones that require a comma is to determine the status of each in describing the noun. If neither adjective is subordinate to the other, the comma is needed. Therefore, if you can switch the adjective order in the sentence without changing the meaning of the sentence, the comma is needed.

> **Needed (coordinate):** Bertha was a dynamic, informative speaker.
> **Needed (coordinate):** Your cousin has an easy, happy smile.
> **Not needed (noncoordinate):** Murray has short black hair.
> **Not needed (noncoordinate):** Alec ate a big greasy hamburger.

A sentence can contain both coordinate and noncoordinate adjectives:

> The (1) informative, (2) insightful (3) grammar book became a best seller. (1 and 2 are coordinate; 2 and 3 are noncoordinate.)
> The (1) insightful, (2) informative, (3) compelling book became a best seller. (1, 2, and 3 are all coordinate.)

AFTER -LY ADJECTIVES USED WITH OTHER ADJECTIVES

When an -ly adjective is used with other adjectives, use a comma. (You can test to see if an -ly word is an adjective by checking whether it can be used alone with the noun. If it can, use the comma.)

---
e.g.

Taylor is a **lovely,** young lady.

Working in **dimly** lit areas can cause eyestrain.

In the last example, "dimly" is not an adjective because it cannot be used alone with "areas."

ISOLATE WORDS THAT INTERRUPT

Commas are used to set off expressions that interrupt the flow of a sentence:

Rhyming poetry, **as you may recall,** can sometimes include stilted language.

PROCEED WITH CAUTION

Remember:

e.g. means "for example"

i.e. means "that is"

When either of these is used in a sentence, it should always be followed by a comma.

You need to master a variety of things before you can reliably use proper grammar; e.g., parts of speech usage, punctuation practices, and proper sentence construction.

Learning the basics of good grammar is easy if you take the right step; i.e., study this book one hour at a time.

SEPARATING NONESSENTIAL WORDS

When someone or something is understood or identified within the context of the sentence, the description that follows is considered nonessential and should be surrounded by commas:

Matt, **who works at the car wash,** is still in college.

The young man who works at the car wash is still in college.

In the last example, we would not know to which young man the sentence refers without the description; therefore, that sentence doesn't require the commas used in the first example.

TASK: NONESSENTIAL WORDS TEST

Here are some hints to help you recognize nonessential words. First isolate the words in question (within the sentence) and ask yourself the following about those words:

1. Can you leave out the clause, phrase, or word and still have the sentence make sense?

2. Does the clause, phrase, or word interrupt the flow of words in the original sentence?

3. Can the clause, phrase, or word be moved to a different position in the sentence and have the sentence still make sense?

If the answer to one or more of these questions is yes, the clause, phrase, or word in question is nonessential and should be set off with commas. This sentence is correct: **With the exception of when he yodels,** Homer has a melodic singing voice.

EMPHASIZE WORDS IN A DIRECT ADDRESS

A comma is used to set apart the name and title of the person spoken to directly at the beginning of a sentence:

"**Doris,** could you set up a meeting with Professor Freeman for me?"

Commas are used when the name and title appears within the sentence:

"I contacted you, **Professor Freeman,** because I'm curious as to how you arrived at your conclusions."

A comma is also used to set off a name when it falls at the end of a sentence:

"Do you have sufficient data to back those conclusions, **Professor Freeman?**"

DIRECT QUOTATIONS

A comma is used to introduce direct quotations:

Professor Freeman said, **"I'll need to refer to my notes."**

Commas also are used to interrupt direct quotations:

"Okay," I said, **"Take all the time you need."**

"I'm not going," Kay replied, **"And that's my final answer."**

(See Hour 19, "The Ins and Outs of Italics, Parentheses, Quotation Marks, and More," for a review of how to quote others.)

JUST A MINUTE

Capitalize the title when you're directly addressing someone:
"Thank you, **Professor,** for your time."

RULES FOR COMMA USAGE WITH DATES

The following rules apply to comma usage with dates:

- A comma separates the day of the month from the year and also appears after the year. (Use of the comma after the year is now considered optional.)

    We agreed to meet on **December 31, 2001,** in New York City.

- Forego the comma if any part of the date is omitted.

    We plan to meet in **December 2001** atop the Empire State Building.

- Do not use commas when a date is written as day, month, and then year.

    31 December 2001

GEOGRAPHICAL NAMES

Formal usage still dictates that you use a comma to separate the city from the state and use another after the state; however, it's becoming standard practice to eliminate the comma after the state.

With a comma after the state: I've lived in **Podunk Junction, Ohio,** most of my life.

Without that comma: I've lived in **Podunk Junction, Ohio** most of my life.

GEOGRAPHICAL ADDRESSES

A comma is used to separate the elements of a geographical address:

The White House is at **1600 Pennsylvania Avenue, Washington, DC.**

Wendy lives at **123 South Park Drive, Amish Village, Indiana #####.**

PROCEED WITH CAUTION

 The ##### in the last example indicates the zip code. Do not place a comma between the state name and the zip code.

DEGREES OR TITLES

Commas are used to surround degrees or titles used with names:

Norville Bartholomew Smith**, Ph.D.,** is the son of John Smith**, Jr.**

Note that, in the last example, the period used with the abbreviation of "Junior" suffices for the end sentence punctuation.

Mimic the usage style of the person bearing the name title. Some use the comma after the surname and before the title; others don't. Likewise, some spell out the title rather than use the abbreviation.

e.g.

John Smith Jr.

John Smith, Jr.

John Smith Junior

John Smith, Junior

All of the preceding examples are correct.

However, when you are uncertain as to the person's preference, use a comma and the abbreviated form of the title.

COMMA SPLICES

A *comma splice* is another variation of the run-on sentence. (Refer to Hour 2, "Mastering the Basic Parts of a Sentence," for a review of run-on sentences.) A comma splice is a bit more ambitious than a run-on sentence, however, because the writer at least uses *some* punctuation and separates the two sentences with a comma. It doesn't matter, though; it's still wrong.

---

e.g.

Incorrect: Martin went to the **movies, Cara** stayed home.

JUST A MINUTE

For the record, the grammar check in Microsoft Word 2000 did not pick up the comma splice error.

Moral: You can't rely on machines to do everything. Some things you need to learn how to do yourself.

Keep in mind that any time you correct a sentence by rearranging the words, you need to ensure that the sentence meaning remains clear. Without addressing any ambiguity issues that may result, there are five ways to correct that sentence:

1. Go with two sentences separated by a period.

   Martin went to the movies. Cara stayed home.

2. Replace the comma with a semicolon.

   Martin went to the movies; Cara stayed home.

3. Go with the comma where it is, but add an appropriate coordinating conjunction immediately after it.

   Martin went to the movies, **and** Cara stayed home.

4. Begin the sentence with a coordinating conjunction.

   Although Martin went to the movies, Cara stayed home.

5. Use a coordinating conjunction in the middle of the sentence.

   Martin went to the movies, **although** Cara stayed home.

A COMMON ERROR WITH ESSENTIAL ELEMENTS

Essential elements of the sentence should not be set off by commas.

"That" clauses after nouns are always essential:

The dress *that Eva made for you* is beautiful.

The software *that came with this computer* isn't the greatest.

"That" clauses following a verb expressing mental action are always essential:

Greg **thinks** *that he can finish the proposal by noon.*

Sharon **wishes** *that her vacation would never end.*

Refer to Hour 5, "Elementary Sentence Components III: Verbs," for additional information on linking verbs that use a complement.

COMMA CONFUSION

Proper comma placement adds clarity to a sentence. Therefore, it's understandable that a comma in the wrong place can cause an illogical break and add confusion because of the unnecessary and unexpected pause.

We've covered the things to do with a comma. Some of the things you need to remember are

- Never use a comma to separate the subject from the verb.
- Never put a comma between the two verbs or verb phrases in a compound predicate.
- Never put a comma between the two nouns, noun phrases, or noun clauses in a compound subject or compound object.
- Never put a comma after the main clause when a dependent (subordinate) clause follows it (except for cases of extreme contrast).

  Marie was still in a good mood, despite losing the race. (This sentence is correct because of the extreme contrast; however, the comma is optional in informal usage.)

SEMICOLON

A *semicolon* is the form of punctuation used to

- Divide the independent parts of a sentence that contain commas indicating omitted words.

  The first part of Justin's book has eight **sections;** the second, **five;** the third, ten.

- Present a stronger break than the one provided by a comma before explanatory phrases introduced by words such as "for example," "that is," or "namely."

  Ashley enjoys many things about her current **career;** namely, the company car and her expense account.

JUST A MINUTE

It's okay to use a comma when fewer than three items follow these introductory words:

Sabrina may ask that we bring some refreshments, *namely,* *chips and dip.*

- Separate two independent clauses when they are not joined by a coordinating conjunction (**and, but, for, or, nor, yet**) or to join two related sentences (when the coordinating conjunction has been omitted).

e.g.

Heidi recognizes the importance of good **grammar;** she believes it will assist her in presenting a more professional appearance in both her speech and her writing.

The connectives "consequently," "however," "like," "moreover," "nevertheless," "still," and "then" are not coordinating connectives; therefore, main clauses that are joined using them are separated with a semicolon.

e.g.

Christy had planned to **attend;** however, something else came up.

Do not use a semicolon in front of those words, however, if they do not connect two complete sentences or if they are used as interrupters.

Kyle is, therefore, hoping for first place.

Ken, however, will be happy as long as he places in the yodeling competition.

- Separate items in a series when the items already contain a comma or another form of internal punctuation.

Dwayne lost his last three games with scores of **13:15; 10:15;** and **14:15.**

Faith can't decide whether she wants to decorate her room in **mauve, fuchsia, and orange; burgundy, scarlet, and chartreuse; or ebony, taupe, and fawn.**

Q&A

Q. Why do commas cause so many problems?

A. Most commas reflect the natural pauses people take when speaking. However, commas also provide a grammatical function that isn't heard in speech. You have learned in this hour that commas have specific uses in a sentence to separate certain sentence components. Mastering the comma will enhance the clarity of your writing and will also help you identify various parts of a sentence.

Q. How can you tell if part of a sentence is essential?

A. If a sentence changes meaning when part of it is removed, that part is essential and should not be set off by commas. If the meaning of the sentence doesn't change, commas are used because it is not essential to the sentence's meaning. The sentence won't change without it.

Q. When do you use a semicolon?

A. The primary use for a semicolon is to use it instead of a comma to separate two main clauses that don't use a conjunction to join them. Sometimes your inner voice will tell you which to use: Listen to the pause. The pause after a semicolon is longer than when a comma is used; you can often hear the longer pause in your mind.

HOUR'S UP!

Choose the sentence with the most appropriate punctuation:

1.　**a.** If you, bring the popcorn, I'll bring the drinks.

　　b. If, you bring the popcorn. I'll bring the drinks.

　　c. If you bring the popcorn; I'll bring the drinks.

　　d. If you bring the popcorn, I'll bring the drinks.

2.　**a.** I visited Boise, Idaho, but I was very young.

　　b. I visited Boise Idaho … but I was very young.

　　c. I visited Boise, Idaho but I was very young.

　　d. I visited Boise Idaho. But I was very young.

3.   **a.** Jessica got married; on September 12 1992.

     b. Jessica got married, on September 12 1992.

     c. Jessica got married on September 12, 1992.

     d. Jessica got married on September, 12 1992.

4.   **a.** Professor Irvine who owns a farm, teaches law.

     b. Professor Irvine, who owns a farm, teaches law.

     c. Professor Irvine who owns a farm teaches law.

     d. Professor Irvine, who owns a farm; teaches law.

5.   **a.** Angela, a nurse was late, for her shift.

     b. Angela a nurse, was late for her shift.

     c. Angela, a nurse, was late for her shift.

     d. Angela a nurse, was, late for her shift.

6.   **a.** The new improved, version will sell better.

     b. The new improved version will sell better.

     c. The new, improved, version will sell better.

     d. The new, improved version will sell better.

7.   **a.** The assignment, as you may recall, was due yesterday.

     b. The assignment as you may recall, was due yesterday.

     c. The assignment, as you may recall … was due yesterday.

     d. The assignment as you may recall; was due yesterday.

8.   **a.** June won, two awards at the spelling bee; Emma won four.

     b. June won two awards at the spelling bee; Emma won four.

     c. June won two awards at the spelling bee, Emma, won four.

     d. June won two awards, at the spelling bee; Emma won four.

9.   **a.** On my trip I will visit New York New York, Chicago Illinois, and Los Angeles California.

     b. On my trip I will visit New York, New York, Chicago, Illinois, and Los Angeles, California.

     c. On my trip I will visit New York, New York; Chicago, Illinois; and Los Angeles, California.

     d. On my trip I will visit New York; New York; Chicago; Illinois; and Los Angeles; California.

10.　　a. Three people are ready to leave, Keith, Allan, and Michael are waiting by the door.

　　　　b. Three people are ready to leave; Keith, Allan, and Michael are waiting by the door.

　　　　c. Three people are ready to leave; Keith; Allan; and Michael are waiting by the door.

　　　　d. Three people are ready to leave Keith; Allan and Michael are waiting by the door.

ANSWERS

1. d		**6.** d	
2. a		**7.** a	
3. c		**8.** b	
4. b		**9.** c	
5. c		**10.** b	

RECAP

This Hour covered commas and semicolons. You should now understand some of the problems presented by commas and how to work around them. Now that you have mastered the comma and the semicolon, let's move on to Hour 12 and learn about some of the other forms of punctuation.

HOUR 12

Other Forms of Punctuation

CHAPTER SUMMARY

LESSON PLAN:

In this Hour, you'll learn how to use many of the other forms of punctuation.

Among the things we'll cover are

- More about how to properly punctuate your sentences.
- How to handle lists.
- The rules for period usage.
- How to avoid the appearance of amateur writing.

The *period* is the form of punctuation whose most common use is to mark the end of a declarative or imperative sentence or an indirect question—in other words, a sentence that isn't an exclamation or a question.

e.g.

> Cody asked how many were expected to attend.
>
> A period will soon mark the end of this sentence.

A period ends a quotation when the quotation is also the end of the sentence. In this case, the period goes inside the quotation marks.

e.g.

> Nikki said, "And you can quote me on that."
>
> Simon says that everyone should "take a moment to ponder punctuation."

(See Hour 19, "The Ins and Outs of Italics, Parentheses, Quotation Marks, and More," for a review of quotation marks and for information on using quotations.)

Periods are also used

- After the letters in initials and some acronyms.

   Mrs. L. Sutton once worked as an **R.N.** at **J.T.D.M.** Hospital.

- To end abbreviations.

    Stir in a **lb.** of butter and a **tbs.** of vanilla.

- To form leaders that link information such as in a table of contents.

    Hour 11: Controlling the Comma and the Semicolon … Page XXX

- To indicate several different functions when used with numbers.

    1. For decimal points: **99.9%**, **17.6°C**

    2. To separate dollars from cents in monetary expressions when the dollar sign is used: **$9.95**, **$.42** (to indicate 42 cents or 42¢).

    3. To show the multiplication function in mathematical expressions:

        15 . 5 indicates 15 times 5.

    4. To terminate numbers or letters tabulating a list.

        1. First List Item

            a. First Subitem

            b. Second Subitem

        2. Second List Item

- To signal the omission of words, sentences, or paragraphs. (Ellipses are discussed later in this hour.)

When the last word in the sentence is an abbreviation or another form that ends in a period, do not follow it with another period:

I'm proud of that B.S.N. She is my daughter.

I need to diet, exercise, **etc.** Someday I will.

QUESTION MARK

A *question mark* is the form of punctuation used

- After a direct question.

    Are you **ready?**

- At the end of each item in a series of interrogative expressions.

    Has Nicole decided on the church for the wedding? the reception **hall?** the **caterers?** the **musicians?**

- Between or within parentheses to show uncertainty.

    Fawn thinks Michael's birthday is December 3**(?).**

    The Grand Poobah (**1086?**–1134) ruled during the Poobahtan Period.

In formal writing, do not use a question mark in parentheses to indicate sarcasm:

Incorrect usage: Wasn't that a good **(?)** use of our production budget?

Do not use a question mark to end an indirect question:

Correct usage: Lorrie asked Walter when she could expect him for dinner.

- After an interrogative sentence even when it is part of a larger sentence.

  What is this supposed to **mean?** Jordyn wondered.

- Within a parenthetical question either set off with dashes or within parentheses.

  It's already time (can you believe **it?)** for another presidential election.

  Our new accountant Fred Fussbudget—can you believe that's really his **name?**—says we have to trim our expense accounts.

- When within a sentence, a question mark and a parenthesis fall at the end of a sentence, the question mark is placed inside the parenthesis if the question only applies to the parenthetical material:

  Ernie **(isn't it a fun coincidence that his dad's name is Bert?)** won the blue ribbon for the best paper-clip collection.

- If the question applies to the entire sentence, the question mark goes outside the end parenthesis:

  How many times has Nadine sung on television (I mean on the national networks, not local **stations)?**

- If both the complete sentence and the parenthetical material are questions, only use one question mark outside the end parenthesis:

  Is it true that the Redneck Bar and Grill has a good chef (that is, can we count on them to cater the meal for such a grand **affair)?**

- When a declarative or imperative sentence is intended to be interrogative.

  This is what everybody's so excited **about?**

A question mark goes inside the quotation marks when it is part of the quote and goes outside when the quote is within the question.

Jessica asked, "Is that all there **is?**"

Who sang the song about "is that all there **is**"?

EXCLAMATION MARK

An *exclamation mark* is the form of punctuation used with a word, phrase, or sentence to indicate emphasis or show surprise:

Oops!

Son of a gun!

That's ridiculous!

PROCEED WITH CAUTION

 Avoid the overuse of exclamation marks! It's the sign of an amateur writer! This is especially true in formal business letters! It's far better to use action verbs and appropriate writing to paint the picture you wish your reader to perceive than to rely on an exclamation mark to make your point!

COLON

A *colon* is a formal punctuation mark used to direct attention to what follows it. Common uses for the colon are

- After the salutation in a formal or business letter.

    Dear Renee:

    Dear Ms. Bykofsky:

    Gentlemen:

    (Refer to Hour 11, "Controlling the Comma and the Semicolon," for a review of comma usage in the salutation of an informal or personal letter.)

- Before a series of instructions in tabular form.

    To install the hoochie to the **whatchamacallit:**

    1. Remove thingamabob from housing.

    2. Insert it in the bracket marked sprocket.

    3. Fasten with doofus calibrated to the dinglehopper.

- Between Bible chapter and verse.

    John 3:16

- Between clauses of a compound sentence when the second clause or phrase explains or illustrates the first clause.

    The committee has one purpose thus **far:** reaching an agreement on when to hold the committee meetings.

JUST A MINUTE

When a colon is used between two complete sentences of a compound sentence, capitalize the first word in the second sentence:

Complete, complete: That agreement may be **difficult: N**obody on the committee works the same days or hours, and all of the designated meeting rooms are booked for the next year.

Complete, incomplete: The committee members remain determined in their **goal:** to make the committee a success.

- Between hours and minutes.

    9:00 a.m.

    12:00 noon

    9:00 p.m.

    12:00 midnight

    at 9:00 in the morning

- Between magazine volume and page number(s).

    The Grammar Gazette, 12:6

    The Grammar Gazette, 12:6–12

- To indicate ratios.

    At a ratio of 5:1

- To introduce a formal or long direct quotation in factual writing.

    In her essay "How to Vegetate," Elaine **says:** "Learning how to efficiently do nothing is an art in itself. It requires a total lack of dedication. Sitting around in a vegetative state may look easy, but it isn't."

- Prior to a series or list within a sentence.

    There are three colors in the American **flag:** red, white, and blue.

- Prior to a list in tabular form, regardless of whether the list is preceded by a complete sentence.

    There are three colors in the American **flag:**

    red

    white

    blue

Capitalization and punctuation are optional in a list done in tabular format; however, both should be consistent.

- For title and subtitle separation.

  Hives: A Memoir of Allergic Reactions

APOSTROPHE

The *apostrophe* is used to

- Form contractions (for informal writing) by marking character omissions in contracted words and dates.

  Michele's worked for me since **'98.**
  (**Michele has** worked for me since **1998.**)

PROCEED WITH CAUTION

Do not use an apostrophe in abbreviated names and titles. Most common abbreviations also do not use an apostrophe to signify the omitted letters.

Sgt. Wm. Grunden, **ret.,** is my good friend.
(**Sergeant William** Grunden, **retired,** is my good friend.)

- Form the plurals of symbols, abbreviations, and some dates and numbers.

  1. When clarity is needed (i.e., the word is referred to only as a word).

     Check your wording because the excessive use of **and** in one sentence can mean it's a run-on sentence.

  2. When the plural of an uppercase letter could be misunderstood.

     The Roman numerals for the number 27 are two **X's** and a V followed by two **I's.**

PROCEED WITH CAUTION

Do not use an apostrophe when a word reflects its meaning in a sentence:

There are no **ifs, ands,** or **buts** about it.

When a date, number, or acronym ends with an uppercase letter, it does not require an apostrophe with the **s:**

How many **Ph.D.s** did it take to screw in a light bulb in the **1990s?**

- Form the possessive case of indefinite pronouns and nouns, using the following rules:

    1. Use an **'s** to indicate possession for a singular noun and indefinite pronouns:

        Kathan's artwork is innovative, creative, and pleasing to the eye.

        Jill is asking for volunteers; she needs **someone's** help if she is to finish the project.

    2. When nouns in a list all demonstrate possession of an item, use the **'s** on the last noun in the list:

        John, Paul, George, and **Ringo's** music marked the beginning of the popularity of rock groups.

    3. To indicate individual possession of similar items, apply the **'s** to each noun:

        Scott's and **Mike's** cars are both for sale.

(Refer to Hour 3, "Elementary Sentence Components I: Nouns," for a review of the rules for forming possessives for nouns ending in *s*.)

Apostrophes are not used

- With possessive pronouns to indicate possession; they do so automatically because of their function.

    Edith, **whose** rocking chair sits on the porch, is glad that the chair is **hers.**

- With names that signify a place, institution, or certain awards to designate possession.

    Mike got his **Masters** degree at Johns **Hopkins** University.

- With plural proper nouns that are used as labels.

    Channel 35 will televise an interview of the *Ohio State **Buckeyes*** dodge ball coach at 11.

Compound nouns, however, do receive an apostrophe; the **'s** goes on the noun closest to the object to indicate possession:

The *prosecuting **attorney's*** review of the evidence will determine if the case will require the *grand **jury's*** decision.

A noun or pronoun that precedes a gerund should be possessive and, therefore, use the **'s** when appropriate.

Elaine's *understanding* of grammar is one of her assets as an excellent employee.

ELLIPSIS

An *ellipsis* is a series of three periods (which are sometimes separated by spaces before, after, and between the periods, but the extra spaces are optional) used to indicate word omission:

1. Omitted words from the beginning of a quotation are indicated by three periods used as the ellipsis; the first word after the ellipsis will be lowercase:

   " … to fetch a pail of water."

2. Omitted words in the middle of a quotation are indicated by the ellipsis (three periods) to mark the omission:

   Jack and Jill went … to fetch a pail of water.

3. When the omitted words are at the end of the sentence, use the ellipsis (three periods) followed by the appropriate end punctuation:

   Jack and Jill went up the hill …

4. When the words are omitted at the end of a quoted sentence, use the ellipsis (three spaced periods with one space before and after each period) followed by the necessary end punctuation:

   In his most-famous speech, Martin Luther King said, "I have a dream …."

5. When sentences are omitted between other sentences within a quotation, use three spaced periods after the ending punctuation mark of the preceding sentence:

   The popular nursery rhyme says, "Mary had a little lamb …. The lamb was sure to go."

6. The omission of one or more paragraphs is designated by ellipses in the form of a single row of periods:

   This is the first paragraph.

   . . . .

   This is the third paragraph.

When the paragraph before the omitted one ends in the middle, use four periods to indicate the absence of the remaining words:

This is ....

....

This is the third paragraph.

When the paragraph after the omitted one starts in the middle, use three periods to indicate the omitted opening words of the paragraph:

This is the first paragraph:

....

... is the third paragraph.

7. Speech hesitation is indicated by the use of an ellipsis (three periods) between words to signify where the natural flow of speech has been interrupted:

"Please ... please help me," she begged.

HYPHEN

A **hyphen** is the connecting mark used between words or parts of words.

Words formed by adding prefixes are not hyphenated unless

They are compounds formed with **all-, ex-, quasi-,** or **self-.**

all-inclusive

ex-husband

quasi-professional

self-explanatory

The hyphen is needed to distinguish the word from a homonym.

re-cover (hyphenate to mean "cover again")

The letter of the prefix is the same as the first letter of next word.

pre-**e**xisting

sem**i-i**ndependent

There is a repeating sequence of letters that would be confusing or unattractive.

non-obligatory (would look like "no no bligatory" otherwise)

The prefix or suffix is added to a name, number, proper noun, or symbol.

post-**Newtonian** theory

pre-**1970** rock music

pro-**American** sentiments

Pb-free paint (stands for lead, an element in the Periodic Table of the Elements)

FYI   The final authority on use of the hyphen in formal English is *The Chicago Manual of Style;* however, it is becoming more and more acceptable—especially in technical writing—to limit the use of the hyphen to only those times when it is necessary to avoid ambiguity.

A hyphen is used to

1. Combine most compound adjectives that immediately precede the noun they modify.

   post-game party

   well-known fact

PROCEED WITH CAUTION

Do not use a hyphen when the compound modifier comes after the noun:
The *party* will be held *post game.*

2. Create compound words that contain numbers or combine with -half.

   8-bit computer

   first-time buyer

   one-half cup

PROCEED WITH CAUTION

Adverbs ending in -ly that are used as adjectives do not form hyphenated compounds.

fully functional design

highly irregular procedure

3. Differentiate compound words formed by two words with equal functions so that the newly created compound is a single word with a different meaning.

blue-green walls

one-to-one ratio

state-of-the-art design

4. Form all compounds created by adding -free.

fragrance-free detergent

5. Divide words (between syllables) that fall at the end of a sentence in typeset documents. Such words are divided unless

- The word is a contraction or a one-syllable word.
- Two consonants or two vowels are pronounced as one sound.
- The division means that a single letter will stand by itself.

Otherwise, words are divided according to common rules stating that you divide

- After a prefix: **non-traditional**
- Before a suffix: **help-ful**
- Between double consonants unless those consonants fall at the end of the root word: **bat-ter, yell-ing**
- Between two consonants between two vowels when each consonant is pronounced separately: **tan-gent**

JUST A MINUTE

When a single consonant falls between two sounds, the word is usually divided before the consonant: di-van.

However, if the initial vowel is short and accented, the word is usually divided after the consonant: haz-ard.

- Between two vowels when the vowels are pronounced separately: bi-ology
- Between compound words: bed-spread

JUST A MINUTE

When the compound word is also a hyphenated word, divide the word at the hyphen that's already part of that word.

DASH

A *dash* is used to add special emphasis beyond that which is provided by other forms of punctuation. For example, a dash is used

- To signal an abrupt change in the notion of the sentence.

    I suppose we could—no, that just won't work.

- To set off asides, explanatory comments, or parenthetical expressions apart from the general flow of the sentence.

    We thought Grandma's earrings were costume jewelry, but—can you believe it?—they're a pair of 10-caret diamonds set in platinum.

PROCEED WITH CAUTION

 The first letter of the first word set off by a dash is not capitalized, even when it is a part of a complete sentence.

- To add emphasis to nonrestrictive modifiers normally set off by commas.

    Jack Spratt—as tall as his wife was wide—could eat no fat.

- To explain a preceding list.

    Red, white, and blue—all are colors in the U.S. flag.

- To mark a passage of interrupted conversation. Two dashes are sometimes used in lieu of an ellipses and end-of-sentence punctuation.

    Henry had what sounded like a good excuse for his tardiness, but——

HOUR'S UP!

Choose the sentence with the most appropriate punctuation:

1.   **a.** Are you ready, or do you need more time?

    b. Are you ready … or do you need more time!

    c. Are you ready or do you need more, time?

    d. Are you ready, or do you need more time.

2. **a.** Hey! Stop, that thief!

    b. Hey; stop that thief ...

    c. Hey stop, that thief!

    d. Hey! Stop that thief!

3. **a.** The doctor said, you have nothing to worry about.

    b. The doctor said; "You have nothing to worry about."

    c. The doctor said, "You have nothing to worry about."

    d. The doctor said, "You have nothing to worry about?"

4. **a.** You have only one task: learn everything in this book.

    b. You have only one task: learn everything in this book?

    c. You have, only, one task: learn everything in this book.

    d. You have only one task, learn everything in this book.

5. **a.** Shirleys work is impeccable; she's very organized.

    b. Shirley's work is impeccable; she's very organized.

    c. Shirley's work is impeccable, she's very organized.

    d. Shirley's work is impeccable; shes very organized.

6. **a.** The cat ran away, howling, after I stepped on it's tail.

    b. The cat ran away, howling; after I stepped on its tail.

    c. The cat ran away, howling after, I stepped on its tail.

    d. The cat ran away, howling, after I stepped on its tail.

7. **a.** Apostrophe's are my favorite form of punctuation.

    b. Apostrophes are my favorite, form of punctuation.

    c. Apostrophe's are my favorite-form of punctuation.

    d. Apostrophes are my favorite form of punctuation.

8. **a.** Many programs are considered must, see television.

    b. Many programs, are considered must see television.

    c. Many programs are considered must-see television.

    d. Many programs are considered must ... see television.

9. **a.** "The wind," he said, "is blowing in a north-easterly direction."

    b. "The wind" he said, "is blowing in a north-easterly direction."

    c. "The wind," he said, "is blowing in a north easterly direction."

    d. "The wind," he said "is blowing in a north-easterly direction."

Quiz

10.   **a.** My friends aunt's neighbor won the lottery.

b. My friend's aunt's neighbor won the lottery.

c. My friends, aunts neighbor won the lottery.

d. My friend's aunts neighbor won the lottery.

ANSWERS

1.	a	**6.**	d
2.	d	**7.**	d
3.	c	**8.**	c
4.	a	**9.**	a
5.	b	**10.**	b

RECAP

This Hour covered other forms of punctuation used in the English language. You should now understand periods, exclamation marks, question marks, colons, and the other forms covered in this hour. Now that you have mastered some of the other forms of punctuation, let's move on to Hour 13 and learn about the rules of grammar.

PART III
Setting Your Style

Hour 13 The Importance of Knowing the Rules

Hour 14 Forego the Fluff

Hour 15 Getting the Job Done

Hour 16 Leads and Closings

HOUR 13

The Importance of Knowing the Rules

CHAPTER SUMMARY

LESSON PLAN

In this Hour, you will learn about the challenges presented when using the English language. Rules provide a commonality of understanding in language and make it functional. Rules give us standards by which we can better communicate. However, English is a tricky language, as we will discover, so mastering the rules can be equally complex.

Among the things we'll cover are

- The importance of correct spelling.
- The need for precise expression in writing or speaking.
- How to pare down your writing so it says the most with the fewest number of words.
- How to think and write clearly.

The great news about English as a language is that it is vast and expressive. Drawn from many other languages and cultures, it is continually evolving to meet current communication needs.

Unfortunately, that is also the bad news about English.

The problem facing everyone who uses English is that the language has more than half a million words designed to say just about anything a person might need to explain; however, mastering that many words is a life's work.

WHAT SPELL CHECKS CAN'T TELL YOU

Some English words are spelled with just one letter (I, a), whereas a word such as the medical term "pneumono-ultramicroscopicsilicovolcanoconiosis" can take up almost a line by itself.

Spelling revokes most of its own rules.

PROCEED WITH CAUTION

 Most of us were taught a little phrase that went, "I before e, except after c, or with a long a, as in neighbor or weigh." Well, that covers about 90 percent of all words but not such everyday words as "weird" or "codeine" or even a proper noun like "Einstein" that breaks the rule twice.

Spelling is further complicated by the fact that English is filled with *homonyms:* words that sound exactly alike when spoken, although they can be spelled as many as three or four different ways.

Homonym Examples

Variation 1	Variation 2	Variation 3
air	ere	heir
aye	I	eye
bowl	bole	boll
rain	reign	rein
rode	rowed	road
sees	seize	seas
to	too	two

Conversely, words that are spelled very similarly often do not sound at all alike. "Pay" may rhyme with "say," but that doesn't mean all words will follow the same pronunciation rule.

Same Spelling, Different Sound

Variation 1	Variation 2
cow	low
dose	lose
horse	worse
paid	said
sew	few

Many of our so-called "English" words land directly into our dictionary from other languages and gain acceptance as common usage without the necessity for translation. Spanish words used in English include taco, burro, lasso, poncho, and sombrero; French words include ambiance or resumé.

The number of words in the modern dictionary continues to increase at an astounding rate. Here are a few words that have entered the language since the post-Vietnam era:

- acid rain
- caplet

- granola
- instamatic
- Muppet

New technologies also bring us new words and phrases, many of which change as our understanding of the terms evolves.

The Evolution of Terms from New Technologies

As a New Term	Accepted in Common Usage
Internet	Net
on-line	online
World Wide Web	Web

Technology changes our perception of some words, too. In the 1960s, the popularity of Beach Boys music reflected that "surfing" meant riding the waves. With the introduction of the television remote control, channel "surfing" became the new rage. Since the advent of the Internet, "surfing" now means embarking on a search on the World Wide Web.

 See Appendix B, "Resources," for a list of recommended dictionaries.

Never take a chance on the spelling or current meaning of a word: Look it up!

MUTABLE MEANINGS

One serious problem in trying to master English is that words can be altered in meaning or in their "social acceptability" from one generation to the next. For example, in the 1950s, all working men were called "professionals." During that same era, however, to call a woman a "professional" was to imply that she was a prostitute or a streetwalker. By the early 1980s, the role of working women had changed drastically from previous decades, and the term "professional" had lost all of its negative connotations. Numerous other examples exist of words that were reinvented with the passing of time.

Making things even more confusing are words that can have opposite meanings. "Wind up" means to start a watch or to finish a speech. The "commencement" of an education ends it, but the "commencement" of a battle begins it.

Words that have numerous meanings can only be defined when heard in context. Different definitions of the same word become especially hard to follow when you attempt to convey one meaning and your audience assumes you mean the other one. For example, if someone writes "The boat is fast," he or she may know perfectly well what the sentence means. Yet the reader or listener could be confused. A boat that is "fast" can be a boat that is tied to the dock with ropes; however, it can also be a boat that moves across the water at a high rate of speed. Since one of these interpretations of "fast" is the opposite of the other, the reader could be left wondering what the boat is actually doing or capable of doing. Be sure the words you use have the same meaning to your audience so you can avoid the phenomenon known as "a failure to communicate."

HISTORY, ATTITUDES, AND HABITS

Language history is interesting. As noted previously, language evolves from one decade to the next. However, the very *way* people talk also evolves. Most people fall into speaking habits and use expressions that they seldom really think about. Because some English words or concepts have no neuter form, it is very common for a woman to walk up to a small group of women and say, "Hi, guys. What's going on?" Now, she does not mean "Hi, you *males*." The catchall word "guys" is just functional in all situations.

GENDER-SENSITIVE WRITING

In order to reflect that men are now more involved in what used to be female-dominated occupations and vice versa, language has evolved to include a neutral reference to all occupations as well as aspects of culture. Here are examples of ways to alter language so as not to imply a sex either way:

Nonsexist Terminology

Term	Nonsexist Alternative
businessman	businessperson
cameraman	camera operator
chairman	chair, chairperson
maid	domestic help
man-hour	work-hour

Term	Nonsexist Alternative
mankind	the human race
manmade	handmade
salesman	salesperson, sales representative
steward/stewardess	flight attendant
watchman	guard, security officer

TASK: EVALUATE YOUR AUDIENCE

When you're communicating through speech, it is important to consider the people you will be addressing. To help evaluate your presentation and make sure it touches on the key points necessary to maintain your audience's attention, there are some questions you should ask yourself.

Focus on an oral presentation that you expect to be or could be making in the future. Ask yourself the following:

1. Do I fully understand what I'm going to say?
   - Are my objectives clear?
   - Am I sure that my objectives match those of the firm or person I'm representing?
   - If there are guidelines established for the presentation, am I following them?
   - Can I reduce what I want to say to plain, direct language?

2. How well do I know my audience?
   - Can I anticipate my audience's nonverbal signals or reactions?
   - Am I sure I haven't made uninformed assumptions or judgments about my audience?

3. How will I get their attention?
   - Have I created a good rapport?
   - Does the audience trust me and have confidence in my abilities?
   - (If speaking) Am I going to vary my voice sufficiently to keep people interested?
   - Am I offering a solid set of facts?
   - Have I verified that my statistics are current and correct?

4. Am I correctly gauging their level of understanding?

- Are the vocabulary and professional terms appropriate for the audience?

- Am I remembering to conclude or summarize key points before moving on to a new topic?

5. Am I factoring in audience feedback and how to respond to it?

- Am I using open-ended questions to discover people's thoughts and feelings and to provoke opinions?

- Can I anticipate what feedback, suggestions, and ideas I'll receive from the audience members and have a clear idea of how I'll respond to them?

Use this checklist when you prepare any type of oral presentation. You can also adapt it for use in preparing written presentations. Also refer to Hour 15, "Getting the Job Done," for advice on adapting to your audience.

NOUNS AND VERBS

Now that you have considered language in general and have given thought to assessing your audience, let's look at specific ways to use the parts of speech most effectively. Because nouns and verbs are the foundation elements of any sentence, your speech and writing will benefit if you choose them wisely. (Refer to Hour 3, "Elementary Sentence Components I: Nouns," for a review of nouns.)

Use nouns that are visual and specific; they should make it easier for your audience to grasp your topic of discussion.

The word automobile is a noun, but it does not put a specific image in anyone's mind. However, the words "jalopy," "coupe," "junker," and "limousine" do. Ask yourself how you can make the image or meaning sharper by substituting one noun for another. Your first choice may not be your best choice.

Verbs are words that depict action or being. As with nouns, the more specific the verb, the quicker it will convey its exact meaning to the audience. Your job as a communicator is to use the verb that best conveys your precise message. Suppose you want to use a verb that means "wrote quickly." You have to be careful. If you say "jotted" or "dashed," it would imply that the writing had been done hastily yet clearly. However, if you said "scribbled," it would imply that the writing had been done in a fast and perhaps indecipherable manner. It is important to select your verbs carefully. Your audience will pick up every nuance and shading of a word's meaning.

VERBALIZING NOUNS

In selecting verbs, make sure you avoid forcing nouns to serve as verbs. Some words, such as "parade," are acceptable as either a noun or a verb, depending on their context. Others do not make the switch as easily.

"Verbalizing" can be downright funny if it is carried too far.

e.g.
___

If we can *water* the horse, can we **milk** the cat?

This example is obvious, but others may not be—so be careful. Stick to established, strong verbs. (See Hour 24, "Problem Words and Expressions," for a review of verbalizing nouns.)

ACTIVE AND PASSIVE VOICE

In using verbs, don't confuse *voice* with *tense*. (See Hour 5, "Elementary Sentence Components III: Verbs," for a review of verbs and verb tense.) Whenever possible, try to stay in the active voice.

Active and Passive Voice

	Active Voice	Passive Voice
Present tense	see	is seen
	design	is designed
Present perfect tense	have seen	have been seen
	has designed	has been designed
Past tense	saw	was seen
	designed	was designed
Past perfect tense	had seen	had been seen
	had designed	had been designed
Future tense	will see	will be seen
	will design	will be designed
Future perfect tense	will have seen	will have been seen
	will have designed	will have been designed

ADJECTIVE AND ADVERB OVERUSE

A precise noun will put a clear image in the mind of the audience. Communicators who are not in the practice of using precise nouns will often use adjectives as literary crutches. Instead of simply saying, "It was a mansion," a weak communicator will say, "It was a very big house." Similarly, people who are not in the practice of using precise verbs will often use adverbs as literary crutches. Instead of simply saying, "She whispered to her," a weak communicator will say, "She spoke quietly to her." Consider revamping your material if you find too many uses of adverbs such as "truly," "very," "totally," "completely," "really," and "amazingly." Using strong nouns and verbs not only will reduce the number of words you have to use, it also will make the meaning clearer.

GRAMMATICAL AMBIGUITY

You've learned a great many rules and guidelines by which to craft your communications, but you also have to make some allowance for the "common sense" aspects of getting your message across. Consider a parallel situation. In the law, there is the *letter* of the law and the *spirit* of the law. The letter of the law may say that it is illegal to drive down a city street faster than 35 miles per hour. However, the spirit of the law says that you may exceed that speed limit to rush an injured child to the hospital. Likewise, the common sense aspects of communicating can sometimes supersede the rules of grammar. Here is an example:

The word "everyone" is singular. As such, it requires a singular pronoun for proper agreement, as in, "Everyone has *his* book." However, how logical is a sentence that says, "Everyone waved to the President, and the President waved back to *him?*" You know logically that "everyone" at the beginning of the sentence refers to a group or a crowd. Therefore, it is more rational and correct to say "them" instead of "him." Let's see how we can put this rational thinking to further use.

WORKSHOP: LOGIC AND CLARITY

The idea of using common sense can help you improve your communication whenever something just doesn't "ring true." If something sounds wrong, even if you cannot decide exactly why, it probably *is* wrong. Yes, the grammar and punctuation may be correct, but the *logic* of what is being said just doesn't make sense. Here are things to check whenever this occurs:

1. **Do the math:** Consider these lines: "I was the middle guy they hired. Tommy came on first, then me, and then the Johnson twins." If there are a total of four people, how can you be the "middle" guy? It doesn't add up (or divide properly).

2. **Don't mix two different elements:** You've heard someone counter an argument by saying, "You're mixing apples and oranges." Avoid doing the same thing. Consider this line: "Last year our college had 200 students, but this fall we have expanded to 310 different classes." The number of enrolled students is not the same as the diversity of class offerings. In fact, just because the classes are offered does not mean they will have enough students to fill them. Thus, the sentence proves nothing.

3. **Avoid euphemisms:** Audiences get confused when communicators hide the meaning of a word or sentence by creating a euphemism for it. Instead of admitting that a college's grant application was turned down, the college will announce, "The grantor rejoined in the negative." Sometimes a euphemism is used as a way to "spin" the press; however, in most instances, it is best to say what you mean and mean what you say.

4. **Be sensitive to time sequences:** One writer used "oh fudge" as a sample obscenity substitute for a historical novel that theoretically was written more than 100 years before the 1847 English company process that resulted in the first chocolate confections. If you use a time comparison, it has to be in the proper sequence of events.

5. **Evaluate your word order:** If you say, "He gave her cat food," does that mean the man fed the woman cat food or that the man gave food to the woman's cat? Or is the cat a female? Make sure the word order in your sentence is such that the words say what they are supposed to mean.

6. **Try not to tip your hand:** When you frame a question or present a problem in a way that influences the thinking of your audience, you are disrespectful of the audience's ability to decide for itself. For instance, you might say, "Can we expect our school's tuition, which has skyrocketed from $14,000 per year to $26,000 a year, to keep increasing at these incredible rates?" Phrasing the information that way implies that the audience should be against this trend. Unless you are writing an editorial or a position paper or running for office, you should be a presenter of facts, not opinions.

PERSPECTIVE AND POINT OF VIEW

The angle and focus you decide on for your material needs to be limited to a topic that can be covered in the amount of time and space allotted. For instance, a vast topic such as "The History of the Guitar" would require a 300-page book to do it justice. However, a more limited perspective of that topic, such as "Leading Jazz Guitarists of the 1950s," would be manageable. Next, you need to see if you can capture the essence of the entire piece in one thesis or topic statement, such as "Django Reinhart of France and Les Paul of America developed distinctive jazz styles for the guitar in the 1950s that are still influencing musicians today." From this, you should write a lead paragraph that will captivate the audience. Don't forget when doing so that a *topic* is not an *angle*. ("Guitar Players of the Fifties" is a topic, but "Reinhart and Paul, Still Setting the Style for 21st Century Jazz" is an angle.)

Once the angle has been established, you need to provide a perspective that will "voice" your insights about the topic. Stringing together a series of statistics pertaining to numbers of records sold and numbers of people attending concerts will bore your audience. However, explaining how Les Paul figured out ways to rewire his amplifiers so he could invent echo chambers will help your audience understand *why* people bought his records and attended his concerts. He was someone who had created a totally new sound!

Let the style of your writing reflect the energy of the topic. Because the topic is music, there should be a lilt and rhythm to your words, not a plodding and stumbling of erratic sentences. Quote the musicians themselves to lend authenticity, both to the two musicians you are focusing on and to contemporary musicians whose styles have been influenced by your subjects.

If you have the misfortune of having to write about a topic that is far less compelling than music, treat it as a challenge to your presentation skills. Use the advice in this book and in the references you'll find in Appendix B to create and hold the attention of your readers. Make sure your point of view is always evident in the presentation. Use anecdotes and examples that demonstrate by illustration the points you are making. Make everything work together in such a way that the audience will come away knowing what your point was in presenting the information and fully understanding your perspective on it.

Hour's Up!

1. In gender-sensitive writing, which of the following are most appropriate?

   a. businessperson, letter carrier

   b. chairman, mailwoman

   c. chairperson, stewardess

   d. flight attendant, chairwoman

2. What is it called when words have different spellings, though sound the same when spoken?

   a. synonym

   b. homonym

   c. antonym

   d. acronym

3. Which of the following are examples of the active voice?

   a. has been seen, wrote

   b. has written, saw

   c. sees, writes

   d. will see, has been written

4. Choose the most appropriate word to complete this sentence:
   A _____ will assist you with your purchase.

   a. salesperson

   b. sales associate

   c. salesman

   d. either a or b

5. Choose the most appropriate sentence to include in a memo to your company's Computer Network Administrator:

   a. Can you list my Internet mail address on the World Wide Web site?

   b. Can you list my e-mail address on the Web site?

   c. Can you list my electronic mail address on the Internet site?

   d. Can you list my Internet e-mail address on the Web site?

6. Choose the most appropriate revision for the following sentence to avoid the passive voice: All travel claims must be authorized by your supervisor before travel occurs.

    a. Your supervisor must authorize all travel claims before traveling.

    b. Before you travel, your supervisor must authorize all travel claims.

    c. Your supervisor must authorize all travel claims.

    d. The supervisor must authorize all travel claims before you travel.

7. What refers to the process of turning nouns into verbs?

    a. gerundizing

    b. verbalizing

    c. nounification

    d. participilization

8. Choose the most appropriate phrase to complete this sentence: We should hire a _____.

    a. night watchman

    b. night watchwoman

    c. security guard

    d. a or b

9. Choose the most appropriate revision for the following sentence to avoid the passive voice: Your success will be determined by hard work and attention to detail.

    a. Attention to detail and hard work will determine your success.

    b. Your success will determine your hard work and attention to detail.

    c. By your hard work and attention to detail, your success will be determined.

    d. Attention to detail and hard work will be determined by your success.

10. What are important considerations when preparing for an oral presentation?

   a. understanding the subject

   b. using simple language

   c. verifying data

   d. a, b, & c

ANSWERS

1.	a	**6.**	b
2.	b	**7.**	b
3.	c	**8.**	c
4.	d	**9.**	a
5.	b	**10.**	d

RECAP

During this hour, you gained an understanding of how using nouns and verbs in a precise way and applying some logic to your presentation plans will help make your communication clearer. You examined the complexity as well as the richness of our English language, and you gained knowledge about how to use it effectively. Now that you are aware of the importance of these rules, in Hour 14, "Forego the Fluff," you will learn some more of these helpful rules by which to improve your communication skills.

HOUR 14
Forego the Fluff

CHAPTER SUMMARY

LESSON PLAN:

In this Hour, you will learn 16 contemporary rules of writing that can help make it easier for you to write, read, and remember.

Among the things we'll cover are

- Selecting words with the greatest impact.
- Holding your reader's attention.
- Simplifying complex material.
- Enhancing your first draft.

Whether you realize it or not, you have a goal with everything you write. Writing isn't just about authoring the great American novel. Writing and its subsequent objectives can include the following:

Your Writing Objectives

Writing Type	Desired Response
article	informed readers
business report	recognition
e-mail	favorable reply
loan application	extended line of credit
memo	positive feedback
novel	best-seller list
thank-you note	appreciation for your thoughtfulness

As you can see, regardless of what you write, your objective is to evoke the desired response from your reader.

THE RULES OF EFFECTIVE COMMUNICATION

The great British author W. Somerset Maugham once said, "There are three rules for writing a novel. Unfortunately, no one knows what they are."

Maugham's words ring true for other forms of writing as well. All writing presents a challenge, whether it's a novel, short story, business letter, or annual report. However, there are some basic rules that will help you not only in writing but also in everyday communication.

Use Everyday Language

In everyday communication, most people tend to use a working vocabulary of about 650 words. It's not that they don't know more words; it's just that that's all people need to use to communicate at the supermarket checkout or at the car wash.

Does this mean we can never use big words? Quite the contrary. Just remember that you help others understand unfamiliar words when you make an effort to place them in the right context.

Suppose you need to prepare a newspaper ad in which you describe a kitchen. Your ad could say, "The kitchen comes equipped with state-of-the-art appurtenances for implementation of the various items and accessories in making a culinary repast of impressive proportions an ecstatic phenomenon." English professors don't move very often, so you're probably better off saying that it "comes equipped with all features, utensils, and appliances." If you insist on using non-everyday terms in your ad, you'll at least establish the context for the reader to understand what you mean if you follow the original sentence with one that states something about "these state-of-the-art appurtenances …"

Don't throw people a curve. Speak to them in the traditional language of a circumstance so they will understand you immediately.

When you communicate, your job is to do so in a fashion that is clear and understandable.

Performance Art

Look at the nouns you use to see if they create a picture. Then check your verbs to see if each accurately conveys what you had in mind.

TASK: WRITE IT RIGHT

To add depth to your writing, ask yourself how a better word might be used in a particular sentence. Notice how the sentence "She read a book" does not put a very vivid picture in your mind. However, by writing "She read a biography" or "She read a novel," you are able to create a better visual image. Best of all, you did it without using more words; you simply did it using better words.

Next take a look at your verbs. Would "She walked" be better conveyed as "She limped"? A child would most likely "run" or "skip"; someone with less enthusiasm might "amble" or "stroll." Choose your verb to portray the appropriate action.

Go through your initial draft and examine the nouns and verbs. If you don't "see" or "feel" what is supposed to be portrayed, the reader won't either. Find replacement words.

CAN THE CLICHÉS

JUST A MINUTE

Rule #3: Avoid tired, worn-out expressions and phrases.

When descriptive phrases are used over and over, they lose their zest and impact. They waste space in a sentence because they make no impression on a reader who has "tuned out" these phrases due to repeated exposure.

Just as people who live near an airport become accustomed to the sound of airplanes flying overhead, people who hear or read the same recurring clichés and well-worn phrases ("clean as a whistle," "works like a charm") thousands of times don't pay attention to them anymore. Your job is to spot those clichés and eliminate them. Replace them with more vibrant writing.

FRUGAL, YET FORCEFUL

JUST A MINUTE

Rule #4: Use short words whenever possible.

Strive to use shorter words. Of course, there are some words, such as "unquestionably," that may not have an easy shorter substitute. In that case, consider using two shorter words ("no doubt").

Consider the impact of the following one-syllable words:

brief	bright	clear	cold
crisp	joy	sting	stone
taste	truth		

There is a punch and a vibrancy to these one-syllable words. Don't overlook the power they can add.

KEEP IT SIMPLE

JUST A MINUTE

Rule #5: Use simple sentences.

All great communicators across time have known the value of the simple declarative sentence. Consider these examples:

- On D-Day morning, when everyone was waiting for President Eisenhower's orders to come down to launch the attack, it was expected that he would send a long elaborate proclamation. Instead, he sent one simple sentence: "You will enter the continent of Europe and undertake operations aimed at the heart of Germany and the destruction of her armed forces." The men who had been training for months for this day only needed the go-ahead from the commander. Ike knew that and gave it.
- When General Douglas MacArthur left the Philippine Islands, his farewell address was one sentence: "I shall return."

Simple, direct sentences are easily understood and are more readily remembered than long, rambling diatribes. Get to the point.

VERSATILE VARIABLES

JUST A MINUTE

Rule #6: Vary the length and style of your sentences.

Have you ever listened to a monotonous talker who drones on and on and on until you find yourself falling asleep? When you're the speaker, you can prevent this from happening if you keep your presentations lively by varying the syntax, style, and length of your sentences.

Change the length of your sentences to create rhythm, pace, and momentum. Occasionally insert the surprise of a two- or three-word sentence.

PRACTICAL PARAGRAPHS

JUST A MINUTE

Rule #7: Keep paragraphs short.

Readers love white space on a page.

Children's books usually have nice artwork on a page along with one or two sentences of the story. Most of us learned to read that way. The books appealed to the eye. Most of us still like to turn a page and see short, non-intimidating paragraphs.

There are several ways to go about keeping paragraphs short:

- Use dialogue, starting off a new paragraph each time you switch to a different speaker.
- Break long paragraphs into smaller ones when a sentence begins to introduce additional material or gives specific examples that amplify the topic sentence.

You can also make a page more visually appealing to a reader's eye by using the following:

- Block quotations
- Inserts
- Lists (such as this one)
- Sidebars
- Subheadings

Word Position to Emphasize Meaning

Rule #8: Put the key words you want to emphasize either at the beginning or at the end of your sentences.

When you hit a word hard at the start of a sentence or make it the main thought at the end of a sentence, it is more emphatic. It carries importance. The word dominates all the other information in that sentence.

For example, suppose you want to stress the importance of time. Your solution is to put your time words at the beginning or end of your sentence. Notice how the emphasis on "now" is obvious when it is placed at the start or finish of this sentence:

e.g.

Now is the time for every good man to come to the aid of his country.

It is the time for every good man to come to the aid of his country **now!**

Notice, however, that you can provide the exact same information, yet lose the emphasis on immediacy, when you bury the word "now" in the middle of the sentence:

e.g.

It is the time **now** for every good man to come to the aid of his country.

It is the time for every good man **now** to come to the aid of his country.

True, the same information is there, but it doesn't convey the same urgency.

Whenever you have a fact, date, number, or message that you want someone to remember, start or end the sentence with that information.

Keep Things Active

Rule #9: Use the active rather than the passive voice whenever possible.

You will recall from earlier lessons in this book that passive voice involves the use of helping verbs. (Refer to Hour 5, "Elementary Sentence Components III: Verbs," for a review of verb voice.) The passive voice has its time and place; however, there are two reasons why readers prefer to read material written in the active voice:

- It conveys the same information in fewer words.
- It draws the reader closer to the events taking place (hence the term "active voice").

Take a look at the following sentences:

e.g.

Passive voice: The book **was given** to Tom by Bill.

Active voice: Bill **gave** Tom the book.

The first sentence uses eight words, and the information seems distant. The second sentence uses only five words, and the information seems to draw the reader into what is happening.

Unless you have a specific need to use the passive voice, try to avoid it. In cases in which the actor or performer is not known, the passive voice provides an excellent option: The book **was given** to Tom.

Here, the person who gave the book to Tom may be unknown, or it may be unimportant. The same thing could be conveyed by saying: Someone **gave** the book to Tom.

You don't need to avoid the passive voice entirely, but you should use it only when it's appropriate and makes sense with the rest of what you are saying.

PROCEED WITH CAUTION

Don't confuse the passive voice with past tense. You can still use the active voice to describe events that took place in the past. Using the active voice does not mean you cannot write in past tense. It just means that you eliminate the helping verbs. (Refer to Hour 5 for a review of helping verbs.)

Clutter-Free Commentary

JUST A MINUTE

Rule #10: Cut needless words, sentences, and paragraphs.

Get right to the point. Most people appreciate that, especially in news items, business reports, and other types of nonfiction writing. People who can get to the point in everyday communication are more easily understood and appreciated. Remember this simple guideline: If something doesn't move the action forward or provide vital information, cut it.

Beginning writers abuse this most commonly when trying to quote dialogue. They think that it doesn't matter what the people quoted are saying as long as they record what was said. This, however, is wrong.

Quotations need to do one of two things:

- Move the writing forward
- Fill in needed information

See Hour 19, "The Ins and Outs of Italics, Parentheses, Quotation Marks, and More," for a review of using quotations.

Task: Cut, Don't Paste

Go through your material and decide the following:

1. Would a stronger verb allow you to delete several adverbs?
2. Would a more visual noun enable you to cut some adjectives?
3. Could you cut a full page of background material if you dropped the same information into a short passage of dialogue (fiction) or used an appropriate quote (nonfiction)?

Look for ways to "tighten your writin'."

Conversational Narrative

JUST A MINUTE

Rule #11: Write it the way you would say it.

Avoid artificial, plastic language. Have you ever heard anyone but a lawyer use words and phrases such as "per" or "pursuant to"? Never, right? The thing to keep in mind is that these words carry a specific meaning for people of that profession. These words have their time and place. Unless you're a lawyer, if you try to use these words, you probably won't know what you're talking about.

Here's a simple rule of thumb for most writing:

If you would never say it, don't write it either.

If you do, it won't sound like your voice; even worse, the reader may not have any idea what you are trying to say.

Remember that, in your writing, you want to be natural. Read your material aloud and ask yourself these questions:

- Does it sound real or false?
- Does it sound as though I am genuinely trying to communicate? Or does it sound like I am trying to imitate some style of writing that I deem formal enough for the content?

Don't be stuffy. Good writing flows naturally, the same way good conversation does.

RESEARCH, THEN RECORD

JUST A MINUTE

Rule #12: Know your material thoroughly before you try to write about it.

If you were asked to give a lecture on sociopath profiling, would you feel ready to do it? Probably not. You'd have to do research. You'd have to talk to some experts. You'd have to find out some basic information.

You can't explain something unless you understand it yourself, whether it's an accounting procedure, a government policy, or advances in understanding the criminal mind. Ask questions, seek examples, insist on definitions, and request demonstrations until you understand the topic. Then—and only then—are you ready to explain it.

TASK: GET THE PICTURE

When you're interviewing someone or going over new material during your research, determine whether it would help your understanding of a subject if you

1. Put things into your own words. (In the case of an interview, ask for specific spellings of any words with which you are unfamiliar and consult your dictionary when you return to your office.)

2. Draw a diagram or put the data into a chart.

3. Compare it to things you already understand.

You have nothing to feel self-conscious about in asking questions. Just keep probing, researching, and double-checking facts until the matter is clear in your mind. Then you can do the amazing: explain the subject in language anyone can understand.

FIND YOUR OWN VOICE

JUST A MINUTE

 Rule #13: Be original.

Beginning artists often imitate the masters until they develop their own style. There's a difference, however, between studying the work of others and being a copycat. You want to emulate another person's work, not copy it.

Most great communicators become that way by reading a lot. Reading about how to write, however, can only provide so much benefit. You also need to read other good writers. Doing so will help you develop a sense of the pacing, logic, and phrasing that get a message across to others. You want to have a good story to tell and be able to tell it well.

People often think that, if they can copy the style of someone who is successful, then they, too, will become successful. The reason writers like Jane Austen, Charles Dickens, Ernest Hemingway, Laura Ingalls Wilder, Jack London, and Virginia Woolf are still read today, many years after their deaths, is that they had a distinctive voice, a unique style of writing that made their works fresh, vibrant, and intriguing. More contemporary writers, such as Stephen King, Mary Higgins Clark, Frank McCourt, Alice Hoffman, Sue Grafton, and John Grisham, stay on the best-seller lists because they, too, write in unique styles.

There is no room for a copycat writer, but there is always room for a fresh voice. No one else in the world will have read exactly the same books you have read, worked in the same jobs, lived in the same homes, traveled to the same places, watched the same movies, and experienced the same relationships. You are original, and your ideas are just as important as anyone else's. You can tell it your way. Stay distinctive.

PEDESTRIAN PATTER

JUST A MINUTE

Rule #14: When writing for the general public, avoid shoptalk and jargon.

Although the people you work with in your field speak your "lingo" all day long, the rest of the world may not be familiar with these catch phrases and trade references. Remember our discussion of lawyers in Rule #12? Just as you shouldn't try to use words you don't understand, you shouldn't use words that other people won't understand.

A young couple buying a first house may not understand common real estate terms such as "earnest money" and "point spread." A person making his first stock trade may not comprehend phrases such as "on margin" or "zero coupons." People not yet working with computers may not understand typical references such as "RAM" or "zip drive" or "OS."

Nobody is an expert at everything. Keep that in mind. Write in general terms. If you need to use a technical term or a business phrase, be sure to define it. Do not assume that, because medical, legal, or carpentry terms are familiar to you, they will be to everyone else as well.

When it doubt, explain it.

TIMING YOUR EDITS

JUST A MINUTE

Rule #15: Don't rush to revise.

Quite often, when you're working intensely on a project, you become so close to it that you find it hard to approach it objectively. This is a very common problem. Fortunately, there's an easy solution that works for most people.

If you set the work aside for a day or two, you can pick it up and look at it with a more critical eye.

PRACTICAL PUNCTUATION

JUST A MINUTE

Rule #16: Use punctuation wisely.

Some beginning writers are not confident in their use of punctuation. To compensate for this, they often choose one specific point of punctuation and use it almost exclusively. If you have ever read a short story written by a 9-year-old child, you might recall that nearly every line ended with an exclamation point! The child was convinced that this would make the story more exciting. Of course, it only served to show the child's inexperience as a writer.

Likewise, a page filled with ellipses looks like the paper has been riddled with machine gun fire.

Punctuation marks are like salt. A little bit is good, but if there's too much, you might not be able to identify anything else. Use of the question mark, exclamation point, ellipsis, colon, semicolon, and dash should be blended to enhance the flavor of your writing. Sprinkle them so they do their jobs without drawing attention to themselves.

You don't want people to notice your punctuation. You want them to understand your ideas. (Refer to Hour 1, "Understanding Grammar," for a review of punctuation.)

HOUR'S UP!

1. An effective way to emphasize a point is to put the key words:

   a. at the beginning of the sentence

   b. at the end of the sentence

   c. in the middle of the sentence

   d. a & b

2. An excellent way to develop your own style is to:

    a. copy other writers

    b. study other writers

    c. be original

    d. b & c

3. What techniques can you use to enhance your communication and make your language more illustrative and meaningful?

    a. visual nouns

    b. passive voice

    c. action words

    d. a & c

4. A good rule of thumb when trying to convey meaning is to:

    a. use long, fancy words

    b. borrow words from other languages

    c. use simple language

    d. use clichés everyone understands

5. When writing for the general public, you should always:

    a. use simple language

    b. use very technical terms

    c. explain technical terms you use

    d. a & c

6. When writing, you should:

    a. use as much punctuation as you can

    b. use only the punctuation that is necessary

    c. frequently use dashes, ellipses, and exclamation points

    d. a & c

7. Which of the following help to keep a reader's attention?

    a. long paragraphs and long sentences

    b. short paragraphs and long sentences

    c. short paragraphs and varied sentences

    d. long paragraphs and short sentences

8. Pages can be made more visually appealing by:
   a. using sidebars and lists
   b. using block quotations
   c. using subheadings
   d. a, b, & c

9. The active voice is preferred because it:
   a. uses less space
   b. brings the audience closer to the action
   c. a & b
   d. b only

10. When revising, which of the following are excellent techniques?
   a. a cool-off period before resuming edits
   b. cut information that does not move the writing forward
   c. change passive constructions unless they are necessary
   d. a, b, & c

ANSWERS

1. d		**6.** b	
2. d		**7.** c	
3. d		**8.** d	
4. c		**9.** c	
5. d		**10.** d	

RECAP

This Hour covered the 16 rules for effective communication. Once put into practice, they can immediately improve your ability to communicate more precisely and more succinctly through the written and spoken word. Now that you know all about the rules for effective writing, let's move on to logic and clarity in the next hour.

HOUR 15
Getting the Job Done

CHAPTER SUMMARY

LESSON PLAN:

In the world of business writing and speaking, communicators are called upon to prepare a wide variety of materials. In this Hour, we address the specifics of preparing many of these particular assignments and learning how to focus on the target audience for each one.

Among the things we'll cover are

- Determining your target readers or listeners.
- Writing ad copy and sales materials that will sell.
- Using press materials to make the public aware of your business or group.

Consider the different ways you address people in everyday life. If you pick up a 2 year old, you'll speak in simple sentences and small words, and you may even find yourself using "baby talk." If you speak to your spouse, you will talk on an adult level, but you will be casual and relaxed to the point of using slang, sentence fragments, and even grunts or mere nods of the head as responses. If you speak to a customer, you will be friendly and enthusiastic, and your choice of words will show respect and an eagerness to please. If you address a group of executives in your field, your presentation will be formal, you will use the terminology of your profession, and you will try to be concise so as not to waste the valuable time of your colleagues.

In each instance, you are the same person talking, but you adapt your presentation style to whomever is on the receiving end. In preparing materials that "get the job done," you must have the same adaptability.

TASK: ADAPTING TO YOUR AUDIENCE

Adapting your presentation style to a particular audience is an easy enough process to follow if you consider some basic questions before you write:

1. What is the age or age range of the person or people I will be addressing?

2. Is my audience female, male, or both genders?

3. Am I addressing fellow professionals or lay people?

4. What is the education level of my target audience?

5. What are the interests and "hot buttons" of the people to whom I will be communicating?

6. Do I know my audience personally or is it made up of strangers?

7. How much does my audience probably already know about the subject(s) I will be addressing?

8. What sort of response do I want from this audience?

9. Does my audience have any ethnic, racial, religious, political, medical, or social issues that I need to address or be sensitive to in my presentation?

JUST A MINUTE

When an audience feels you are knowledgeable about the desires, needs, and goals with which it is concerned, that audience will give you its attention.

Thinking through these nine questions and perhaps even jotting down a few notes or doing follow-up research to find answers will help you "see" whom you are addressing. The more narrowly focused you can become, the more specific your materials will be.

SELLING IDEAS

Based on a recent study by Dartnell's Institute of Business Research, it is estimated that the average business letter costs companies nearly $19.92 to prepare and mail. The stationery and stamps cost money; the executive who writes or dictates it is on salary while preparing the letter; the administrative assistant is on salary while typing and mailing it. Thus, a poorly written letter that does not "sell" something is a financial burden to a company or organization.

But what do we mean by "sell" something? It should be remembered that a business letter serves as the first, and often the only, means a business has of making an impression on a customer. The letter needs to "sell" professionalism, accuracy, and concern. It may take 15 to 60 minutes to compose a letter; yet oddly enough, if it succeeds in its mission, the reader should be able to read it in less than 60 seconds. The "quick sell" takes some time.

A letter, whether written on e-mail or stationery, is a very versatile aid to business. It can be used to confirm, deny, request, inform, promote, remind, suggest, describe, or even congratulate. Its ability to "sell" each of these processes depends on how well it is written.

APPEALING PRESENTATIONS

We are going to talk about a variety of sales letters, but let's first review some ground rules for all letter writing.

- **Don't complain, just explain.** Try to use a letter or memo to tell readers what you want them to do. Don't get bogged down in explaining what has gone wrong in the past. Instead, focus on what will work best now.

- **Make sincere comments.** Letters that are stilted and stiff because they are comprised of stuffy phrases ("my dear sir," "for the goodwill of the company") will not have a positive impact on readers. You should say what you mean and mean what you say. Be genuine. Tell the truth. Let your natural voice come through in your writing. Avoid starchy, unnatural phrases. Let the reader feel as though he or she has just had a nice visit with you when he or she finishes the letter.

- **Avoid jargon and technical terminology.** A letter is not meant to be an instruction manual, a warranty, or a sales brochure. Therefore, don't drop into shoptalk or technobabble. Keep your communication on a general level.

- **Use opening and closing remarks that make a favorable impression.** Just as your first impression when meeting someone (your smile, your handshake, your first words, your attentiveness, your body language) will make a lasting impression on an individual, so, too, will the opening and closing words of your letter. Decide carefully whether your tone should be casual (as in writing about setting up an annual golf outing for company executives) or more formal (as in expressing condolences on the loss of someone's family member or a professional colleague). Weigh carefully how you will conclude your letter. You may need to be gracious but straightforward (as in dealing with a delinquent account), or you may want to present a subtle yet specific message (as in a sales pitch or a request for an interview). Leave people with no doubt regarding the point of your letter, yet do not make people feel trapped or affronted by your words.

- **Read the letter from the reader's point of view.** When you finish your letter, let it "cool" for a little while. Then go back to it and pretend you are the recipient. Would you want to receive this letter? How would you respond or react to what it has to say? Is it clear enough, interesting enough, and precise enough? Are there any phrases, expressions, or implied meanings that could be taken offensively? Putting yourself in the position of the reader will help alert you to any weaknesses the letter may have.

SALES LETTERS

Each year, dozens of opportunities arise in which a business can make powerful use of super sales letters. The sales letter can be used to increase business by announcing a special sale, introducing a new staff member, publicizing the grand opening of a new outlet, or inviting customers to a convention or trade show. Virtually anything in the way of promoting a business can be done by a sales letter.

Sales letters can be reproduced inexpensively and can be mailed at a discount bulk rate, usually making them less expensive than radio or newspaper advertising. Even better, they can be targeted to a specific clientele or a known market of patrons. As such, their response rate is better than that of a newspaper ad, which goes to people who may neither need your services nor live near your business. The only catch to this advertising bliss is that your letter must be well-written. Many managers and supervisors who fear they might not have the skills to write a good sales letter shy away from this form of advertising. Actually, they needn't be so concerned. After mastering a few basic concepts about sales letters, anyone can learn to write them (including you).

TASK: PREPARING SALES LETTERS

Before you begin to worry about how to word a letter, think about what its contents should be. Once you determine what the letter should accomplish, the writing part will be much easier. Jot down some quick answers to the following questions, which you should ask yourself each time you prepare to write a sales letter:

1. **What am I offering my customers in this sales letter?** Make a note of the special offers you plan to present. They may include product samples, discount coupons, holiday specials, professional advice, or an hors d'oeuvre tray for patrons who drop by during lunch hour.

2. **What news should I announce?** Make a list of special information to give to the customer, such as new hours of business, new locations, an additional phone or fax number, new personnel and their specialties, a new selection of products, the creation of a new after-hours emergency service, your Web site address, or the remodeling of your store's interior. Remember to note when these new services will be available.

3. **What do I want the reader to do?** Each sales letter should have a single important objective. State that objective in one statement to yourself. It may be for people to call for appointments, to mail back an enclosed postcard, or to visit the office for a cup of coffee during an open house. Whatever it is, establish it clearly in your mind so you can highlight it in the letter. Remember that your goal is to *sell* something.

4. **What particular benefits will my clients gain?** Your objective is not to brag about your beautifully remodeled store or office, but to explain how that remodeled location will benefit the client. You have to come up with a list of benefits for the people you are trying to service. Make a list of what you can do for the client and then emphasize that in your letter.

Having answered the preceding four questions and settled on your letter's content, you need to write the letter itself. Each sales letter should contain the following sections: a headline, an attention grabber, a notice of the time frame to which the letter applies, a mention of the benefits offered to the client, and a closing sales pitch. If there is room in the letter for an appropriate announcement (one that ties in with the general content of the letter), add that as well.

- **The headline** should be a definite banner across the top of the letter. It should contain no more than five words, set in oversized bold type. Your word processor should be able to provide this option, or you can consult with a quick-press business to assist in this process.

- **The attention grabber** should be a short lead-in paragraph of about three or four sentences. This paragraph should hook the reader by making a promise, telling a secret, announcing an opportunity, or offering something for free.

- **The time-frame notice** should specify how long the readers have to take advantage of the offer being made. Don't be ambiguous. Make everything obvious. Instead of "We are having a Christmas sale," say "Our pre-Christmas sale will last from December 15–23." Instead of

"Please drop by at our open house this weekend," say "You're invited to our open house from 1–5 P.M. on Saturday, March 5."

- **The benefit to the clients** should be mentioned throughout the letter. Each time you mention "free coffee," "ample parking," or "baby-sitting provided," you add a reason for the client to continue reading. Keep in mind that the client is wondering, "What good is this offer to me?" If you can satisfactorily answer that question, you'll win the client.

- **An announcement** should be no more than one paragraph (unless the whole purpose of the sales letter is the announcement itself). Rather than some offhand bit of office news, announce something that ties directly into the theme of the letter. For example, if the letter is about the opening of a new boutique to be run as a companion operation to your hair salon, it would also be appropriate to announce a new credit-card service that would apply to both the salon and the boutique.

- **The sales pitch** is a short final paragraph that asks for the client's business. Your letter will have been hard-hitting about benefits. Now tell the client what to do to gain these benefits. It's time to make your letter pay for itself by closing the deal. Don't be afraid to lead the customer by the hand. Use phrases such as "Call us now" or "Just send back the enclosed postcard." Most readers will do what you ask if you've convinced them that such an action will be in their best interest.

The sales letter is a cost-effective business tool. It's easy to prepare and is reliable in its impact if you follow these steps:

1. Use this section to guide you when you write your next sales letter.

2. Keep a sample sales letter on file. You can update it and use it again every other year.

3. Keep a careful record of the responses each letter receives so you will know what sort of offers your particular clientele responds to most strongly.

Never worry about bombarding your clients with too many sales letters during the year. If each letter uses a different approach or offers a different deal, your clients will most likely take advantage of one or more of your offers.

FUNDRAISING LETTERS

Second only to the sales letter is the fundraising letter. With hospitals, colleges, summer camps, churches, and special appeals groups all competing for available charity money, a fundraising letter must be distinctive and poignant to stand out in a stack.

The objectives of a fundraising letter fall into three categories:

- An appeal for funds
- A request for volunteers to join or assist an organization
- An invitation to attend a benefit at which an organization will be able to explain its mission and seek donations

The more credible your organization, the more seriously your appeal will be considered. Certain organizations, such as the American Heart Association, the Lion's Club, the Salvation Army, and Boys' Town, have proven their legitimacy for many decades. They have a trust factor working for them. Your organization may lack such credibility. If so, your letter will have to be all the more dynamic to convince the reader that he or she needs to support your group's objectives.

Among the tried-and-true methods of successfully wooing supporters by way of fundraising letters are these practices:

1. **Relate a story.** People like to know specific ways in which past donations have been used to make a difference in people's lives. Anecdotes about crippled veterans being given artificial limbs that enabled them to become employed, stories about flood victims being provided food and shelter, or testimonials from folks who were able to go to college thanks to minority grants are all good examples of direct ways in which organizations put donations to good use. Don't expect statistics to move people. They won't. You can say that 2,700 flood victims were given a hot meal every day for a week, but it won't have the same emotional impact as one story of a specific family being fed. Be point-blank with examples.

2. **Convey a sense of urgency.** Explain that action must be taken *now.* Point out that the matching grant funds will not be available after May 10, that the supplies have already been donated for the disaster victims but that shipping costs are holding up immediate delivery, or that 98 people now on a waiting list for heart transplants could be saved if the hospital can purchase new equipment this month. Don't let readers feel casual about responding. Put pressure on them to respond today!

3. **Begin hard and fast.** Research shows that most people consider fundraising letters to be junk mail, so you must do something fast to

grab the reader's attention. A clever turn of phrase, a photo on the top of the letterhead, a promise of a tax break when needed most, or some form of personalization ("Your donation of $50 last year helped send 10-year-old Lonnie Jensen to camp for the first time, Mr. Samuels.") is needed to keep the reader from throwing the letter away.

4. **Don't open the door for argument.** Don't put debatable passages in your letter such as, "You know that this is the best way to donate your money, right?" (Maybe the reader isn't truly convinced of that, so why bring up the subject?)

5. **Focus on outcome, not on brow beatings.** Don't harass the reader for not having donated to his or her alma mater for the past eight years. Instead, tell the reader how his or her donation will help complete the new dormitory or will add needed science books to the library. People cannot be shamed into giving donations.

6. **Use a P.S.** The eyes of readers are drawn to a post script. This can be used as a "close" for the donation "sale" or as a gesture of appreciation.

7. **Find a celebrity to endorse your cause.** If your letter can be signed by a high-profile person in your community or, better yet, on the national level, it will be read more carefully.

8. **Enclose a return envelope.** The easier you make it for people to respond, the more likely it is that they will.

As with all letters, the fundraising letter needs action verbs, powerful metaphors, graphic images, and fast sentence pacing. The "pitch" may be for a worthy cause, but it is still a form of sales letter.

PRESS RELEASES

One of the keys to gaining high visibility for your business or organization without having to spend a lot of money is to make use of free publicity. This is often garnered through the use of press releases. Here are some of the most common ideas for press release topics:

- Policy statements that affect the community
- Business anniversaries
- Recent moves, new land purchases, or building upgrades
- Promotions, newly hired personnel, personal education

- Assistance to a worthy charity or community group
- Solving a problem common to many people
- Something routine done in a new or unusual way
- Something local linked to an item of national interest
- In-service training
- New looks at routine businesses
- Future challenges facing a business
- A record set, a survey announced, or an award received

Newspapers are 35 percent news and 65 percent advertisements; magazines are 45 percent news and 55 percent advertisements. This means editors in both of these media are eager for news tips and story leads. Your goals in providing material to these media outlets (and don't forget that press releases can also be sent to radio and television stations) will be to make yourself and your business better known in the community and to gain this exposure by spending as little money as possible. Let's dissect a small press item that you might submit to your local newspaper. Of what value is it?

Middletown, Ohio—The office of Eye Care and Wear, 2020 Main St., announces the addition of Mary M. Marydale as head receptionist effective August 14. Miss Marydale is a local resident who graduated from Middletown High School in 2001 and also attended Ohio Secretarial Business School. She is the daughter of Mr. and Mrs. Frank Marydale, 321 Farm Rd.

The preceding press release may seem to be short and unimportant, but don't let its size fool you. When this item appears in print, it will accomplish three major things:

- It will remind people of your business name and will advertise its address.
- It will show that you are supporting the local economy by hiring local residents instead of outsiders.
- It will give you the support of the entire Marydale family and all of the family's friends.

Best of all, it costs you nothing but a little time in typing and submitting the release.

The components of a press release are very basic:

1. Submit your release on letterhead stationery that has a contact phone number and an address in case verification of the news item is needed or amplification of the information is required.

2. Date the release.

3. Use a "slug note" that lists the town and state to which the release applies.

4. Stick to one specific point but supply all the basic facts that would be of interest to an editor and his or her readers (who, what, when, where, why, how, how much).

5. Label the release "FOR IMMEDIATE USE" or "FOR IMMEDIATE RELEASE" if it is of time-limited value or "FOR USE ANYTIME" if it is just general information.

6. Abbreviate the words "street," "road," and "avenue"; all state names when they follow the name of a city (unless they are extremely short such as Ohio or Iowa); days of the week; and months of the year.

7. Centered below the last line, type "end," "###," or "30."

 Among the useful guides to writing press releases are *The New Publicity Kit* by Jeanette Smith. John Wiley & Sons, 1995. ISBN: 0471080144; and *Six Steps to Free Publicity: And Dozens of Other Ways to Win Free Media Attention for You or Your Business* by Marcia Yudkin. Plume, 1994. ISBN 0452271924.

PREPARING A PERSONAL BIOGRAPHY

Sometimes, when you are asked to make a speech, you will need to provide the host with some information that can be used to publicize your appearance in advance as well as to introduce you at the event. Other times, if you gain a reputation as an expert in a field of endeavor, you will be asked to prepare a personal biographical profile of yourself for members of the media. You will need to include information such as your legal name, professional affiliations, and other pertinent details. Refer to the earlier Biblio File on publicity manuals; they include instructions on preparing your personal biography as well.

TASK: REFLECT YOUR PERSONALITY

Students of literary analysis quickly develop an ear for the writing styles of well-known authors. Ernest Hemingway's use of short sentences, powerful verbs, and strong visual images makes his writing distinctive. Conversely, William Faulkner's use of long, carefully balanced sentences and the Southern sound of his word choices make his writings very different from Hemingway's but no less distinctive.

The way you write should reflect your personality.

Every writer has a special advantage over all other writers. Since no two people ever have identical experiences in work, family, travel, reading, and hobbies, each person is unique. This uniqueness, as it applies to one's role as a writer, means there is no other person in the whole world who could express something exactly the way that writer could.

What about you? When you need to prepare personal written materials, think about the following:

1. Can you recognize what makes your writing unique to you? Often, writers who lack confidence in their abilities to write will "overcome" this fear by buying workbooks with fill-in-the-blank form letters. Thus, every letter "written" by this writer sounds like all the others. There is no vitality or originality.

2. There are ways you can discover your personal communication strengths. You can tape yourself giving a speech and play it back. Where did the audience laugh or applaud? What did you say, how did you say it, and why did it trigger these responses? Can you repeat that in similar ways in other speeches?

3. Which of your sales letters drew the best response from clients? What did they tell you about your letter that "sold" them on your ideas or offers? Can you develop that same delivery for other pieces of writing?

4. What sort of writing or speaking techniques do you admire in other people? Have you tried to adapt these techniques to what you write, yet add your own "spin" to them?

Review this section whenever you're ready to start writing. You'll see your writing reflect more of your personal style every time.

ADD FLESH TO THE SKELETON

One of the best ways to ensure that what you write "sounds" like you is to pare down the information to its barest elements and then reconstruct everything using anecdotes, illustrations, metaphors, similes, and examples that come naturally to you. Your speech, business letter, or newsletter article may be in front of you, reduced to a basic outline of key points and a few supportive phrases.

Fine. Now, as you look at this, ask yourself, "If I were in conversation with someone regarding this topic, how would I explain this first point?" Jot down the arguments, anecdotes, and illustrations that come to mind. Move to the next point doing the same thing and then to all the other points. When you finish, you will have the workings of something that will read, sound, and ring true as something written by you. It won't seem plastic or contrived or artificial or "ghostwritten." It will be the real you, and that is what people will appreciate.

ESTABLISH YOUR VOICE

As you continue to communicate as a writer and a speaker, you will discover a certain rhythm to your delivery that works best for you. You will gravitate to vocabulary words that resonate with your audience. You will rely on a set kind of presentation outline that fits you best. All of these factors will combine to make you comfortable with your "voice." Just as a comfortable lounge chair consists of a soft headrest, back-supporting cushions, and an elevated footrest, so, too, does a piece of writing consist of those stylistic elements that make you comfortable as a communicator.

AIM FOR SIMPLICITY, NOT SIMPLE

Being comfortable in your presentation is not the same as being loose or unfocused. Actually, the ability to hold an audience and teach that audience through natural, easy-to-follow presentation skills is something that takes practice and skill. Your goal will be to make things simplistic, not simple-minded. You will want to explain and define matters without talking down to your audience. As you've discovered in this and all the other hours in this book, there is a big difference between the two.

Hour's Up!

1. An audience's attention is fleeting unless you:
    a. distribute your speech beforehand
    b. offer cake and doughnuts
    c. are knowledgeable about the subject
    d. use charts and graphs

2. Effective letters:
    a. don't lay blame
    b. don't dwell in the past
    c. are sincere
    d. a, b, & c

3. Some techniques for fundraising letters include:
    a. conveying a sense of urgency
    b. relating a story
    c. begging and pleading
    d. a & b

4. Why is a press release an effective tool?
    a. reduces advertising costs
    b. raises company profile
    c. gets current information into the hands of the public
    d. a, b, & c

5. One way to put your personality into your communication is to:
    a. mimic other writers
    b. follow ready-made forms or checklists
    c. recognize what makes your communication unique
    d. avoid originality

6. What techniques can you use to add personality to your communications?
    a. anecdotes
    b. metaphors
    c. examples
    d. a, b, & c

7. Personal biographies should include:

   a. name, education, business background

   b. age and salary

   c. professional affiliations and areas of specialty

   d. a & c

8. "Establishing your voice" refers to the process of

   a. expanding your style, vocabulary, and confidence

   b. studying other writers

   c. observing presentations

   d. taking notes

9. Why should form letters be avoided?

   a. they are cost-effective

   b. they are impersonal

   c. they save time

   d. a, b, & c

10. How are letters similar to meetings in person?

    a. first impressions

    b. informal

    c. structured

    d. organized

Answers

1. c		**6.** d	
2. d		**7.** d	
3. d		**8.** a	
4. d		**9.** b	
5. c		**10.** a	

Workshop

Take time to listen to audio tapes of your speeches. Watch videotapes of yourself before an audience. Discover which phrases, anecdotes, or expressions you use resound most positively with your audience. Make an effort to go more in those directions when you write or speak.

RECAP

This Hour examined how to get the job done in regard to specific formats of writing, including sales letters, fundraising letters, and press releases. It also showed you how a writer can make his or her writings true to his or her voice and style. Now that you know about some of the key forms of writing on the job, let's enhance your skills in the next hour by focusing more on those important leads and closings.

HOUR 16

Leads and Closings

LESSON PLAN:

In this Hour, you'll learn about leads and closings and how to use them to grab and hold attention.

Among the things we'll cover are

- Ten attention-getting fiction techniques.
- Four nonfiction attention grabbers.
- Five reasons why endings and closings fail.
- Five techniques for writing effective endings.

Grabbing attention quickly is a necessity in our modern, frenzied society. Leaving the reader feeling satisfied at the conclusion of a piece of writing is just as important. In this Hour, we will discover ways to write leads and closings that will accomplish both of these goals.

SOLID FROM START TO FINISH

According to author Mickey Spillane, "The first chapter sells the book, and the last chapter sells the next book."

What he was stressing was the importance of leads and closings. Regardless of your communication forum, it's important to create an immediacy so that your audience will want to stick with you to hear what you are going to say. It makes sense that your ideas will have a greater impact if people are interested in learning more about them. The beginning of your presentation or report should have a "hook" that will grab everyone's attention and pique the audience's interest. It's the *lead* that will do this for you.

You want your lead to have some sort of emotional impact:

More and more Americans are smoking today, and they are finding it socially acceptable to do so.

You can probably imagine the first-impression reactions triggered by a lead like that:

- **Misunderstanding:** More people are smoking? I thought those numbers were down.
- **Outrage:** How dare anyone promote that nasty habit?
- **Curiosity:** Why would anyone promote that nasty habit?

The steps it takes someone to reach that curiosity state may vary—and they occur in far less time than it took you to read the preceding bullet points—but that curiosity is necessary if you're going to capture your audience and hold its attention. A lead is successful when it begins in a way that pulls in your listeners, viewers, or readers and holds their attention as you continue. You want them "hooked" so that, in the case of the preceding sample lead, you can continue to hold their attention.

LEAD ME, AND LEAD ME NOW!

We live in an impatient society. Back 165 years ago, people used to wait five days for a stagecoach to show up. Today, they get upset if they miss one section of a revolving door going into a bank. As one bumper sticker puts it, "We want instant gratification, and we want it NOW!"

Knowing this, you cannot delay "gratification" for too long, or you risk losing your audience.

TASK: TAKE IT FROM THE MOVIES

For the MTV generation with its multisurface images on movie and television screens, computer graphics that flash and move, and interactive videos, getting to the point is of the essence. People today don't want to spend 10 minutes building up to the main point of a report or presentation. They want to get into it immediately.

Here's an experiment you can do that will prove how very limited the attention span of today's audiences is as compared to previous generations:

1. Go to your local video store and rent two movies: *Gone with the Wind*, made in 1939, and any one of the numerous James Bond movies made during the 1990s.

When you put in the *Gone with the Wind* video, it begins with 10 minutes of film credits telling you such things as the name of the movie; the names of the actors, director, and producer; and even the name of the author who wrote the book on which the film is based. Finally, after what seems like an eternity, the camera goes from a long shot of the plantation to a sweeping, slow close-up of Scarlett O'Hara on her porch entertaining two young gentlemen callers. At last the story is underway.

Why did this take so long? In 1939, no one had a television set. So when someone went to see a movie, it was expected to be a full night's entertainment. The order of the day was to just settle back, be patient, and wait for events to unfold.

2. Next, replace that video with a James Bond film and look at the difference in the opening.

Why is there a need for all these immediate dramatics? It's because of television. After a movie runs its course at the theaters, it will be sold to the television networks. When the movie is shown on television, its viewers will be sitting in recliners holding remote controls. If the movie does not grab them right away—click!—they will start channel surfing to see what else is on. And with more than 100 channels to surf these days, it's unlikely they will ever get back around to the original movie they just abandoned. So the movie producer has no choice: either make that opening scene phenomenal or assume the movie will never have a second life on TV.

3. Use your movie-opening experience to influence the way you plan your leads.

LEADS FOR NONFICTION WRITING

Just as the movie producer and scriptwriter have to work purposefully to grab the reader's attention quickly, so, too, do you. If you are writing a news report, an interview, a profile, or even a sales brochure, your nonfiction writing has to have the same capability as the movie script to "hook" its readers. Let's look at four ways this can be accomplished:

1. **The shocking statement:** This is an opening designed to grab the reader's attention:

How would you like to age 20 years in just five hours?

That's not something you would normally want to do unless you're having a rough day and hoping for early retirement. But if you work for a company that distributes theatrical makeup and you're giving a sales presentation, that's a pretty effective hook, isn't it? It raises a lot of questions and makes people want to know more.

By starting your piece with an absolutely jolting statement, you will arrest your listeners' attention and will probably motivate them to listen further. This is the technique suggested in the "smoking" example we used at the beginning of this hour.

PROCEED WITH CAUTION

If you choose the shocking-statement method, make sure the statement relates directly to your topic. Otherwise, you'll lose the listener/reader—he or she will be wasting too much time trying to figure out what one has to do with the other. You won't have his or her full attention, and the impact will be lost.

2. **The direct statement:** This statement recently appeared on the cover of a corporate newsletter:

   It will be the only chance you will have this entire decade.

   My only chance? All decade? For what? Once you read more, you discover that the article discusses the census and its importance.

   By starting off with something that speaks directly to someone, you grab his or her attention. That is what is known as being "hooked."

3. **Clever use of quotations:** Using another person's words can sometimes help you draw attention. There are several ways you can go about it:

   • **Use familiar lines.** You can just use a line that everyone knows ("An Apple a day keeps the doctor away") and have it lead into your topic (a speech about an online medical database or a popular type of computer).

   • **Quote from a known work.** You can use a line that readers may not immediately recognize. You can then cite your source (the Bible, Shakespeare, the Constitution) and immediately show how this has a bearing on what you are saying.

   • **Use creative alterations.** You can take a familiar quotation and change it slightly, surprising your audience. Erma Bombeck used this technique in her book title *The Grass Is Always Greener over the Septic Tank.*

Any of these uses of quotations can hook your listener, making him or her want to hear more.

4. **Employing powerful descriptions:** Vivid description can serve to build tension at the beginning of an article or speech. It draws the audience into the setting by promising that there is something unusual here or that some catastrophic event is pending. It adds force to the impact of your words. For example, if you were going to report on a devastating hurricane that severely damaged a city, you might want to begin by describing the tomb-like silence that reigned over the city during the hour just before the hurricane came ashore. You could draw attention to the fact that cars had not been moving on the streets, telephones hadn't been ringing, birds hadn't been chirping, and children were not playing in the schoolyard. Everyone, instead, had been huddled into storm shelters, anticipating the terrible winds and slashing rains.

JUST A MINUTE

After this pensive lead, you could switch to very graphic descriptions of the onrush of wind and the uprooting of trees as the hurricane then came punching its way through the vulnerable city. The contrast from the earlier quietude to the subsequent cacophony would hold the readers or listeners in rapt attention.

In Fiction, Lead with Your Write

Because fiction writing is primarily a form of entertainment, its leads must be even more captivating than in nonfiction. Nevertheless, in fiction writing, a lead must also help the reader understand what is going on in the plot by revealing key facts about the story. Let's examine the duties of a well-written fictional lead.

Establish the Locale

Readers immediately want to know not only where they are but also when the story is taking place. The *where* may be obvious since the setting is described as a passenger ship, but a crucial part of the plot is *when* this ship is setting to sea. Is it during modern times with the worry of being lost in the Bermuda Triangle? Is it in 1912 when the *Titanic* went down? Is it during World War II when German U-boats were patrolling the oceans? It is important to establish the setting as soon as possible so readers won't feel uneasy or confused. Yes, readers don't mind being flexible. They will go back to Robin Hood days with you or ahead to the future, but you have to let them know where and when the events of the story are occurring.

Set Up the Story Setting

A story's title doesn't always indicate what sort of story is about to be told. The title *Catch-22* gives no indication that the novel is about World War II bomber aviators. *Angela's Ashes* no more indicates that it is a story about poverty-stricken Irish peasants than *The Thorn Birds* indicates that it is about Australian sheepherders. Knowing this, the writer has to indicate quickly through other stylistic means what kind of story it is. If it is a mystery, then a theft or murder needs to be committed. If it is a comedy, then something funny needs to happen right away. If it is a romance or a melodrama or a western or a spy story, indication of this needs to be cued to the reader at the outset. (This is not to say that two genres cannot be combined, such as a western/comedy or a mystery/romance.)

Introduce the Main Characters

Readers need to start bonding with the central characters as early as possible in the story. To do this, the characters have to be "visible" to the readers. They need to know the characters' names, physical descriptions, occupations, general ages, and personal interests. The challenge comes in trying to convey this information without just "reporting" it to the readers.

A short but active opening scene can give a lot of information about the characters, such as what they look like, what they do for a living, and what their personalities are like. Insert some subtle pieces of information. Stated and implied information help readers relate to the central characters.

Set the Tone

Readers usually come to a piece of writing with no preconceived notions as to what it will be like. As such, they try to pick up from the text what sort of attitudes they should have toward the characters and the story. Should they be respectful of the characters or should they be ready to laugh at them (or laugh *with* them)? The tone of a police procedural novel might be serious, businesslike, even dramatic. However, the tone of a comedy novel would be lighthearted, whimsical, and humorous. Your job as the writer is to establish the mood and set the tone of the story at the beginning. Use words, scenes, episodes, and character behavior to portray the "atmosphere" of the story.

GET TO THE CONFLICT QUICKLY

As noted earlier, modern readers are impatient. They want something to occur very early in a story to raise their curiosity, to give them a reason to turn the page, to cause them to stay with the story. If you wait too long to provide such events, you risk losing your reader's interest. We will next look at 10 processes by which successful writers can snare their readers.

IN THE BEGINNING

As we look at these 10 techniques for grabbing the attention of readers, keep in mind that some will have crossover applications. Many of them can also be used as openings for speeches, sales pitches, or scripts for training films.

JUST A MINUTE

No matter what kind of communicating you are doing, if you don't first grab the attention of your audience, you won't succeed in your overall presentation.

1. **The absorbing action scene:** As noted earlier in the James Bond example, a fast-paced action scene can rivet people to a movie or book. Knowing this, you might want to think about your overall plot and choose to open with a storm at sea or a gun fight or a high-speed auto chase.

2. **A strong descriptive passage:** Just as we discovered that descriptive passages work effectively for nonfiction articles or speeches, they also can work effectively in fiction. You may want to open your story with a detailed description of a spooky old house that your characters are going to have to enter. You could make the readers smell the mildew in the air, feel the cobwebs on their faces, hear the rotting boards crack under their feet, and see the sagging shingles and gutters. With just a few brief paragraphs, the readers would "be there."

3. **An opening dialogue challenge:** To draw readers immediately into the conflict of a story, you can open with two people having a heated argument, a drowning teenager screaming for help, or a prosecuting attorney pointing a finger into the face of a defendant and asking a series of

blunt questions. Just by overhearing these words, the readers will know what the conflict is about. The readers will be intrigued enough to want to see how the situation is resolved.

4. **The pending action sequence:** By opening a story with a promise that something monumental is about to occur, readers will be eager to stay and see how the event culminates. In Edgar Allan Poe's short story "The Cask of Amontillado," the author begins the story by saying, "The thousand injuries of Fortunato I had borne as I best could; but when he ventured on insult, I vowed my revenge." The readers immediately assume that the narrator is going to do something terrible to Fortunato, so they continue to read to see what that will be. They aren't disappointed. The narrator eventually lures Fortunato into a cavern and seals him alive in a tomb. The opening lines promise some sort of action, and the author delivers on that promise.

5. **The suspenseful introduction:** Suspense is created in the opening of a story when the readers are aware of what is happening in the story but the characters in the story are not. Thus, if the Lone Ranger and Tonto are riding quickly down the trail and are unaware that an ambush is waiting for them at the next bend, the all-knowing audience will be compelled to stay with the story to discover whether the heroes will escape their pending doom. This is why the opening chapter of Peter Benchley's novel *Jaws* is so terrifying. The readers know that the giant shark is swimming in the shore waters, but the teenage girl going for a night swim does *not* know this. The result: gulp!

6. **The humorous introduction:** Stand-up comics win audiences by coming on stage and immediately saying something funny. The late Jackie Vernon was once told to wear a cowboy outfit for a skit on a television variety show. He employed what is known as the "reverse," surprising the audience with an unexpected twist in his dialogue, when he walked out and said, "My grandfather was an old Indian fighter. My grandmother was an old Indian."

JUST A MINUTE

Writers can use this same gimmick to open a story or a speech. The funny lines need to be tested on a preview audience of listeners or readers. Something isn't funny until it actually makes someone laugh.

7. **The appeal to the senses:** By making a reader or listener aware of the sensory aspects of a scene or circumstance, the writer will help him or

her "fit" into the story. For example, if you want to help someone know what pioneer living was like, you could present the positive sensory aspects of that life: the fresh scent of pine trees, the clean taste of water from a mountain stream, the shrill caw of an eagle flying overhead, and the vision of beautiful snowcapped mountains in the distance. You could also present the negative sensory aspects: the foul smell of laboring oxen, the gritty taste of dried and stale corn during winter, the touch of picky mattresses made of straw, and the lonely wail of a hungry coyote. By combining the two, the overall experience will become vivid and will draw the reader into the story.

8. **The shocking scene:** Just as in nonfiction, in which a shocking statement can grab a person's immediate attention, a shocking scene works effectively in fiction writing. Horror writers such as John Saul and Stephen King use this technique frequently. By opening a story with a description of a very graphic knife fight in a prison yard or a vicious rape in a city alley or an abduction of a child from a playground, the reader will be horrified yet mesmerized. Granted, this sort of lead will certainly not appeal to all readers, but it can be effective if written well.

9. **Start in the middle:** There is no law that says a story has to be told in chronological order. Sometimes it is more effective to start in the middle, come back to the beginning, and then go to the ending. For instance, you might want to open your story with a private detective coming upon a murder scene, then flash back to how the detective was hired earlier to protect the woman who was killed, and then conclude by having the detective track down the murderer. Instead of a 1-2-3 order, it's a 2-1-3 order. It works.

10. **Begin two plots simultaneously:** Although difficult to pull off, there are times when telling two stories simultaneously in sequential passages can be very powerful. A love story might begin with a man starting his day in one part of the city and a woman starting her day in another part of the city. The man reads the morning paper and sees a job opening advertised at a certain store. The woman reads about the same job. They each decide to go for an interview. The writer continues to move the readers back and forth from the man to the woman, getting the readers to like both characters while also making it obvious that only one will be able to get the job. What will happen when the two plots finally converge as both characters arrive for the same interview? Therein lies the suspense and the cause for the readers to continue to turn pages.

ALL'S WELL THAT ENDS WELL

Now that we have learned how to write leads for fiction and nonfiction that work effectively, let's go to the other side of the bookends and take a look at closings and why they're important.

If a reader finishes a piece of writing feeling that it was worth his or her time and that it was informative and/or entertaining, he or she will be inclined to read additional material by the same writer. However, if either the lead (sometimes spelled *lede*) or the closing disappoints the reader, the entire piece of writing will have failed.

You've probably had that experience yourself. You've been watching a movie for 90 minutes when suddenly it builds to its climatic ending, but instead of turning out logically, the whole story ends on a bizarre note. You are left wondering, "What was that all about?" Later, when people ask you if you would recommend the movie, your answer is, "Naw, it's not worth the time." In effect, because the ending failed, your opinion is that the whole movie failed.

Most of the time when a memo or a business report or even a short story closes poorly, it is because of one of five specific reasons. Knowing what they are will help you avoid them.

1. **Prejudicial material:** Trying to mandate how a reader must feel about an issue will usually alienate the reader. Sending around a company memo letting employees know that they can leave work early to go out and vote is fine, but ending it with an endorsement for a specific political party is not acceptable. Likewise, writing a company report about the tightness of the annual budget is all right, but not if it concludes with a statement such as, "So, if we want better profits next year, let's make sure we remain a nonunion company." Just present the facts. Don't add your opinion or personal judgments regarding a matter. (Save that for political speeches or newspaper editorials.)

2. **Redundant material:** If you have explained your points well in a business letter, e-mail message, or corporate report, it just wastes time and space to write, "In summary … " and then start restating all of your points. If the reader has missed a point, he or she can go back and read the material again. The only exception to this rule is in speech writing. Since the audience may not have a copy of your speech outline, it

would not hurt to do a very brief summarization of your key points (without amplification or detailing).

3. **Unresolved issues:** Stories that stop without solving a crime or without telling who won the sporting event leave the reader hanging. That's unfair. Similarly, reports that stress the need for budget cuts yet offer no suggestions regarding how this can be done or how soon these cuts need to be made will just frustrate the reader. All writings need to be concluded, and issues need to be resolved; otherwise, your writing has been for naught.

4. **Listlessness:** Some writers get it into their minds that they need to write a "one-page letter" or a "half-page memo" or a "1,500-word term paper." Once this spatial obligation has been met, the writer stops writing. That is called "stopping," not "closing." The reader needs to know that something has been concluded, ended, completed.

PROCEED WITH CAUTION

 A writer cannot just slow down and then stop, as though he or she has run out of steam. An ending must be a strong finish, not a listless collapse.

5. **Unrelated material:** If a memo has the heading "Staff Picnic," that is what it should be about. Getting off topic and ending with an appeal for everyone to be part of the annual blood drive diverts the reader's attention from the primary topic. Even worse, people interested in donating blood might not be interested in attending the staff picnic, but if they ignore the memo because of the heading, they'll never get the news they needs. Stick to the topic at hand and bring it to a specific conclusion.

THE FINISHING TOUCHES

Now that we know what *not* to do, let's learn what techniques *should* be used in writing effective closings.

1. **The echo effect:** Although a piece of writing should not repeat what has already been stated, the use of a response echo can be effective. When your lead statement calls out a problem and your closing statement echoes back an answer, the reader is left feeling informed about an issue.

A short e-mail memo might begin by stating that leaving lights on in offices and rooms not being used costs the company an extra $1,000 annually in electric bills and replacement bulbs. The memo might conclude with a solution: "So please just remember to 'click and close' as you walk out the door." The reader is both informed of the problem and given a suggestion as to how to correct it.

2. **The agreement affirmation:** If an editorial or personality profile has depicted a strong message that virtually all readers can identify with, the only thing the closing statement needs to be is a flat statement of what already has been proven. The reader will nod as if to say, "I agree wholeheartedly with that."

If a story has been written about an American POW in Vietnam who confused his captors for five years and finally escaped to freedom, a good closing statement would be: "The enemy interrogators had taken away Captain Wilson's freedom, his uniform, his food, and his proximity to the other soldiers. The thing they were never able to take away from him, however, was his determination to survive!" The reader will agree and will feel satisfied with this sort of conclusion.

3. **The ironic twist:** Readers will accept a surprise ending to a story as long as it makes sense within the context of the story. A news article about a prisoner who served six years busting rocks and filling sandbags might also relate how the man went to school while in prison and got degrees in accounting and computers. However, the twist ending to the story would be the fact that, once the man was released from prison, no one would give him a job handling money because he was a convicted felon. As a result, the only job he could secure was a position with a gravel company—busting rocks and filling sandbags. The reader will not expect this ending but will accept it because it is believable within the context of the overall story.

4. **The joke or pun:** There is an old Vaudeville adage that says, "Leave 'em laughing." That's not bad advice. If you can conclude your press release or sales letter or convention speech with a little levity, most people will enjoy it. It doesn't have to be a knee-slapper of a joke. Anything that evokes a smile will be sufficient. A savings and loan company recently sent out a promotional letter that ended with a pun: "Our products and services are things you can *bank* on." (Hey, for bankers, that's not too bad.)

5. **A powerful quotation:** We saw earlier how three variations of quotations can be used as effective leads. An all-inclusive summary statement from a person being interviewed can likewise be an effective closing. A pledge by a college president to take his or her school boldly forward into the realm of advanced technology would make a good closing quotation.

A convincing prediction by a manager about the optimistic prospects of his corporation would also be a good closing. This "voice of authority" conclusion carries weight with readers and listeners.

HOUR'S UP!

During the next two weeks, make a point of listening to the ways people initiate conversations, sermons, speeches, and news reports. What techniques do they use to capture your attention? Similarly, pay attention to the ways they conclude their presentations. How did you feel afterward, informed or confused? Draw personal applications from these examples.

1. In order to grab your audience's attention, you can use:
    a. a lead
    b. an index
    c. an illustration
    d. a, b, & c

2. What are some of the techniques you can use for effective fiction leads?
    a. tone
    b. setting
    c. characters
    d. a, b, & c

3. What kind of lead grabs the reader's attention by jolting him or her?
    a. shocking statement
    b. powerful description
    c. direct statement
    d. quotation

4. What kind of fiction lead starts off in the middle of a conflict?

    a. action scene

    b. humorous introduction

    c. descriptive passage

    d. dialogue

5. What kind of close gives the reader a surprise ending?

    a. echo effect

    b. powerful quotation

    c. joke or pun

    d. ironic twist

6. What kind of lead sets the stage and makes the reader or listener expect something important?

    a. quotation

    b. shocking statement

    c. powerful description

    d. direct statement

7. What is a close called that answers a problem mentioned earlier?

    a. powerful quotation

    b. echo effect

    c. agreement affirmation

    d. joke or pun

8. What kind of lead speaks directly to the reader?

    a. shocking description

    b. direct statement

    c. powerful description

    d. quotation

9. What kind of close sums up the points already made?

    a. joke or pun

    b. agreement affirmation

    c. echo effect

    d. ironic twist

10. What kind of lead uses a joke or funny story to catch the audience's attention?

    a. strong descriptive passage

    b. suspenseful introduction

    c. pending action sequence

    d. humorous introduction

ANSWERS

1.	a	**6.**	c
2.	d	**7.**	b
3.	a	**8.**	b
4.	a	**9.**	b
5.	d	**10.**	d

RECAP

This Hour's lesson focused on leads and closings. You now should understand how to use leads in both fiction and nonfiction. You should also understand what causes closings to fail, how to avoid these problems, and how to write closings that succeed. Now that you have mastered leads and closings, let's move on to Hour 17 and learn how to develop ideas.

PART IV

Putting Your Style into Practice

Hour 17 Developing Ideas

Hour 18 Managing Your Research

Hour 19 The Ins and Outs of Italics,
Parentheses, Quotation Marks,
and More

Hour 20 Remain on Task

Hour 21 Getting Beyond Your First Draft

Hour 22 Putting Your Style into Practice I

Hour 23 Putting Your Style into Practice II

Hour 24 Problem Words and Expressions

HOUR 17
Developing Ideas

CHAPTER SUMMARY

LESSON PLAN:

In this Hour, you'll learn about ways to come up with and develop ideas.

Among the things we'll cover are

- Where to look for ideas.
- Scrutinizing the ideas you find.
- How to gather idea information.
- Ways to maximize the creative process.

Mind mapping is a process in which you can quickly organize your thoughts before beginning the actual writing process.

TASK: MAKING A LIST

The procedure is simple:

1. Write the main topic of your letter or report in the middle of a piece of paper and draw a circle around it.

2. Using word association, jot down any random ideas that might relate to the key topic and then connect these words or phrases to the main topic with lines.

3. When you are through brainstorming, evaluate the ideas you have jotted down and cross out the ones that don't really apply or aren't all that important.

4. Number the remaining ideas according to their importance or according to what the natural order would be if you were discussing them with someone.

5. Use your numbered list as the foundation for an outline.

Task: Mind Mapping

Here is a sample mind-mapping procedure for the subject "Improved Customer Service":

1. Write "Improved Customer Service" in the middle of a piece of paper and draw a circle around it.

2. Surround the circle with words and phrases such as "helpful attitude," "heavy competition," "clean delivery vans and trucks," "faster response time," "cheerful smile," "falling stock market," "lower prices," and "efficient paperwork."

3. Extend a line from each phrase to the circle that surrounds the words "Improved Customer Service."

4. Evaluate each item in your brainstorming list. Chances are, you will cross out some words that don't apply to your objective.

5. Number the remaining items in what you now perceive as their logical sequence.

JUST A MINUTE

A mind-mapping session might go something like this: Imagine a customer walking through the front door of your place of business. What should be the appropriate actions? You would probably begin by greeting the customer with a smile on your face and in your voice to welcome him or her to your business. Your imagined steps would continue all the way through to the point where you obtain the payment and hand the customer his or her proper receipt. Now number those imagined steps according to the order in which they're performed and you're done.

6. You're now ready to use this numbered list to prepare your outline. Follow a similar mind-mapping session for each of the numbered points, coming up with key points for each item on the resulting list.

You will find that taking five or ten minutes to use this mind-mapping technique will actually help you save much more time once you start to do your work.

Discovering What's News

If you ever find yourself staring at an empty computer screen or at a blank piece of paper with no idea what to write about for your term paper, your column for the local newspaper, your company newsletter, or an after-dinner speech at the Rotary Club, it is not because you are not a creative thinker. It probably just means you need to learn more about the way to channel your creativity so you can come up with a steady flow of ideas. This is an easy problem to fix, fortunately. You need to learn the ways to help yourself become inspired. In fact, by the time you finish this hour, your new problem will be how to live long enough to tackle all your newfound inspiration.

It helps to know which topics people find most interesting.

THE NEVER-MISS CATEGORIES

Experience shows that the most popular topics are ones that either impact people's lives directly or provide information for enhancing their lives. These topics fall within seven major categories and four secondary categories.

1. **Money:** People never tire of learning about money—how to make, save, collect, invest, and spend it. Share new insights about these facets of this standard topic and you will garner audience interest.

2. **Physical fitness:** People are living longer and, therefore, want to know more about dieting, exercise, plastic surgery, medical cures, and vitamins.

3. **Mental health:** In today's fast-paced and hectic world, people are anxious for help in learning to cope with stress, gain confidence, be assertive without being aggressive, and work within dysfunctional relationships.

4. **Lifestyles:** People find the lifestyles of others to be fascinating, especially if they are unusual or offbeat.

JUST A MINUTE

The more you "practice" your English skills and put them to use in writing and other presentation preparations, the more you will develop your personal style. Consider keeping a journal and use the forced daily writing to keep it up-to-date as a way to hone your skills and develop your voice. If you prefer a less-structured program to develop your style, record family stories or anecdotes about others you know.

5. **Personal advancement ideas and plans:** No matter how many how-to books and self-help articles are published, everybody is interested in new ways to improve his or her life. Your way of doing something is a new way for somebody else.

6. **Activities:** Explore how clubs and organizations provide the impetus to make people want to devote some of their leisure time to them and how such activities impact members' lives.

7. **Entertainment:** Discover new information on places to go, people to watch, and things to do; look for innovative ways to tell others about how to have a great time without spending a fortune.

THE FAIRLY-SAFE CATEGORIES

The preceding seven categories are the sure bets. They touch everyone's lives. However, four other categories, while not universal, are still of interest to a vast number of people:

1. **Crime:** Gone are the days when people didn't lock their doors. People's security consciousness today verges on paranoia. Antitheft devices on cars, home security systems, and neighborhood crime watch patrols are now an everyday fact of life. Still, even with all these precautions, people don't feel completely secure. They want more information about how to prevent crime from disrupting their lives. Crime avoidance tips, lessons, or experiences and personal crime stories are all subjects worth exploring.

2. **Schooling innovations:** How do home schooling, magnet schools, busing, tracking, distance learning, and online education impact or confuse parents about the best ways to educate their children today?

3. **Unusual events:** Educate yourself about a recent phenomenon, such as online investing and the "day-trader" hoopla, the launching of a space station in the 21st century, the threat of biological warfare in the Middle East, or the cloning of large mammals, and figure out ways to explain these events in lay terms.

4. **Profiles of interesting people:** This appears to be the age of the memoir. People never seem to tire of reading about how someone overcame a great obstacle, achieved success, or discovered a way to reach personal serenity.

SOURCES OF IDEA STIMULATORS

Now that you know about the general areas in which people are most interested, how can you use this information to help trigger your own ideas? First, you need to discover how to find innovative material related to these topics. Here are some ideas of where you can look.

DISCOVERING THE "GOLD" PAGES

Suppose you are a columnist who covers news of local interest for the city newspaper. Your job is to come up with fresh articles about newsworthy topics within your limited region. As a novice writer, you go for the obvious stories first: an interview with the mayor, a profile of a retiring fire chief, and a groundbreaking for a new school. However, it does not take long for all the "obvious" leads to dry up. This is when you need a nose for news to survive. It's a good time to open the Yellow Pages of the phone book.

JUST A MINUTE

The classified-ad section of the newspaper is another source you can use to prompt new ideas. The help-wanted section can show you which services people need. Job listings can indicate which areas of business are doing better than others, which jobs are hard to fill (making you question why that would be), and which types of industries are new to your area.

Here are five ways a novice reporter might mine "golden" topics in the Yellow Pages:

1. Find out more about businesses that offer usual services.

e.g.

Do they make fortune cookies in your town? How do they get the fortune inside the cookie? Is there a gunsmith in town who specializes in the making and repairing of muskets for Civil War reenactment groups? How did he learn his trade? Look for any offbeat businesses or nontraditional service companies.

2. Check display ads for companies celebrating their 25th and 50th business anniversaries and then write profiles of those places. Has the business been owned by the same family all these years? How many local residents does the business employ? In what ways does the business expect to expand or change during the coming years? Why did the business locate in this town? Has it opened branches elsewhere?

3. Send a postcard at the beginning of each year to every entity listed under the categories of "Organizations" and "Associations," asking to be placed on the group's active mailing list for press releases, media

kits, and newsletters. As this printed material subsequently arrives, the cub reporter could comb it for potential story ideas to follow up on—everything from fund-raisers to contests to community projects and more.

4. Develop new slants on routine businesses. Visit the local florist and ask him or her who orders meat-eating plants (high school biology classes? college botany classes? private collectors?). Go to an army surplus store and ask about what survivalists buy to store in their basements (weapons? freeze-dried food? military uniforms?). Keep in mind that the best ideas don't always come from the obvious story. Seek the story behind the story.

5. Combine two topics. If you first do a story about egg and poultry farmers in your county and later do a story about hog producers, you can combine the total information into a new article called "Ham and Eggs, the Breakfast Business." Take a look through some of your other research and start playing mix 'n' match.

Each year when the new phone book comes out, new businesses will be listed, different businesses will celebrate their silver and golden anniversaries, new officers will be elected to head the local clubs—everything will become "fresh" news again. Even if you do nothing but plumb the resources of the local Yellow Pages, you will never lack for topics to trigger your ideas.

JUST A MINUTE

Add a new twist to an old topic. One fall, while writing features for the local newspaper, Pam contacted the teachers and asked them: "How did you spend *your* summer vacation?"

GETTING AN EXPERT OPINION

What if you don't want to limit yourself to local news? What if you need to write or speak about statewide or national events and you need to speak to those issues with authority? That's no problem either. Find experts in the field to interview. Interviews can provide you with much of the data and background you require—if not directly in the way of quotes (see Hour 19, "The Ins and Outs of Italics, Parentheses, Quotation Marks, and More," for a review of quoting others), at least indirectly by clueing you as to where else you need to look to gather your facts.

There are any number of ways to set about finding experts. Many can be found via the World Wide Web: Describe your project in an e-mail to profnet@profnet.com and request that people with credentials and expertise in a particular area contact you. You are likely to hear from college public-information directors who will recommend members of their faculties. You can then communicate by e-mail or phone call.

JUST A MINUTE

Visit the ProfNet Web site at http://www.profnet.com for a review of its policies and procedures. People without online access can contact the group directly at ProfNet, 100 North Country Rd., Suite C, Setauket, NY 11733, 1-800-PROFNET or 631-941-3736, fax: 631-689-1425.

Another alternative is to gather a stack of college catalogs from area trade schools and universities and make your own calls to the experts.

You can also visit university Web sites. Many post information online about current research programs and special events taking place on campus.

Ideas are out there once you decide to go look for them.

You can reverse this process, too. If you are in need of something to write about, open the back of the catalog and examine the "faculty biography" section. Discover what the professors have expertise in and then contact them for interviews. State universities can have as many as 3,000 professors. The information available from that many experts could keep you busy for a very long time.

TICKLE YOUR FANCY

One of our friends once said, "My muse amuses herself by avoiding me." You're no different than our friend. You can't depend on inspiration to strike when you need it. That's why it will help if you keep what many people refer to as *ticklers*—files and reminders of important events and possible ideas to develop further. Having ticklers on hand means that you don't have to start with a blank slate each time you need a new idea. Here are some ways to set up and maintain your tickler files:

- **Save business cards.** Record the names, addresses, e-mail addresses, phone numbers, and fax numbers. Cross-reference the names to each person's area of expertise. Sometimes ideas can be triggered by something as easy as shuffling the cards.

When you send someone a thank-you note, write a small message asking the person to keep you informed of any new developments or good news. It's a convenient and thoughtful way to show your appreciation and to make sure people keep you in mind the next time.

- **Fill file folders.** Set up some manila folders in your filing cabinet (for magazine articles and other clippings) and create an "ideas" folder on your hard drive (for your notes or other files such as copies of articles found online). Label separate file folders and create separate folders inside the "ideas" folder on your hard drive for general topics such as women, men, children, hobbies, space, pets, and so on. Once a file gets too large, you can then break it into subcategories (women in business, women in sports, …).

- **Keep a sample supply.** Brochures, newsletters, magazine ads, annual reports, and other commercial publications can be used as sources for content ideas as well as for possible design and layout plans for those times when you need to organize an entire presentation.

- **Prepare a personal portfolio.** Preserve copies of your previous work such as interview tapes, photos, press releases, brochures, and other work materials you may want to refer to at a later date. This work not only can provide you with things to trigger new ideas ("I announced 'A' in that press release, but I didn't say a thing about 'B'"), seeing a finished product can be inspiring: It's your proof that you successfully tackled the job in the past, so you can do it again! (You can also use these examples of your work to show to prospective employers or clients during interviews.)

You can use dry-erase boards with Write-On Cling Sheets and erasable markers, or you can use them as portable bulletin boards for Post-it notes. The sheets come in tablets of 35 per pad and are small enough that you can have one for each project. Each "board" is easy to store between work sessions because you can remove it from the wall, roll it up (with the Post-it notes still inside), and rubber band it shut until you need to retrieve it from your storage shelf and use it again. Made by Avery Label Company at 1-800-GO-AVERY (1-800-462-8379).

STORYBOARD IT

Some people like to write blocks of text and then use the cut-and-paste feature to rearrange the sections in order. Others like to see a project unfold.

A storyboard is one way to help you see what you're thinking. A storyboard is a technique that film directors use to preplan each shot in a scene or sequence. Each shot receives some sort of graphic representation on the board—ranging from a simple stick-figure drawing to an elaborate drawing of the scene showing lighting angles and other minutia. Each image can be repositioned until the director arrives at what he or she believes is the best start-to-finish flow for the scene.

The advantage of using a similar system for your project is that you don't have to "see the filmstrip played out in your mind." It's there in front of you on the board. You don't have to use images to accomplish the same results. A Post-it note for each key word will suffice. Write the key word in bold on the note and stick it on whatever you're using for your board. The parts to a storyboard aren't exact jigsaw puzzle–style pieces; their positioning on the board is fluid until you arrive at an order that you decide best fits your needs.

THE TICKLING CONTINUES...

You can use your tickler files to help you generate ideas in a number of ways:

1. Get in touch with family members, friends, or your business-card contacts and ask them for anecdotes. Cab drivers, police officers, physicians, barbers, bank tellers, and others who deal with the public often have a variety of human interest stories—both funny and dramatic.

2. Cross-check items in your idea folders against information on national news radio and television broadcasts or related Web sites and then localize the event. For example, is there a local allergist or environmental-illness specialist treating people suffering from Gulf War Syndrome? What are the latest developments regarding that condition? Check with your local VFW and American Legion halls to see if they will release the names of any local vets who are dealing with this condition. Once you've conducted some informational, informal interviews, contrast the data you've gathered regarding exposures believed to have caused that syndrome with the everyday chemical exposures everyone encounters.

3. Check Facts On File publications.

See Appendix B, "Resources," for the Facts On File publications and Web site. You can use these resources to cross-check information kept in your ideas folders.

4. Look at the most recent list of best-selling books to get a feel for what is currently attracting people's interest. *Jaws* sparked an interest in sharks; *The Godfather,* curiosity about organized crime, especially how it relates to the Italian-American culture; *Angela's Ashes,* the Irish; and the *Goosebumps* and *Harry Potter* series, sorcery and witchcraft. Find the similarities between current trends and your project and see how they relate to one another.

5. Learn to listen. Pay attention to what others are saying. Sometimes a bit of overheard conversation or a single quote in someone else's speech can generate an idea for the workable solution you need.

It Works for Fiction Writing, Too

You now have an assortment of ways to come up with ideas for term papers, speeches, newspaper and magazine articles, company newsletters, and any other project you might encounter. If, however, you also have an interest in writing novels or short stories, there are some easy ways to come up with ideas for plots, too.

Take another look at your daily newspaper. There are half a dozen ways you can find "plots" in those pages.

1. Advice columns: Read the letters to "Ann Landers," "Dear Abby," and other syndicated columnists and try to retell the problems as short stories. Before reading the response letters, imagine how your story would resolve itself. Many best-selling books, such as *Kramer vs. Kramer, Ordinary People, When Pride Still Mattered,* and *Snow Falling on Cedars,* have plots not unlike problems discussed in advice columns.

2. Comic strip shuffle: Take five dramatic comic strips, cut all the squares of the various panels, and shuffle them. Flip them up at random, lay them end-to-end, and read the story. You'll wind up with something like Rex Morgan, M.D., appealing to Daddy Warbucks for funds to keep Mary Worth's retirement community from being closed. That's not a bad plot, actually: A concerned physician helps change his capitalistic father's ruthless corporate image by convincing him to help senior citizens from being evicted from their apartments; the industrialist meets a gracious lady at the apartments in the process, and Daddy and Mary live happily ever after.

3. **Comic strip rewrites:** Cover up the word bubbles in the comic strips and try to put your own story to the visual scenes. Ask yourself, "Why would a strong Kerry Drake be tackling a helpless child?" Is Kerry a bully? a child molester? a kidnapper? all of the above?

4. **Horoscopes:** Instead of predictions, let horoscopes be plot summaries. You might read, "Leo: Today you will encounter several strangers, and you will also be involved in several money transactions. Be on your toes." Strangers, money, toes? Ah-ha! Here's the plot: A struggling ballerina who has failed at several auditions is suddenly approached by three so-called "booking agents." Each offers her a large sum of cash to join a ballet troupe scheduled for a tour of the Middle East. Why? Is it a case of white slavery? Is the girl the illegitimate daughter of a sheik who fathered the child when in the United States as a student years ago? Does the girl have real dancing talent ... harem style? The plot twists are limitless, and best of all, there are 12 new horoscopes to use every day.

5. **Movie reviews:** Turn to the arts pages and read a review of a movie you have not seen. Most reviewers will not spoil a movie for you by revealing the ending. Take the skeleton of the review and use it to outline a similar story that you can develop your own way. Your original ending and your story's different locale and characters will ensure its uniqueness.

6. **Letters to the editor:** A "public forum" or "letters to the editor" column can produce a variety of ideas. They will also give you a sense of how others with political leanings different from your own think and feel about a topic. There's the added bonus that almost any local controversy can be fodder for plot or subplot scenarios, too. These print resources will include personal details you probably won't hear about on the local radio or television news. (Just remember to fictionalize the locale in your story.) You can imagine how a letter to the editor about cancer awareness could trigger the plot idea for a novel in the order of *One True Thing* by Anna Quindlen (Dell Publishing Company, 1998. ISBN: 044022103X.).

These tips can help get you started. With careful exploring, you may be able to find other plot ideas hidden in various places in your daily newspaper. So be careful not to line the birdcage with your next bestseller.

WORKSHOP: TURNING NONFICTION INTO FICTION

As you apply the lessons you have learned in this Hour about nonfiction writing, take time to imagine how your research might also be used as fiction. An interview of a local artisan about her stained glass reproduction designs could provide you with the background necessary to write a story about the historical and sentimental significance of ornamental windows, the stresses and frustrations involved in a restoration project, or the financial considerations somebody encounters when faced with the decision of whether or not to preserve a landmark or simply repair a façade. Play with these ideas.

HOUR'S UP!

1. An excellent way to develop your personal style is to:

    a. read newspapers

    b. keep a journal

    c. write descriptive grocery lists

    d. write letters to celebrities

2. If you are trying to organize your ideas, a good exercise is:

    a. reading other writers

    b. watching television

    c. shopping

    d. mind mapping

3. What topics interest people a great deal?

    a. money

    b. physical fitness

    c. lifestyles

    d. a, b, & c

4. Where is a good place to consult for ideas?

    a. hairdresser

    b. yellow pages

    c. police department

    d. a, b, & c

5. A good idea is to save clippings and other idea triggers in a:

    a. shoe box

    b. mason jar

    c. tickler file

    d. glove compartment

6. An excellent way to plot your ideas graphically is to use a:

    a. storyboard

    b. computer

    c. video camera

    d. a, b, & c

7. You may be able to get ideas for design, layout, or content from:

    a. brochures

    b. magazine ads

    c. reports

    d. a, b, & c

8. Fiction writers can sometimes get excellent ideas from:

    a. advice columns

    b. movie reviews

    c. letters to the editor

    d. a, b, & c

9. What can sometimes be an effective tool when approaching a subject?

    a. pretending

    b. consulting an expert

    c. renting a video

    d. a, b, & c

Quiz

10. Fiction writers can also get ideas by:

    a. copying other writers

    b. reading horoscopes

    c. reading comic strips

    d. b & c

ANSWERS

1. b		**6.** a
2. d		**7.** d
3. d		**8.** d
4. b		**9.** b
5. c		**10.** d

RECAP

This Hour focused on how to master techniques that will enable you to come up with new ideas to write about. Before you put your ideas into words, remember to review the various hours, keeping the rules and lessons clear in your mind. Practice will make perfect.

HOUR 18

Managing Your Research

CHAPTER SUMMARY

LESSON PLAN:

In this Hour, you will learn how to prethink projects so they will be creative and interesting. You will also learn how to plan, organize, and present your material in the most logical and interesting way possible.

Among the things we'll cover are

- The art of creative thinking.
- Procedures related to research.
- How to prepare an outline.
- Methods of organizing your materials.

Company reports, business speeches, grant proposals, and various other types of presentations usually begin with somebody having to do some research. Knowing how to save time during this process will make your work easier. The first step is to engage your mind in prethinking exercises. Your audience—whether it is your boss, a customer, or a larger group of interested parties—will be judging your work in four specific ways:

1. The relevance of what you produce
2. The originality of your thoughts, ideas, and plans
3. The scope of your talents
4. The complexity and accuracy of your presentation

Your ability to think creatively will be crucial to the success of each of these four aspects of any project.

Let's review some of the ways you can open your mind to be creative in the thinking and subsequent investigative phases of your research. Here are some exercises you can put into immediate practice:

1. **Expand the boundaries.** As you begin researching your topic, go beyond the existing limits. Find the alternatives and explore them to see where they take you.

2. **Change your perspective.** If you are doing research on customer service, look at your business

through the eyes of the customer. Start looking at everything from the outside rather than just from the inside.

3. **Discover new applications.** Take a look at your products or services and start researching ways they might be used in different applications. Recycle and diversify.

4. **Pretend you are someone else.** Take on a different persona before initiating your research and planning. Consider how Thomas Edison, Madame Curie, Bill Gates, or Martha Stewart would tackle the problem. Follow the direction you think one of these people would take and see where it leads you.

5. **Work backward.** Start with the end result and work back to the start.

6. **Ask enough questions.** Before you head to the library or schedule an interview with an expert, decide first what you need to uncover in your research. Make a list of pertinent questions and then narrow your initial list to those most appropriate for the research needed.

When you use these prethinking procedures, you will narrow the focus of where you should start your research. This helps you determine how you should concentrate most of your time.

THE RANGE OF RESEARCH

There are many avenues available for research today. Give consideration to what advantage each might be to you. Here are some ways to start:

- Books
- Current newspapers, back issues, clipping files
- Professional journals and trade magazines
- Television and video documentaries
- Radio talk shows
- Editorials from radio, TV, newspapers, and the Web
- Historical records, photographs, illustrations, cartoons
- Museums, national parks, science exhibitions
- Dictionaries, books of world records, almanacs
- Newsletters, club histories
- Family albums
- Web sites

- Toll-free numbers for corporations and organizations
- Colleges, universities, trade schools
- Government offices and government publications
- The Yellow Pages of the phone book
- Biography indexes
- Encyclopedias
- *Who's Who* publications
- *Reader's Guide to Periodical Literature*
- Churches, synagogues, mosques
- Pamphlets, maps, posters

NARROW THE TOPIC

After you assess the amount of research material available, start to narrow the focus of your topic. Set out to solve one specific problem or address one key issue; do not speak to all the ancillary aspects of your topic. Focus, reduce, realign, and condense your research materials. Stay on the main topic.

Similarly, condense your time frame for completing the research. Set a specific date when the research must be gathered and the writing must be started to allow you ample time to complete your work before your deadline.

TASK: OVERALL RESEARCH PLANNING

To make your research and writing deadlines compatible, you should lay out a six-step organizational plan. Ask yourself the following:

1. What steps are necessary to accomplish the desired results?

   What activities (in detail) are to be done?

   What sequence of activities will you need to follow to keep things moving on schedule?

2. Why must each step be taken?

   Ask continually, "Is this step necessary?"

   Ask, "Is this step being taken in the right sequence?"

3. When must each step be taken?

   What is the date or time for the accomplishment?

   How much time will be allotted for each part of the research and writing processes?

4. Who will take each step?

   Will secretaries or research assistants be involved?

   What will the chain of command be for this project?

   Which parts of the research should you do yourself?

   Which parts should you delegate?

   What procedures are in place should one link in the chain be a weak (unreliable) one?

   What factors related to the research may be beyond the abilities of your assistants?

   Have you made provisions for aspects of your research (and the interpretation of that research) that are beyond your own expertise?

5. Where will each step take place?

   Will you work onsite?

   Will you go offsite to libraries and other locales?

   Will you visit other sites of your own company?

6. How will each step take place?

   Go back through the preceding five points and look for any loose ends or unanswered questions.

   Build in checks for the accuracy of all findings.

Add it all up and you have a grand scheme for your research project.

GETTING TO WORK

With your game plan now outlined, it is time to kick into gear. Begin by making a list of significant words related to your research topic. For example, if you want to research the women's liberation movement of the 1960s, you might make a list that would include these words: women's liberation, equality, sexism, good old-boy network, Equal Opportunity Act, pink-collar workers, and feminism. These generalized terms could then be narrowed to subheadings such as military sexism, business sexism, educational sexism or radical feminism, militant feminism, and feminism in the arts.

JUST A MINUTE

For those times when you have problems thinking of related topics and synonyms, consider checking a thesaurus. Book indices and tables of contents also can be used to trigger ideas to aid you in your research.

TAKING YOUR RESEARCH ONLINE

Internet search engines (such as AltaVista, Profusion, or Google) or directories (such as Yahoo!) can help you locate the online references available to aid you in your research.

You reach an "address" on the Internet by way of the uniform resource locator (URL); e.g., www.ricehahn.com. Although there are always exceptions, you are more apt to discover reliable information on sites on a Domain Name System (DNS) as opposed to the ones maintained on online "public pages" such as those with "geocities" or "tripod" in the URL.

The three letters that follow the period will indicate the source of the data. These are the most common:

- **.com**   Indicates commercial and for-profit groups
- **.edu**   Indicates colleges, universities, and educational research organizations
- **.gov**   Indicates government agencies
- **.mil**   Indicates the branches of the U.S. military
- **.net**   Indicates a computer network such as an Internet service provider (ISP)
- **.org**   Indicates not-for-profit groups or organizations

In conducting initial research, you can narrow your topic by combining two headings such as "feminism, historical" or "feminism, contemporary." In fact, you can even specify the time frame you wish to stay in such as "feminism, 1963–1975."

OTHER INTERNET OPTIONS

Appendix B of this book includes a list of online resources. Be sure to spend some time exploring these options. However, don't overlook these other options:

- **Chat rooms** are where people of like interests gather to talk online; some provide "scheduled" chat sessions that can be great places for you to probe the mind of an expert.

- **Direct inquiries** can be sent via e-mail to professors.

- **Newsgroups** and lists provide the forums for posting news items related to specific topics.

LIBRARY SPEAK

If you are working with hard-copy materials in the library or are running data searches on the library's computer, you will need to understand "library speak." For example, a *magazine* is a periodical (weekly, monthly, quarterly) that is produced for general readership (such as *The Saturday Evening Post* or *Time*). A *journal* is a professional publication written and read by people in a designated discipline of study (such as *The Pacific Historian* or *Modern Fiction Studies*). Determining your audience's level of understanding about your topic will often determine from which periodicals you will cull research.

As you examine various articles, take notes from or make photocopies of only the articles that have solid information related to your research topic; highlight the specific information that will help you most.

Two basic guides on research methods are the *MLA Handbook for Writers of Research Papers,* 5th Ed. by Joseph Gibaldi and Phyllis Franklin. Modern Language Association of America, 1999. ISBN: 0873529758; and *The Craft of Research* (Chicago Guides to Writing, Editing, and Publishing) by Wayne C. Booth, Gregory G. Colomb, and Joseph M. Williams. University of Chicago Press (Trade), 1995. ISBN: 0226065847.

To determine whether a book will fit your needs, check the title page for the date of publication, look at the table of contents to see if the whole book or only specific chapters relate to your topic, check for information about the author's credentials to determine his or her experience in the field, and use the bibliography and works-cited pages as leads for further research.

JUST A MINUTE

 Some libraries keep their previous editions of encyclopedias on hand. So if you need to research a topic from the past, don't dismiss the dog-eared texts on the library shelves.

MEDIA MERIT

When using an article, a book, or the Internet, use discernment in the material you incorporate into your research. Stay with writers, publications, and institutions that are reputable. Avoid public-relations hype. Try to verify your facts with more than one source. Check out people's credentials before quoting them. Just because something is in print or on the Net doesn't make it true, reliable, or valuable.

PROCEED WITH CAUTION

 Research data is only as good as the researcher who compiled it. Although an advanced degree or licensing designation can't guarantee that the person knows and understands his area of expertise, such "expert identifiers" usually indicate the authorship of reliable information.

TASK: RECORDING SOURCES

Maintain a "running bibliography" as you do your research. Record all the bibliographical data of any online source, book, or magazine from which you draw information in a notebook, on a designated disk, or in a designated hard drive folder.

1. Write down the author's name (last name first), the title of the article, the periodical, its volume and issue number, the date of publication, and the page numbers of the article. If it is in a newspaper, note the section of the paper from which it came. For a book, note the chapter, pages, city of publication, publisher, and date of publication. (Sample bibliographical models are provided later in this hour.)

2. Double-check all addresses, phone numbers, statistics, records, dates, and the spelling of names.

3. If you make photocopies of articles or book pages, mark all the bibliographical data directly on those pages. This will prove valuable should you need to verify what you have quoted or cited later.

4. Give credit to your references either by quoting the material in quotation marks and then citing it or simply by citing it (even if it is paraphrased) so that the right source will get documentation credit (and you avoid plagiarism).

Along with your running bibliography, also keep a brainstorming notebook or an ideas folder on your computer hard drive. There you can record all the sudden insights related to your topic that come to you, new areas to explore, or ideas on how best to present the material you've gathered.

CONDUCTING THE PROFESSIONAL INTERVIEW

Interviewing an expert in the field you are researching will give your research originality, credibility, and format variety. Here are some guidelines on how to set up and conduct such interviews in a professional manner:

- When you set up the interview, tell your subject what you want to discuss and how much time you will need so that he or she can pull together any necessary notes, photos, and other materials in advance.

- Do some homework before the interview. Read the interviewee's press kit, personal bio, or *Who's Who* entry.

- Whenever possible, conduct the interview on the person's home turf: his or her office or home.

Do not schedule an interview to take place in a restaurant. The noise there will distort what you tape-record. Even worse, if your interviewee is a celebrity, strangers may come up to your table and ask for autographs, interrupting your time to talk.

- Do not have other people present. You don't need quotations or opinions from others, just from your expert source. Limit the meeting to just the two of you.

- Use a tape recorder but also take notes. As you listen to your questions being answered, take notes about the interviewee's office décor, gestures and mannerisms, physical features, clothes, and other bits of information that will not be on tape. This will later help you put together a full profile of this visit.

Make sure you use a tape recorder that warns you in some manner when it's time to change the tape. Otherwise, as you transcribe the tape, you may discover that you lost track of time during the interview, and your tape ran out long before the person interviewed ran out of what could have been quotable things to say.

- Arrive prepared for the worst. Always bring spare batteries, backup cassette tapes, extra film, extra ink pens, and plenty of notepads. Don't let a technical breakdown make you look like a fool before you even get started.

- Spend the majority of your time listening. Use body language movements that imply you are paying attention, but let the other person do the talking. You are there to listen and to learn. Don't step on the speaker's words. Allow him or her time to pause and think. Lulls in a conversation are part of good interview pacing. Let the speaker remain relaxed and move at his or her own pace.

- Keep your topic narrowed to key points. Unless you are there to get the person's life story, you just want his or her insights on a specific subject. Prepare your questions in advance and have them arranged in a logical order. Work to keep the discussion focused and on topic.

- Although your interview is a fact-finding mission, use some open-ended questions to discover the interviewee's thoughts, opinions, ideas, and feelings on the topic you are discussing. Who better than an expert in the field to ask about the emotional or sociological aspects of a topic?

Use open-ended questions to get a conversation rolling. If you ask, "Your career is in bioengineering?" the person will say, "Yes." However, if you ask, "What made you decide to devote your professional life to bioengineering?" the person will have to explain the answer with background and details. That's a good icebreaker.

- Observe the other person's body language, and make notes of why and when it occurs. Gestures and fidgeting can be clues to that person's "hot buttons."

- Ask one question at a time. Don't ask a multipart question and expect to get a straight answer. Ask about the first aspect of the information you need; once that has been obtained, move to the next point, and then the next, and maintain that pace.

- Save your toughest questions for last. Even if you have to pull a question or two out of normal sequence to time it right, do so.

Don't ask anything too sensitive early in the interview. ("How did you feel when you learned you were under federal investigation?") By the end of the interview, you will have established a rapport with the subject, and he or she will therefore be more apt to answer. Even if the interviewee decides not to give you an answer, you will still have your other interview information.

- Don't grant final approval of the interview to the person being interviewed. You don't want to risk delays in your project caused by waiting for the person to get the material back to you. Even worse, the person may decide to rescind a quote.

  One way to counter a request to view a finished interview is to offer to fax the person anything that may need verification, such as dates, costs, or spellings. This will keep control of the research in your hands (where it belongs).

- Don't wait too long to write up the notes of your interview. Regardless of whether you'll be writing up the interview as an article or as part of the narration for a video presentation, you should get the basics down on paper before the nuances and subtle matters of the conversation begin to fade.

- Avoid problems later by asking the person being interviewed to state his or her understanding of the purpose for the interview. This will give you a chance to correct any misperceptions. Also consider having the interviewee sign a "publication consent agreement."

 FYI For a sample publication consent agreement, see *Write on Target: A Five-Phase Program for Nonfiction Writers* by Dennis E. Hensley and Holly G. Miller. Writer, 1995. ISBN: 087116177X.

Task: Organizing the Material

Now that it's time to organize your research, you're probably faced with interview tapes, photocopied articles, magazines folded open to articles, books marked at various chapters, and computer disk backups of your down-loaded data. It can seem overwhelming. How do you begin to make sense of it all? Start with this simple exercise.

Sit down and summarize in one topic sentence what your entire research project is about. That may sound impossible, but it isn't.

For a report about the lesser-known benefits of the space program, your topic sentence might be, "Although the U.S. space program has provided exciting adventures, more directly beneficial have been its product spin-off develop-ments ranging from freeze-dried foods and vitamin supplements to Teflon surfaces, Velcro, and satellite communications." In this introductory sentence, you will have made a case for proving that the ancillary aspects of the space program have helped thousands of people who have never gone into space. You also will have previewed some of the areas your presentation will explore (food, cookware, convenience, and technology).

With this foundation, you can now start putting together the rest of your pre-sentation. Your next step is to choose the blueprint you wish to use.

There are several options you can consider.

YOUR LEAD

In Hour 16, "Leads and Closings," you learned that you should adapt the way you introduce a passage to fit your audience and the intent for a particular piece of writing or a presentation. Consider the previously mentioned sentence as a possible "mission statement" for research:

> "Although the U.S. space program has provided exciting adventures, more directly beneficial have been its product spin-off developments ranging from freeze-dried foods and vitamin supplements to Teflon surfaces, Velcro, and satellite communications."

Another alternative could be the "strong descriptive passage" approach:

> "Three … two … one." You hear these words, and you know that another mission is about to be launched into space. "Blast off!" You've seen enough such launches that these words alone can cause you to imagine the heat rising in waves off the space craft as the braces that support it on the launch pad fall away and the earth around it trembles from the force of yet another vehicle being propelled into space …."

You could take several approaches if you want to lead with some humor. Here are three:

> "When you're engrossed in a project with a deadline looming just beyond the horizon, the last thing you want to hear a team member mutter is, 'Houston, we have a problem.' Thanks to our space program, we know that phrase isn't one said by a utilities director for a major metropolitan city in a report to the city council (although some thought the Y2K bug could have made it one). We've evolved. Science fiction gave us lines like 'I'm sorry, Dave. I'm afraid I can't do that.' or 'Danger, Will Robinson!' Each of these phrases implies that things are not going well. When it comes to *your* project deadline, if 'not going well' is an understatement, you know you're in trouble."

> "Mothers everywhere sing praises to this country's space program—whether they realize it or not. Forget about nonstick skillets and satellite TV. Those pale when compared to the convenience of Velcro on tennis shoes. The time saved from what was once the daily chore of repeatedly lacing up preschoolers' shoes has been enough for many mothers to embark on a second career and launch numerous (online and traditional) entrepreneurial adventures while still holding down a full-time job."

"I blame NASA for our country's 'thin' obsession. Baby boomers know that it's no coincidence that the waif look began about the time of the first manned space missions. The televised shots of astronauts floating around in a space cabin gave fashion executives worldwide a new way to make women feel inadequate about their bodies. Weightlessness! Twiggy and the countless underfed, surgically enhanced sticks that have followed her down the runway now mean that unless you're a size zero, you weigh too much."

SEQUENTIAL ORDER

Make an outline of major developments in the field or topic you will be discussing.

1. Develop a three-pronged outline of historical background, current developments, and future goals.
2. List historical events in chronological order—dynasties, generations, ruling classes, or sociological eras.

Once you make this decision, you can make a list under these key points of various supportive material you wish to present, and you can label your research information according to where it will fit into the outline.

CAUSE AND EFFECT

Cause and effect is the presentation pattern followed by most scientists: If you put helium in a balloon (the cause), the balloon will rise (the effect).

It can also be used by social scientists: If you crowd too many people into a soccer stadium and arouse them to an angry pitch (the cause), you will cause a riot (the effect).

Similarly, it can be used by political scientists: If the media portrays a president as being unfit for office (the cause), the congress will be pressured to impeach him (the effect).

You likewise can make an outline that presents all the causes of the effects in your topic of research. You then can arrange your research in that pattern: cause and effect #1, cause and effect #2, cause and effect #3, and so on.

COMPARISON AND CONTRAST

This format calls for you to make an outline that shows how elements of your research do or do not resemble other related matters. Your outline will list the key points of comparison and what you have found to support them, and then it will list the key points of contrast and what you have found to support that. Your research will fall in line, and you can develop your conclusions accordingly.

THE SOAPBOX

This is the most direct of all the formats. It calls for you to imagine yourself standing on a soapbox in the middle of a public park, trying to sway a crowd of listeners to believe that your position on an issue is correct. Your "soapbox" presentation will cover your most powerful facts, the names of people who agree with you and what they have to say on this issue, and explanations of what the public needs to know about the topic.

COUNTERPOINT AND REBUTTAL

This format calls for an outline that consists of the arguments against the stance you are taking. Then, under these key outline points, list the elements of research you have found that will refute these arguments. Build your case with facts, interview quotes, and new points of view, all of which will poke holes in the opposing side's arguments.

DEFINE AND EXEMPLIFY

This format works best if your research hopes to break new ground or to establish a new stance in a certain field. For example, you might want to claim that the label "country music" should be limited to songs written strictly for instruments native to the United States. You could then exemplify this by discussing songs composed for the banjo, autoharp, and harmonica.

PROCESS ANALYSIS

This format is the most functional, but often least exciting, of the various presentation formats. It simply calls for you to devise an outline that puts something together or takes it apart in a set way. So if you are trying to explain the best way to set up a dorm room or to arrange a room to be shared by siblings, you just walk through the process from (a) bringing in the necessary functional items of furniture, to (b) adding items of aesthetic taste, to (c) establishing "personal space" boundaries. It can work in reverse, too.

If you want to explain why a division of your company went bankrupt, your research might uncover information about what led to its initial great success followed by an analysis that shows it failed to update its key products, neglected to lure new customers, and finally lacked a good operational plan.

PROPER DOCUMENTATION

Remember that when you take notes, you should put the information into your own words. This is called *paraphrasing*—a form of condensing information so that the gist of it remains. (Refer to Hour 1, "Understanding Grammar," for a review of the meaning of "gist.") This process is effective for when you don't want lots of linked quotes from other people. It also is a way you can demystify technical or scientific information by translating it to a layperson's level. Be sure to identify your source and then document where you found the information. Here's an example:

> "In Jack Smith's biography of Doris Duck (*Wall to Wall,* 1989), he tells the story of Doris' journey from the excavated ancient city of Troy through the sites of many of the great civilizations of the distant past to reach her destination: the Great Wall of China."

The original source for this information might have been a book several thousand pages long; however, you just want to mention the key points about Doris' adventure and the author of the work from which you gathered your information.

Material used in your research presentation should be listed in a "Works Cited" page at the end of your typed research. A standard format is to list the author's name (last name first) followed by a period, the name of the book (underlined or in italics) followed by a period, the city of publication followed by a colon, the name of the publisher followed by a comma, and the date of publication followed by a period. If the information runs to a second line, indent that line five spaces.

e.g.

Hahn, Pamela Rice, and Dennis E. Hensley, Ph.D. *Macmillan Teach Yourself Grammar and Style in 24 Hours.* Indianapolis: SAMS, 2000.

For articles, list the author's name (last name first) followed by a period, the name of the article or the book chapter in quotation marks with a period, the name of the magazine or book in which this material appeared (underlined or typed in italics), the volume number, the date of publication in parentheses, and then the page numbers on which this excerpt appears.

e.g.

Wilson, James. "High School Security in New York." *Sheriff and Deputy Quarterly.* Vol. 22. 2001: 83–102.

As you prepare your paper and refer to another person's writing, you can put a set of parentheses at the end of the quoted or paraphrased material and list the last name of the author and the page number, such as (Hahn, 9). That will refer to the work cited at the end of the paper.

Refer to Appendix B, "Resources," for a list of style guides with additional citation guidelines.

WORKSHOP: HONE TO THE BONE

Take a moment to think about several research projects you need to start investigating. Reduce each project to one succinct topic sentence. Hone and refine that sentence until it says precisely what the research project will specifically focus on. Once you are satisfied with the sentence, get busy with the entire project.

HOUR'S UP!

1. It often helps to change your _____ while you do your research.

    a. slant

    b. dictionary

    c. perspective

    d. shirt

2. Don't overlook consulting _____ when you do your research.

   a. your grandmother

   b. old encyclopedias

   c. Facts On File

   d. b and c

3. A researcher should avoid granting permission to the interviewee to see the final version of the interview because:

   a. it can cause delays while waiting for the interviewee to reply.

   b. the interviewee might dispute which points you believe need emphasized.

   c. the interviewee may want to change his or her answers, which can require yet another "viewing" after you make the requested changes.

   d. all of the above.

4. Whenever possible, it's a good idea to write up your notes from an interview:

   a. within a week.

   b. as soon as possible.

   c. after you've had the chance to ponder everything said.

   d. an hour before your deadline so that your words will be fresh.

5. Once you're ready to begin your research, you should:

   a. make a commitment to yourself to not restrict your study by imposing any deadlines to complete your work.

   b. set a specific deadline for completing your research that fits within the timetable for your project.

   c. limit your research to one reference book so that the research remains focused.

   d. check the television listings to see if you can find a documentary that will answer all of your questions.

6. Data you find on the Internet should always be:

    a. verified, the same as any other research.

    b. assumed to be true because nobody would take the time to post it online if it wasn't.

    c. never used.

    d. considered only if it includes pictures.

7. Librarians only call a magazine a *periodical* if it is:

    a. the current issue.

    b. has pictures.

    c. is published weekly, monthly, or quarterly.

    d. doesn't have pictures.

8. Check the title page of a book to ascertain the:

    a. publication date.

    b. cost of the book.

    c. name of the person who took the pretty pictures.

    d. name of the movie based on the book.

9. Whenever possible, conduct an interview:

    a. when there are a lot of people around so that you can see how the subject reacts to others.

    b. at a restaurant so that you can grab lunch and save yourselves both some time.

    c. as a one-on-one discussion.

    d. when the interviewee's press agent is present.

10. You can grab an audience's attention:

    a. with fireworks.

    b. with backup singers.

    c. by wearing a flashy wardrobe.

    d. with a strong lead.

QUIZ

ANSWERS

1.	c	**6.**	a
2.	d	**7.**	c
3.	d	**8.**	a
4.	b	**9.**	c
5.	b	**10.**	d

RECAP

This Hour covered how to seek, find, and organize research. You now know how to prethink the procedure, narrow a topic, locate information in the library and on the Internet, interview experts, and manage all the accumulated research. Now that you know how to conduct research and prepare a basic outline of what needs to be presented, let's proceed to Hour 19, "The Ins and Outs of Italics, Parentheses, Quotation Marks, and More," where we will explore how to use dialogue properly and how to use quotation marks appropriately.

HOUR 19

The Ins and Outs of Italics, Parentheses, Quotation Marks, and More

CHAPTER SUMMARY

LESSON PLAN:

In this Hour, you'll learn about some other forms of punctuation that can cause problems. Once you learn how to use them correctly, however, they can add personality to your writing.

Among the things we'll cover are

- When and how to use italics.
- Using parentheses.
- When brackets are appropriate.
- The slash and its actual name.
- Using quotation marks and quoting others.

 Italics are the style of type in which letters slant to the right. Italics are not a form of punctuation as much as they are a means to add special formatting to text that adds emphasis to that text. (You may have noticed throughout this book that we use italics to highlight unfamiliar words that are followed by a definition.) Italics can also be used for the following:

(Note that the use of **bold type** in these examples is not related to the use of italics; its purpose is to expedite the reader's identification of the relevant part of the sentence.)

- **Emphasis**

  Just what part of *no formatting* do you not understand?

JUST A MINUTE

The use of **bold type** is another way to add emphasis. Its usage isn't governed by rules as specific as those for italics.

- **Titles of complete works**

  1. Books

     Macmillan Teach Yourself Grammar and Style in 24 Hours is available at your local bookstore.

  2. Film

     According to one survey, the three greatest escape films of all time are *American Dreamer, Creator,* and *The Sure Thing.*

3. Plays

Death of a Salesman is one of the current revival plays on Broadway.

4. Magazines

Frank's first sale to a national magazine was an article that appeared in *A.N.A.L.O.G. Computing.*

- **Abbreviated titles of complete works**

    Bilbo is a featured character in *Tolkien's LoTR.* (*LoTR* is a common abbreviation used for J. R. R. Tolkien's *The Lord of the Rings.*)

- **Unfamiliar words**

    Because of the popularity of Stephen R. Covey's *The 7 Habits of Highly Effective People: Powerful Lessons in Personal Change*, *paradigm* has come to mean a perception or interpretation of how the world works.

- **Scientific and foreign words not yet part of the vernacular (common language native to another group or country)**

    The work was done on a *quid pro quo* arrangement.

PROCEED WITH CAUTION

Never use italics and underlining together when formatting text. Before word processors were invented, manuscripts and documents prepared on typewriters used <u>underlining</u> to indicate *italics* to the typesetter. Since the two forms of typesetting mean the same thing, they should never be used together.

PARENTHESES

Parentheses are the curved punctuation marks used to

- Enclose a *parenthetical expression* (an amplifying or explanatory word, phrase, or sentence inserted into a passage).

    There are divergent opinions among experts as to which computer OS **(operating system)** is best.

- Enclose the independent part of a sentence that is not directly related to the main part.

    Ten books by Taylor Caldwell **(all first editions)** sold at auction recently.

In 2000, the United States celebrated Thanksgiving on Thursday, November 23. (**Thanksgiving never falls on the last Thursday of the month.**)

- Enclose an appositive rather than surround it with commas.

  Renee and Doris (**our favorite editors**) agreed to the changes.

- Enclose numbers of listed items within a sentence.

  Once you learn how to (**1**) leap tall buildings in a single bound, (**2**) change your clothes in a phone booth, and (**3**) disguise your true identity behind a pair of glasses, you, too, can be a super man.

- Enclose words or figures that clarify.

  Henry's paid fines totaling six hundred dollars (**$600.00**) for five (**5**) parking tickets.

- Group units such as those in a mathematical expression.

  You arrive at the conclusion by taking the sum (**a + b**) of the parts.

- Provide a place name that is not part of an official name but is necessary for clarification.

  The Podunk Junction (**Ohio**) Summerfest will be held the second weekend in August.

JUST A MINUTE

Parentheses are often used to convey less emphasis or importance than commas do. Dashes can also be used. Your choice of which to use isn't as much a matter of proper usage as a matter of which seems proper for the tone you want to convey in the passage.

For example, a sentence such as

Because it would take far too long to do otherwise, we decided to stick to our outline and write this book.

could be rephrased for emphasis using parentheses or dashes:

We decided to stick to our outline (**it would take far too long to do otherwise**) and write this book.

We decided to stick to our outline—**it would take far too long to do otherwise**—and write this book.

Here are some rules to remember regarding parentheses:

1. Place end punctuation inside the parentheses only if an entire sentence is inside it.

2. The first word in a complete sentence inside parentheses begins with a capital letter.

3. A phrase inside parentheses does not begin with a capital letter (unless it begins with a proper noun) and contains no punctuation before the end parenthesis.

   This book includes a list of books recommended for *Further Reading.* **(It is in Appendix B.)**

   This book includes a list of books recommended for *Further Reading* **(Appendix B).**

   This book includes a large number of usage suggestions **(tips and cautions).**

4. If a comma, period, semicolon, or other punctuation mark is part of the sentence, it goes after the end parenthesis.

   Don knows how to fix just about any computer problem you can think of (and many you probably haven't even thought of **yet**); he's a true geek wonder.

5. A quote within parentheses maintains its punctuation.

   Martin Luther King, Jr.'s most famous phrase (**"I have a dream …"**) became a rallying cry for the civil rights movement.

6. A question or exclamation inside parentheses receives the proper punctuation.

   I substituted butter for the lard (Do you have a better **idea?**) in this recipe.

   I substituted butter for the lard (and it made it taste so much **better!**) in this recipe.

7. A single parenthesis is not a legitimate punctuation mark.

   Incorrect: Barb gave her son the options of a) cleaning the room himself or b) letting her clean it.

   Correct: Barb gave her son the options of (a) cleaning the room himself or (b) letting her clean it.

BRACKETS

Brackets are the half-box-style punctuation marks used to

1. Insert editorial comments that provide a missing word or words within a quote: "These **[times]** are what try men's souls."

2. Provide the means to distinguish when one set of parentheses would appear inside another: (Candy told me that she'll bring the **[chocolate and peanut butter]** fudge.)

PROCEED WITH CAUTION

Be careful not to add superfluous brackets, especially when the inserted meaning could be considered common knowledge or if the meaning can be determined by the context of the sentence.

THE SLASH/VIRGULE

The slash (/), or *virgule,* is a punctuation mark that is avoided in most formal usage. You can use it

1. If it appears in a trademark.

2. If (and only if) you need to use "and/or" in a sentence in which it can't be replaced by something more elegant.

JUST A MINUTE

Corporate titles such as "vice president/marketing" are usually better written as "vice president of marketing."

The *back slash* (sometimes written as one word: *backslash*) is the slash turned around backward (\). Keep in mind that, with computer filenames on IBM- and Windows-compatible computers, you should use back slashes; uniform resource locators (URLs) and World Wide Web addresses use virgules. For clarity, computer users usually refer to a virgule as a *forward slash.*

---
e.g.

C:\folder\filename.doc

http://www.ricehahn. com/

QUOTATION MARKS

Quotation marks are the punctuation marks used to indicate dialogue in fiction or direct quotes in other writing and presentation formats. They can be used

1. Around the exact words of a speaker.

   Charlie looked in the bag of candy and asked, **"Is** that all there **is?"**

2. To enclose each part of a direct quotation when other words come between those parts.

   "There is more candy in that **bag,"** Charlie's mother told him, **"than** you get to eat **today."**

3. To enclose quoted phrases or words within a sentence.

   Bruce told the audience that they each must be wearing a name tag **"to** qualify for the door **prize."**

4. To indicate a poem.

   One of RJ's recent poems is **"Watching** You **Read."**

5. To indicate a song title.

   "Everyone Knows" is a little-known folk song from the 1960s.

6. Around magazine titles and other titles that comprise less than an entire book (individual chapters from a book, handbooks, lectures, magazine and newsletter articles, pamphlets, sermons, and short stories).

   "Appendix B, Resources" lists other books that will help you increase your knowledge of grammar and style.

7. To emphasize a word or phrase defined or explained in the rest of the sentence.

   A **"mouse"** is a pointing device used to move the cursor on a computer screen.

8. To direct attention to a word in a sentence.

   Investors are taking advantage of the **"portfolio trackers"** now available online.

9. Around a technical term.

   Doctors now believe there may be a link between **"Chiari syndrome"** and "fibromyalgia."

10. Around a trade name.

> **"Alpha"** is the publisher of this book.

11. Before each quoted stanza of a poem and at the end of the last quoted stanza.

> **"Whenever** the moon and stars are set,
> Whenever the wind is high,
> All night long in the dark and wet,
> A man goes riding by.
> Late in the night when the fires are out,
> Why does he gallop and gallop about?
>
> **"Whenever** the trees are crying aloud,
> And ships are tossed at sea,
> By, on the highway, low and loud,
> By at the gallop goes he.
> By at the gallop he goes, and then
> By he comes back at the gallop **again."**
>
> From: **"Windy Nights"** by Robert Louis Stevenson

12. At the beginning of each paragraph and at the end of the final paragraph of continuously quoted material.

> **"I** should not obtrude my affairs so much on the notice of my readers if very particular inquiries had not been made by my townsmen concerning my mode of life, which some would call impertinent, though they do not appear to me at all impertinent, but, considering the circumstances, very natural and pertinent.
>
> **"Some** have asked what I got to eat; if I did not feel lonesome; if I was not afraid; and the like. Others have been curious to learn what portion of my income I devoted to charitable purposes; and some, who have large families, how many poor children I **maintained."**
>
> From: *Walden* by Henry David Thoreau

Rules governing the use of quotation marks with other punctuation marks include

1. In American usage, commas and periods go inside the closing quotation mark.

> The band played **"Stars** and Stripes **Forever,"** and then it played **"The** Star Spangled **Banner."**
>
> The band concluded its performance with **"Yankee Doodle."**

2. A colon goes outside the end quotation mark.

> The preschool dancers performed to selections from "**The Nutcracker Suite**": They pirouetted and almost kept in time with the music.

3. A semicolon goes outside the end quotation mark.

> Janet said, "I'll meet you for **lunch**"; however, she phoned later to say she was unable to make it.

4. When a question mark is part of the quote, it goes inside the end quotation mark.

> Bishop joked about his decision to leave his university position when he mused that "someday came sooner than I expected, didn't **it?**"

5. A quote ending in a question mark never uses a comma in addition to the question mark.

> "Who has seen the **wind?**" Christina asked.

6. When an exclamation mark is part of the quote, it goes inside the end quotation mark.

> "**Whoa!**" said Roy Rogers.

7. Don't add unnecessary commas. Punctuate a sentence with partial quotes and titles of books, movies, plays, and so on as if the quotes weren't there.

> Dennis shut down his computer and said he was going to "call it a day."

> Ann said she recently watched *Practical Magic* and found it "enjoyable."

8. Only use an abbreviation inside quoted material if that is how it is quoted or it is part of a title of address; otherwise, spell out the word.

> **Incorrect:** "Hey, **Mr.**" the gas station attendant yelled. "You didn't pay for your gas!"

> **Correct:** "Hey, **mister,**" the gas station attendant yelled. "You didn't pay for your gas!"

> **Correct**: "Hey, **Mr. Feehan,**" the gas station attendant yelled. "You didn't pay for your gas!"

9. Do not begin partial quotes or full quotes that complete a thought with a capital letter.

   Dawn called Kay **"one** of the nicest people I know."

10. "Said" comes after the speaker's name unless a descriptive element would disrupt the sentence flow by coming between the word "said" and the speaker's name or unless "said" better continues the passage.

    "I quit," Rick **said**.

    "Yeah, yeah, yeah," **said** Baxter. "I've heard that threat enough times before."

    Or: "Yeah, yeah, yeah," **said** Baxter, obviously no longer worried by that threat.

11. Unless the subject is changed or restated, a quote at the beginning of a sentence makes everything that follows it dependent on that quote. The person quoted cannot logically do double duty as the subject of two clauses. If you want to use the same subject for more than one clause, consider using that subject to begin the sentence.

    Incorrect: "I would never use improper grammar," Hazel said, and added: "Not in this lifetime."

    Correct: Hazel said, "I would never use improper grammar," and added: "Not in this lifetime."

    Incorrect: "I'm hungry," George said, and left to go get lunch.

    Correct: George said, "I'm hungry," and left to go get lunch.

Another option is to change or restate the subject:

---
e.g.

Correct: "I would never use improper grammar," Hazel said, and she added: "Not in this lifetime."

Correct: "I'm hungry," George said, and he left to go get lunch.

Only use regular quotation marks with a nickname that's not just a diminutive or one that bears no relation to the real name.

Incorrect: Pamela "Pam" Hahn

Correct: Alfredo "The Cheesy Lasagna" Tortellini

Correct: William "Buddy" Thomas

When a nickname is used without the person's real name, omit the quotation marks:

Pam Hahn

The Cheesy Lasagna Tortellini

Buddy Thomas

Animal and fictional character names do not take quotation marks.

TASK: AVOID INCORRECT RUN-ON QUOTES

A quote—even a partial one—should be closed as soon as the thought is complete:

e.g.

Incorrect: Judy said that outdoor grilling is "wonderful. The meals taste great and the mess is outside instead of in my kitchen."

Can you determine what is wrong with the preceding quote?

What did Judy call outdoor cooking? (She called it "wonderful.") True, she also said, "The meals taste great and the mess is outside instead of in my kitchen." The preceding incorrect example, as punctuated, implies that she said outdoor cooking is "wonderful-the-meals-taste-great-and-the-mess-is-outside-instead-of-in-my-kitchen" as one long thought.

1. You can correct the sentence in several ways:

   a. Separate it into quotes:

      Judy said that outdoor grilling is "wonderful."

      "The meals taste great and the mess is outside instead of in my kitchen," she said.

      or: Judy said that outdoor grilling is "wonderful" and "the meals taste great and the mess is outside instead of in my kitchen."

   b. Move the attribution:

      Correct: Outdoor grilling is "wonderful," Judy said. "The meals taste great and the mess is outside instead of in my kitchen."

PROCEED WITH CAUTION

When you quote someone, just because he or she said something doesn't mean you must use the entire quote. Ideally, a quote should be understandable even without the accompanying text, although this isn't always possible. Even in those circumstances, however, quotes should only be used to stress salient points.

SINGLE QUOTATION MARKS

In American English, single quotation marks are used

1. When a quotation occurs within another quotation.

   "I read the poem **'Hector the Collector'** by Shel Silverstein and loved it," Kamala said.

2. As a matter of typographical style in headlines and other headings.

AND YOU CAN QUOTE ME ON THAT

Now that you know the rules, take a look at how quotation marks, parentheses, and italics were used in this anecdote that Pam wrote for *The Kid Report* about her granddaughter:

My daughter Lara and 4-year-old granddaughter Taylor were here for dinner recently. Lara and I were having a casserole, but because Taylor doesn't like foods mixed together, I made her a toasted cheese sandwich **(which** she assembled on the George Foreman **grill)** and filled the fryer with olive oil to make her some French fries.

I peeled and sliced the potatoes, fried them up just right, and got Taylor some French fries and catsup to go with her sandwich. While she was eating them, I asked her, **"Now** aren't those the best French fries you've ever **had?"** to which she replied, **"No.** McDonald's fries are **better."**

I asked her why. She told me, **"Because** McDonald's doesn't use potatoes in **theirs!"**

(Lara and I decided if that's the case, we don't want to know what McDonald's *does* **use** in theirs.)

Copyright © 1999 Pamela Rice Hahn

Used by Permission

All Rights Reserved

Hour's Up!

Quiz

1. What form of punctuation should not be used in formal usage unless absolutely necessary?

   a. virgule

   b. quotation mark

   c. period

   d. question mark

2. What form of punctuation can be used instead of commas with appositive nouns?

   a. italics

   b. periods

   c. parentheses

   d. ellipses

3. What slanting type style is used to add emphasis?

   a. italics

   b. parenthesis

   c. bold

   d. virgule

4. When you're using quotation marks, where does the period go?

   a. inside

   b. outside

   c. underneath

   d. next door

5. What punctuation marks are used to enclose explanatory statements?

   a. question marks

   b. exclamation marks

   c. quotation marks

   d. parentheses

6. When you put a nickname in between a first and last name, what punctuation should you use?

    a. exclamation marks

    b. quotation marks

    c. periods

    d. italics

7. What kind of punctuation marks are used when people are quoted?

    a. quotation marks

    b. parentheses

    c. question marks

    d. diacritical marks

8. What punctuation marks are used to enclose the numbers of listed items in a sentence?

    a. parentheses

    b. italics

    c. virgule

    d. exclamation marks

9. What punctuation marks are used with technical terms?

    a. periods

    b. parentheses

    c. commas

    d. quotation marks

10. What form of punctuation marks are used for editorial comments?

    a. parentheses

    b. brackets

    c. question marks

    d. periods

ANSWERS

1. a		**6.** b	
2. c		**7.** a	
3. a		**8.** a	
4. a		**9.** d	
5. d		**10.** b	

RECAP

This Hour covered some of the forms of punctuation you can use to add personality and pizzazz to your writing. You should now understand when to use italics, parentheses, and quotation marks. Now that you have mastered the finer points of problem punctuation, let's move on to Hour 20 and learn how to remain on task.

20

Remain on Task

LESSON PLAN:

In this Hour, you'll learn ways to focus on the precise message you want to communicate to your audience. You will learn how to delete superfluous material and stick to the point.

Among the things we'll cover are

- The seven "C's" of writing.
- How to edit your copy before presenting it to others.
- Getting around writer's block.

Focusing your mind on communicating clearly and effectively calls for a game plan. You should begin by reminding yourself how to recognize a professional piece of work once you have it finished. What elements will make it "ring true" with your audience? To make these important elements easier to remember, and because each one begins with the same letter, refer to them as the seven C's:

1. **Clarity:** Paint sharp, clearly worded pictures.

2. **Conciseness:** Make each word count by getting rid of anything that does not move the action forward, provide needed explanations, or entertain.

3. **Certainty:** Accuracy is essential, so check and double-check your facts, figures, quotations, references, sources, and background.

4. **Concern:** Show consideration for others by remaining focused and not straying from your point.

5. **Creativity:** Devise ways to give your words, expressions, ideas, anecdotes, and presentation format pizzazz and flair; you want it to reflect imagination, timeliness, originality, new insights, and focus.

6. **Character:** Identify the strengths of your presentation style and use the originality of your personal voice to enhance the character of what you present.

7. **Completeness:** Tell the full story by mentioning only what is essential.

WORDS TO REMEMBER

You make a greater impact when you carefully choose your words to reflect the meanings you intend.

1. These are the 10 most powerful words in writing copy for direct-mail pieces: free, you, now, new, win, easy, save, today, introductory, and guarantee.

2. These are the 12 most persuasive words that can be used in advertising copywriting: proven, discovery, health, love, new, you, save, money, easy, results, safely, and guarantee.

3. These are the 12 most misused words: dilemma, egregious, enormity, fortuitous, hopefully, ironically, penultimate, portentous, presently, literally, unique, and quintessential. (See Hour 24, "Problem Words and Expressions," for a review of problem words and expressions.)

WHY YOU NEED TAKE-AWAY VALUE

Everybody appreciates value. There have probably been times when you've driven out of your way to get a "good deal." If you are going to give your audience something worth its time and attention, you need to determine what it will want from your presentation.

A presentation of any sort—whether it's an article, a speech, or a sales pitch—that skips from point to point without any logical progression or transitions is one that fails. It's one that fails to deliver any *take-away value*.

STRICTLY DEFINED

Your *take-away value* is the element or message that you wish to convey the most impact. What will your audience "take away" with them once they've heard or read your material?

In the same way that any successful organization operates under a clearly focused mission statement of its plans and objectives, you, too, must remain focused. That doesn't mean you can't have minor digressions here and there. Just be certain that, if you relate an anecdote or include a quote, it can be related back to what you perceive and designate as the take-away value for that presentation.

Task: Guarantee Take-Away Value

The following steps will help ensure that your focus remains on your established take-away value throughout your presentation.

1. **Determine the take-away value.** You must know where you intend to end up (or wrap up) before you can chart your steps on how to get there. You wouldn't accept a job assignment if the boss wouldn't tell you where the office is located. Likewise, you'd be suspect if he said something such as "We like to remain flexible, so we just get in our cars at 8 A.M. and continue driving until we all converge at the same location." Don't expect your audience to ride along if you yourself aren't sure where you're headed.

2. **Slant your lead.** You want your lead to reflect your take-away value. As you learned in Hours 16, "Leads and Closings," and 18, "Managing Your Research," a lead is the way you first grab people's attention and draw them into the material. Your lead should reflect the tone of your presentation and should give some clues as to what conclusions you wish your audience to reach once it has read or heard all your material.

3. **Cover the five W's and two H's.** As you prepare your presentation, make sure it answers the basic questions of who, what, where, when, why, how, and how much. If you've answered all seven, you have a better chance of covering all the important details.

4. **Demonstrate clarity.** Clarity is #1 on the seven C's list for a reason. It's important that you make sure your audience hears what you are trying to say. The message you send is the message received. Avoid ambiguity. Be precise and clear.

5. **Maintain that clarity.** You can do this if you create a strong focus and stay on it. Weave the piece around the one central idea or main theme that is your take-away value. Reflect this theme in a title that contains an action verb. Don't just cover a topic because it exists; describe its merits.

6. **Stay focused on the mission statement for your presentation.** (Refer to Hour 18 for a review of the one-sentence mission statement.) By now you should have summarized your purpose or main idea in one sentence. (If it takes two sentences, you have two themes.)

Knowing your purpose and including the ideas that fulfill this purpose provide the unity necessary to ensure that you remain on topic. That single purpose helps you collect and organize your information effectively so you can reach your goal.

7. **Use specific, concrete language.** Avoid vague generalities. Specific details can make or break your presentation. Whenever you can replace an abstract concept with a specific noun, do so. Employ action verbs. Don't cover broad issues and ideas. Incorporate general ideas and issues into the lives of real people with real quotes, real circumstances with real outcomes.

8. **Show, don't tell.** By using good examples and illustrations, you can paint a picture with your words. If you are covering ways to avoid the perception of sexism, show the unnecessary friction between co-workers that male-to-female-directed comments such as "Don't nag" can cause. If your topic is about how to use the company schooling program, tell about an employee who gained a degree and was promoted as a result. Any time a member of your audience can "see" personal rewards or ramifications because of an action, it has a greater impact than if it were perceived as some mythical infraction or occurrence committed by or happening to "the other guy."

Use real examples discriminately so that you convey a real message. If you are covering intellectual concepts, it may be appropriate to use people's names and their comments. Whenever possible or appropriate, let people talk. As you saw in Hour 19, "The Ins and Outs of Italics, Parentheses, Quotations Marks, and More," direct quotes can breathe life into your presentation and can help maintain audience focus and interest. Endorsements, opinions, feedback, anecdotes, questions, perspectives, and predictions all can be used to work people's words into your letters, brochures, reports, or speeches.

9. **Portray the passion.** Your audience will sense when you have a passion about your topic and will respond favorably to that passion. If you cover the things you care about, chances are your audience will come to care about them, too. Include the heartbeat of your life and you'll tug at the heartstrings of others when you do. Embrace the genuine gusto of your insights and feelings about an issue and your audience will experience it, too.

10. **Maintain accuracy.** Verify all facts. Do your homework. Check every fact, confirm the spelling of every name and place, and validate even the smallest details to make sure everything is correct. Make some extra phone calls or send some e-mails for confirmation if you need to do so. If you aren't sure how to verify some of the information, find out! Don't make excuses; get results. One error can cause your audience to question your ability to cover a topic. If you have several (or numerous) errors, you'll lose them entirely. And you'll lose your credibility in the process.

JUST A MINUTE

Write for the everyday person, not for the intellectual. If the everyday person can understand you, so will the intellectual. However, the reverse isn't true. Great and profound ideas can be communicated in simple, everyday language.

WORKSHOP: BLUEPRINTS AND WORK PERMITS

There will be times when you must be the one who goes out in search of the take-away value. When you're put in charge of a project, adding your style to the end task when working on a team effort is possible if you do all within your power to remain on task. One thing that will help you do just that is to develop a reasonable timetable to ensure that the work gets done. Such a timetable will help you better keep the end goal in mind so you don't get sidetracked by disruptions to your schedule.

TASK: TIMETABLE

You can only add your personal style to a presentation if you have the time to do so. To ensure that you do (have the time), here are some things to ask yourself in this process.

1. What steps are necessary to accomplish the desired results?

   Make a list of the duties and activities that will need to be done.

   Decide who will do them and when.

   Determine the proper sequence of events and when you need them done so you can reach your objective.

   Do the legwork and come up with these answers.

2. Why must each step be taken?

   Each step should lead to the completion of your goals. Make sure that each one is necessary for the project.

   Verify that you've established the correct order of priority for the steps deemed necessary.

3. Should you delegate any of the tasks to others?

   If you decide to delegate, outline and define the chain of command and each person's individual tasks.

   Determine how much time you should realistically allot for each part of each task.

   Note any concerns you have about factors beyond the control of workers that may impact their performance.

4. How will the progress reports of each step take place?

   Scheduled meetings?

   Informal meetings?

   Phone conferences?

   E-mail correspondence?

5. How often should you re-evaluate your progress?

   Establish interim dates to go over your time projections to determine whether they're realistic.

   Make any adjustments necessary.

6. How many changes to your original plans (steps) are needed? How will you incorporate these changes?

   Periodically go back through the preceding five points and note any loose ends.

   Get responses to any unanswered questions.

Make a note of any team members who appear to be falling behind.

Address any other issues that could hinder your ability to reach the project target date successfully.

Negative Realities

Sometimes you have to accept the facts and realize that a team member just isn't an asset to the project. As frustrating as it can be, you may have to pick up some of the slack caused by another person's missed deadlines or failure to grasp the work required. To avoid this type of situation from getting out of hand, here are some things to watch out for:

- Questions that appear to be nothing more than a way to divert attention away from a missed deadline
- Failure to follow instructions
- A member's refusal to adapt work to the style required by the project
- A member's attempts to deflect attention away from him- or herself by complaining about unrelated issues

When this last example occurs, you can save time by doing the following:

Recognizing such behavior for what it is—a way to avoid doing the work or accepting responsibility for work not yet done.

Not getting bogged down in the unnecessary paper shuffle this type of situation can create. You want each piece of paper or task that you personally handle to be one that allows you to organize the material productively according to the style required by the project.

When you give your audience something in exchange for its time, you've successfully supplied a product with value. When you offer the audience something of benefit, it'll embrace your message and take the value of your presentation with it.

Getting Around the Block

Sometimes, despite having all your carefully prepared task lists and project procedures in front of you, you might find that your mind is so full of good ideas that you don't know where to begin. So you don't. Soon you find that you cannot get started because of a fear of breaking some rule or overlooking some procedure. When that happens, it often helps to employ a few tricks to help power-shift yourself into gear.

Do a Free Write

Here's your chance to forget about all the rules for a while. Don't worry about being precise with punctuation or grammar or style. Just start to write. It doesn't matter if you do so in longhand, crayon, or invisible ink. It doesn't matter if you're at your keyboard, away from your desk, or at a picnic table in the sun. Just write as quickly as possible about anything that comes to mind about your topic. "Spill" your thoughts onto the page (or the screen). You can go back and organize your material later. Now isn't the time to worry about any edits. Now is the time to just "do."

Work Backward

You've probably heard someone say, "If you don't know where you're headed, you'll probably end up someplace else." If your presentation involves selling a product or an idea, you already know that you need to end it by somehow asking for the sale. (They don't call it a sales "close" for nothing.) For this exercise, determine the best way to conclude your project (whether it's a letter, a report, or a speech) and write out the ending.

Next, ask yourself some questions about the facts and the background information that would lead to this conclusion. Each answered question will be part of what you now need to add to your first draft. After you have these answers, you can rearrange them later so that they're in a logical order so you can progress from your opening to your close.

Close Your Eyes

Granted, this may not appear to be productive work time if you're leaning back and closing your eyes while you're seated in your cubicle—especially if the boss happens to walk by (which, if you close your eyes, you know he or she will). But sometimes you do need to dream it before you can be it. Athletes practice visualization techniques for a reason: It helps if they can picture themselves achieving their objectives. It doesn't matter which track you're on. The same technique can help in the rat race, too. A mental rehearsal of the reaction you desire from your intended audience can help you frame what is needed to achieve those results.

DRAFT A SEQUENCE OF EVENTS SCENARIO

If your assignment is to write a profile of your company's new president for the annual report or the company newsletter, coming up with a sequence of events will be easy. The chronological sequence will begin with college education, proceed through the person's entry-level work and field experience, and end with details about his or her appointment by the board of directors. When you get in the habit of mapping a sequence of events, you'll begin to develop an intuitive sense of how best to arrange the order to fit the needs of a given presentation.

IMAGINE THE SEQUEL

Hollywood isn't the only place where it's practical to ride on a current wave of success. If you can imagine the things that will result *because of* your successful presentation, you can sometimes better appreciate *why* certain steps are necessary to achieve that success. When you understand why they're important, you can make your decisions on what steps are needed to ensure that you convey the significance of each one. In a manner similar to the one you employ when you draft a sequence of events, Point A will lead you to Point B and so on.

HOUR'S UP!

1. Reading your material out loud helps you:
    a. find awkward wordings.
    b. discover the best voice inflections to use during your presentation.
    c. gauge its flow and rhythm.
    d. all of the above.

2. A presentation is concise when it:
    a. finishes up within the time allotted.
    b. is free of anything that does not move the action forward.
    c. is polite in tone.
    d. is instrumental in helping you get a promotion.

3. Your audience members gain "take-away value" from your presentation when:

    a. you provide them with a tote bag to hold all of the handouts.

    b. you include a box lunch.

    c. you give them something worth their time that includes a message to which they can relate.

    d. you deliver your message over the speaker at the drive-thru window.

4. The one-sentence summary of your project is known as the:

    a. mission statement.

    b. synopsis.

    c. punch line.

    d. manifesto.

4. An efficient presentation:

    a. fits together like a jigsaw puzzle.

    b. meanders around so that you touch on something of interest to everyone.

    c. includes smooth transitions so that it flows from point to point.

    d. a and c.

5. You "show, don't tell" when you:

    a. use hand puppets.

    b. use an overhead projector.

    c. paint vivid pictures with your words.

    d. point to people in the audience and surprise them by telling stories about them.

6. If the everyday person can understand you:

    a. your ideas will seem too simple.

    b. your audience will doubt your education level.

    c. chances are even the intellectuals will understand you, too.

    d. your audience will become bored.

7. The timetable for your project should always include:

    a. the steps necessary to complete the work.

    b. the name of somebody to blame if things go wrong.

    c. a priority order for the necessary steps.

    d. a and c.

8. Some ways you can help decide how to write up your research is to:

    a. do a free write.

    b. work backward, from ending to your lead.

    c. close your eyes and visualize your presentation.

    d. all of the above.

9. Writing things up in chronological order can also be called:

    a. drafting a sequence of events.

    b. preparing the birthday cake fund calendar.

    c. age discrimination.

    d. volunteering an age-old method.

10. Visualizing the sequel can help you:

    a. imagine your next job interview should your presentation fail.

    b. understand why each step in the presentation is necessary.

    c. help you determine which steps are necessary.

    d. b and c.

ANSWERS

1. d	**6.** c
2. b	**7.** d
3. c	**8.** d
4. d	**9.** a
5. c	**10.** d

RECAP

This Hour taught you how to keep focused on your key points and how to remain on task. You now know the importance you need to place on take-away value and how you can include such value in your work. Now that you know how to remain on task, it is time for you to move on to Hour 21, "Getting Beyond Your First Draft," where you'll learn how to edit your first draft and give it the polish it needs.

HOUR 21

Getting Beyond Your First Draft

After you have finished writing the first draft of your article, speech, letter, or story, it is time to go back and proofread it, edit it, and revise it. Yes, what you have written is probably quite good already. Nevertheless, there is always room for improvement.

PROOFREADING TECHNIQUES

Modern technology, with its spelling and grammar check programs, has made some people lazy. They assume that they don't really need to proofread their written material closely, as long as red or green warning lines are not appearing on their word-processor screens. This is dangerous rationalizing, however. Computer spelling programs don't know if you meant to spell "rite," "write," or "right." They don't know if you meant to write "anyone" or "any one." They also don't recognize the latest proper structure for hyphenated and closed versus multiple-word compound word forms.

The computer cannot understand that you may purposely have used a sentence fragment, especially in writing dialogue or in quotes. Computers can process, but they cannot actually think. That's why it's important for you to learn ways to proofread your work.

CHAPTER SUMMARY

LESSON PLAN:

In this Hour, you'll learn how to "doctor" your first draft so that your word choice is more effective and your content says what you want it to say in the most powerful and easily understood way.

Among the things we'll cover are

- How to test your correspondence before mailing it.
- How to edit your written material.
- How to avoid being redundant.
- How to proofread closely and carefully.

Fortunately, proofreading is not very difficult to master, and the benefits it offers in saved time and money make it worth your attention. Here are nine tips that will help you master proofreading:

1. **Read your written material aloud.** Reading something audibly helps you gauge its rhythm, pace, sound, and degree of difficulty. If you discover that certain passages cause you to be tongue-tied or long-winded, rewrite them in more simplified language. Use simple declarative sentences. Keep the paragraphs short. Strive for clarity and power.

2. **Read backward.** If you read sentences in the same sequence you wrote or dictated them, you may read into the sentences things that might not really be there. Since you already know what your business letter, report, or project summary is supposed to say, you may anticipate "ghost" words. To guarantee that you do see each word, try reading backward from the last word on a page to the first. In this way, you will notice if you misspelled a word, forgot a period after an abbreviation, or overlooked a capital letter.

JUST A MINUTE

You know where your strengths lie. Some can work with documents onscreen; however, if you do a better job of proofreading working from a printout, do so. The only wrong way to proofread is to not do it. Use the way that works best for you.

3. **Let it rest.** If possible, let your first drafts or page proofs rest in a desk drawer for a few hours or, better yet, a few days. Later, you can proofread the copy with "new eyes." You will have forgotten the exact sequence you originally used in the written presentation, and you will now be able to judge it as an outside reader.

4. **Juxtapose pages.** As long as the pages of your 20-page report are numbered, there is no reason you cannot shuffle them. Each page can then be analyzed as one unit, and you will not be distracted by your concentration on the overall content. After you've checked for copy errors, you can read the report again later to analyze its continuity.

5. **Vary the routine.** If you come back from a four-day business trip and find your desk burdened with letters, position papers, committee minutes, and staff memos that all need to be proofread by you before they can be issued, do not overload your senses by trying to blitz through everything in rapid succession. Vary the routine. Read and critique all

the letters and then relax and glance through a business magazine. Read and critique the committee minutes and then change the pace by dictating some letters or returning some phone calls. Keep yourself alert and fresh during the proofreading process.

6. **Use a line screen.** When you proofread printouts, a simple line screen made by cutting a 4-mm slit in a 5" × 7" index card can be used as a window opening to run over one line of print at a time. By rapidly moving up the page from the bottom line to the top, you will not be mentally caught up in any sequence of sentencing. You can critique each line for grammar, spelling, and punctuation as it appears before you, verifying context as required.

7. **Delegate.** If you are absolutely too busy to personally make sure your materials are carefully proofread, or if you simply cannot stand to look anymore at what you have been writing and rewriting for the past several days, hand it to someone else. Maybe you can swap something of yours with something of a colleague's; each of you will benefit from a different set of eyes looking at what has been written.

8. **Consult outsiders.** If you work independently and don't have office colleagues to turn to for proofreading help, you can get assistance from outsiders to your business. Some people like to hire people who run typing and transcribing services to do proofreading because these people are trained to spot printed errors. Additionally, there are Web sites that offer tips on how to correct problems you may have discovered when proofreading.

FYI For proofreading and editing help, Jill Frey and Jerry Alexander of the Presbyterian College Writing Center maintain a Web site at http://home.presby.edu/writingc/resources/editing.html. You can also find assistance at Purdue University's OWL (Online Writing Lab) Handouts proofreading strategies site at http://owl.english.purdue.edu/Files/32.html; you can find other articles arranged by topic at http://owl.english.purdue.edu/writers/by-topic.html. In addition, Capitol Community College has a table of Common Proofreading Symbols at http://cctc.commnet.edu/writing/symbols.htm.

9. **Master the art of copy and paste.** When working with information contained in several electronic documents or inserting Web site addresses or copy into your work, you can avoid inadvertent typing errors if you learn how to "grab" that text, copy it, and then paste it into your file.

INADVERTENT ERRORS

Often, while proofreading, you will be so busy seeking mechanical errors that you will sometimes overlook broader-based problems. But you cannot assume that, just because your writings have no mechanical problems, other problems don't exist. Here are some other problems you should watch for:

1. **Misused words.** A *malapropism* is a word that sounds like a word with a totally different meaning; it is used by someone who has mistaken the sound-alike words. For example, if a person runs into a wall and someone else says, "You need to see an *optimist* to get your glasses changed," that is a malapropism. The word "optimist" should have been "optometrist." As Mark Twain once noted, "The difference between the right word and the almost-right word is the difference between lightning and the lightning bug." It is up to you to use a dictionary to make sure you have used words properly.

2. **Crude phrases.** Go back through what you have written and make sure you do not include anything that could be interpreted as off-color language; gender, racial, or ethnic slurs; jargon; clichés; or slang catchphrases that will quickly date themselves. Keep things on a professional level.

3. **Ambiguities.** Make sure that anything you have tried to explain has, indeed, been told clearly.

4. **Redundancies.** Editing onscreen can sometimes introduce redundancies if you copy and then paste words elsewhere rather than "cut" and paste them. Check to make sure you didn't forget to delete any words or phrases you may have moved elsewhere in the document.

5. **Minor discrepancies.** Make sure there are no "changes" that shouldn't be in your report. Statistics stated on one page should agree with those you give on another. Keep your use of spelling and capitalization consistent.

PUNCH THE PUNS

A *pun* is a humorous play on words derived from the similar sounds of words or dual meanings. However, this form of humor can get old fast, so it needs to be used sparingly.

e.g.

Dachshund through the snow ...

Gone with the **Schwinn:** The Epic Story of a Bicycle Race

Intentional puns used in headlines or ad copy are one thing. When they appear due to an accidental arrangement of words, they can create problems that distract from the message being presented.

EDITING

One of the best ways to keep from embarrassing yourself with something you have written is to be your own harshest editor. Here are ten procedures you can follow to help tighten your writing and make your meaning clearer.

PROCEED WITH CAUTION

A line like "I **haven't got** time for the pain" may be okay in a song lyric. There the extra word is needed to maintain the beat. You'll improve your message, however, if you cut superfluous words; because of your busy schedule, you "**haven't** time for the pain."

1. **Cut needless words.** In many cases, you can eliminate one of the words often used with another without changing the meaning. Here is a short list to help you train your ear to hear those extra words that can be cut without changing the meaning of the content.

Needless Words

current trend	finally ended	first began
follow after	free gift	have got
important essentials	local residents	most complete
protest against	specific example	sunset in the west
true facts	very unique	

There will always be exceptions, but by eliminating these redundancies you will often save space, get to your point, and hold the readers' or audience's attention.

2. **Substitute words for phrases.** Here is a list of commonly used phrases that clutter sentences and the words you should replace them with to achieve a more streamlined writing style.

Phrase Substitutions

Phrase	Word to Substitute
prior to	before
on the grounds that	because
in the case that	if
in the course of	during
close proximity	near
majority of instances	usually

3. **Beware of mixed metaphors.** A *metaphor* is a phrase that applies the qualities of one entity to something else to give it a visual or emotional interpretation. (Refer to Hour 1, "Understanding Grammar," for additional discussion of metaphors.) Mike Resnick meant it to be funny when he wrote, "You have to get up pretty early in the morning to pull the wool over my eyes!" Unless humor is your purpose, your message will be lost if you mismatch metaphors. If you create an original metaphor, make sure it follows a logical line of thinking.

4. **Avoid nonaligned thoughts.** Just as one tire on an automobile that is out of alignment can make the entire car ride wobbly, so, too, can one nonaligned sentence cause an entire paragraph to wobble. Read the following sentence and then try to figure out what it means:

e.g.

I've seen a lot of movies lately, which makes me wonder about the so-called unemployment problem.

There is no telling for sure what the sentence in the example means. It could mean that (a) the topics of the movies raised questions about the unemployment problem, (b) too people have money to attend movies for there to be an unemployment problem, or (c) so many people have time to watch movies because they are unemployed. But what if you rewrote it this way:

e.g.

Every time I attend a movie lately, the places are packed; where's the unemployment problem and lack of money I've heard so much about?

Phrasing the thought pattern around one specific theme ensures the precise meaning of the sentence.

5. **Avert ambiguous construction.** The way you choose to word your sentence can make the meaning unclear. Similar to nonaligned thinking, ambiguous construction leaves the reader wondering what the precise meaning of the sentence is. For example, saying "All films are not boring" is wrong since there are many boring movies. Therefore, the sentence should be reconstructed as "Not all films are boring." This implies that, yes, some are boring, but others are not.

   Consider the following:

e.g.

The veterinarian checked two baboons and two sick seals.

In the preceding example, you aren't sure how many sick animals there were. Did the vet check the baboons and find that they were well, but then he checked the seals already knowing they were sick? Or were the baboons and the seals all sick and the vet checked all four? Thus, you need to reconstruct the sentence:

e.g.

The veterinarian checked four sick animals: two baboons and two seals.

Now it's obvious that the adjective "sick" applied to all the animals. Run the same tests on your sentences. Do they say clearly what you meant for them to say? If not, rewrite them.

6. **Prevent illogical phrasings.** Sometimes what is logical inside your mind does not translate itself logically to the printed word. Here's an example: "There will be no admission to the concert tonight." Why have a concert if no one will be allowed inside? "There will be no charge for admission to tonight's concert" states what is really meant.

7. **Watch out for vague references to pronouns.** Misplaced pronouns can cause some of the most hilarious misstatements in writing. Consider this example from a church bulletin:

e.g.

The ladies of the church have cast off clothing of every kind. **They** can be seen in the church basement Saturday.

Chances are that "they" was meant to refer to the clothing, not the ladies; awkward wording of the first sentence caused the pronoun reference to be even more confusing, if not downright embarrassing. (Refer to Hour 4, "Elementary Sentence Components II: Pronouns," for a review of pronouns and Hour 7, "Reaching Agreements," for information on pronoun and antecedent agreement.)

8. **Avoid pretentious language.** In Hour 14, "Forego the Fluff," we stressed the importance of using plain, simple, easy-to-understand words. It's usually best to replace words that may seem artificial, pretentious, overbearing, or pompous with simpler ones. Here is a sample list of the sorts of changes you can make:

Pretentious Word Replacement

Pretentious Word	Preferred Change
behest	request
cognizant	aware
commendation	praise
customary channels	usual ways
instantaneously	now
milieu	surroundings
multitudinous	many
obfuscate	confuse
remuneration	pay
terminate	end
wherewithal	means

9. **Replace long clauses with power words.** Check prepositional phrases and dependent clauses to see if they can be improved by using a stronger noun, verb, adjective, or adverb. If one word can do the work of two or more words, you need to use that word.

    With phrases: The wind, which blew through the cracks, made a whistling sound.

    Improved: The wind whistled through the cracks.

10. **Keep transitions flowing smoothly.** Make sure one sentence flows naturally and logically into the next sentence; the same applies to going from one paragraph to the next. Good communication appears seamless and connects naturally.

WORKSHOP: CHECKING REVISIONS

After you have followed the preceding guidelines for spotting problems in your written material, use the following checklist to judge how well you did on any rewrites.

1. Did you avoid clichés, jargon, vague references, trite expressions, irrelevancies, pretentious language, and any discriminatory expressions?
2. Did you include appropriate details?
3. Did you stay with the active voice as much as possible?
4. Did you use correct grammar and the proper parts of speech?
5. Did you double-check your punctuation?
6. Did you use smooth transitions between paragraphs?
7. Did you indicate any action that needs to be taken?
8. Did you verify your facts and figures?
9. Was your material prepared in the proper format?
10. Was your material specific and straightforward?
11. Was your spelling correct and consistent?
12. Were you careful not to abbreviate unnecessarily?
13. Did you use all necessary capital letters?
14. Was your word choice correct and effective?
15. Was your writing sincere and natural in its tone?
16. Were you careful not to talk down to the reader?
17. Did you use a strong, to-the-point ending?

Although this may seem like a great deal of checking and rechecking, you will discover after a while that it becomes a natural point-to-point procedure.

LEARN FROM OTHER WRITERS

We have stressed that your work should be original. This does not mean you cannot gain insights by studying the "models" of other writers. There is an adage that says, "If you want to know what a crooked stick looks like, find a straight stick. Anything that does not look like that is crooked." A similar lesson can be applied to writing. If you want to know what bad writing is, look at what you consider to be good writing and use that as a measurement.

If you write primarily nonfiction, keep a file of business letters, memos, and reports that come to you. Although you would not want to copy them verbatim, you might highlight a particularly good greeting or closing that you, too, could use sometime. Perhaps someone used an eye-catching layout that you could borrow for material of your own.

JUST A MINUTE

Pull out a couple of manila folders and label them "Items Worth Studying." Fill these files with good examples of letters, brochures, flyers, memos, newsletters, and notes about passages in fiction. Mark the parts of these printed materials that caught your eye. Consider how you might use some of these same phrasings of words or format layouts for writings of your own.

If you write fiction, read novels or short stories with some colored pens or pencils close at hand. Color code the book as you read it. Each time you find a fascinating passage of dialogue, highlight it in yellow. If there is a particularly good description of a setting, highlight it in blue. If you find some very smooth transitions from present time to a flashback, highlight them in green. Then, once you have completed the book, you can go back and reread these specific passages and analyze them again for their effectiveness.

 If you have access to the Internet, you can find a lot of speech or presentation script examples to study. Do a search on AltaVista (www.altavista.com), Google (www.google.com), or your favorite search engine using keywords such as "speech transcripts," "presentation scripts," or "tutorials."

Many companies also now have their brochures online, either as Web pages or available for downloading as Adobe Acrobat (.pdf) files.

READING WITH A PURPOSE

In Appendix B, "Resources," you will find a list of books that will help you think creatively, enhance your vocabulary, experiment with various writing styles, and offer you format guides for how to present your materials.

Make a pledge to yourself that, for the next few months or perhaps even a year, you will mix some of these books into your rotation of reading novels, magazines, and office materials. You don't have to maintain a steady diet of all books about enhancing your communication skills; however, by using the book you are currently reading as a springboard for additional study and by steadily adding to your body of knowledge about writing, editing, and proof-reading, you will soon become an authority in these areas.

JUST A MINUTE

Start building a home reference library of other good books about writing, editing, speaking, and listening. As you read these books, keep them handy for ready use. Review them from time to time to keep your skills sharp.

HOUR'S UP!

1. What is a better choice than "on the grounds that"?

    a. in light of the fact that

    b. because

    c. incidentally

    d. meanwhile, back on the farm …

2. Good writing always has

    a. misused words

    b. crude phrases

    c. ambiguities

    d. none of the above

3. What is a better choice than "obfuscate"?

    a. huh?

    b. tickle

    c. sing show tunes

    d. confuse

4. What is a better choice than "in close proximity"?

    a. yesterday

    b. near

    c. pretty close

    d. a and c

5. If you want a sure way to embarrass yourself, you should

    a. never proofread your material

    b. brush your teeth

    c. wear your seatbelt

    d. watch TV

6. A mixed metaphor should never be used by

    a. oxymorons

    b. someone up the creek without a care in the world

    c. eager beavers who climb the corporate ladder

    d. anyone

7. An important part of editing is

    a. the enduring satisfaction

    b. the social life

    c. cutting unnecessary words

    d. the annual convention

8. What is a better choice than "multitudinous"?

    a. astroturfious

    b. lots and lots

    c. many

    d. an eensy, weensy bit

9. Which is not an important question when making revisions?

    a. Did you stay with the active voice as much as possible?

    b. Did you double-check your punctuation?

    c. Did you remember to lock the door?

    d. Was your spelling correct and consistent?

10. What is a better choice than "majority of instances"?

    a. usually

    b. the odd time

    c. more than once in a blue moon

    d. none of the above

Quiz

ANSWERS

1. b	**6.** d
2. d	**7.** c
3. d	**8.** c
4. b	**9.** c
5. a	**10.** a

RECAP

This Hour showed you that the first draft of any piece of writing is just the beginning of your writing process. You next must use your proofreading, editing, and revising skills to polish the rough copy to make it "shine." Now that you know how to go about revising your first draft, you're ready to learn how to put your style into practice.

HOUR 22

Putting Your Style into Practice I

No matter what form of business communication you're preparing, the language you use can affect the impact of your message. In some instances, formal usage will create a far greater impact for your ideas; in other instances, informal usage will provide a more positive reception for the thoughts you are trying to convey.

Later in this Hour, you'll learn some pointers for specific forms of business communication. For now, here are a few general points that apply to all areas.

ADAPT TO YOUR AUDIENCE

Whenever you're trying to convey information, it's important to keep your audience in mind. You would address a group of first-graders much differently than you would a room full of university professors; you would speak at a different pace and use different words, hoping that the professors still understood.

PROCEED WITH CAUTION

Seriously, how you address your audience can be as important as what you say. If you use words that no one understands, no one can truly appreciate what you're saying.

Choose a level that's appropriate for the group you're addressing, whether it's in a letter, a memo, a presentation, or a speech.

CHAPTER SUMMARY

LESSON PLAN:

In this Hour, you'll learn how to approach various forms of business communication.

Among the things we'll cover are

- How to prepare internal and external office correspondence.
- Points to remember when creating business documents.
- How to add "verb spice" to your resumé.

TASK: MAKING SURE IT FITS

Keep the following points in mind when creating business documents. Ask yourself these questions. If the answer to any of them is "no," you should consider editing until all points are met.

1. Look at what you are writing from the recipient's viewpoint. Is it interesting, tactful, truthful, succinct, and courteous?

2. Is it understandable? Does it over-use jargon or technobabble?

3. Is it accurate?

4. Is the tone appropriate?

5. Is your personality part of the writing? Or are you hiding behind generic terms like "the management wishes" or "company policies state"?

6. Are you conveying important information or using wordy phrases as filler?

After you've completed your draft and have edited it, refer back to this list to be sure you've met all the criteria for a well-written business document.

SOFTENING BAD NEWS

Bad news is a part of life. Just as you've probably already received some yourself, sooner or later, you'll have to give some, too.

Fortunately, you can usually soften the blow when delivering bad news, making the impact a little less severe. Whether it's an employee reprimand or the news of an unsuccessful application for a promotion, there are a few techniques you can use to address the problem at hand while minimizing the chance for hurt feelings.

These tips will help you in all forms of interpersonal relations including conversations with your spouse.

1. **Avoid blaming language.** Don't use phrases that cast blame like "you should have" or "you neglected." You want to minimize the shock and pain involved in receiving the bad news. Casting additional judgment intensifies this rather than reducing it.

2. **Don't be too blunt.** It can be tempting to blurt out negative criticism or bad news, especially when the recipient may be wearing on your nerves. Lashing out won't soften the blow.

Choose your language carefully, using the passive voice when appropriate. Saying "Because the sales report wasn't completed on time ..." is softer than saying "Because you didn't finish the report ..."

3. **Find a positive to emphasize.** Many times, you can use a positive aspect to minimize the impact of a negative one. An ideal example is the manager who must reprimand her staff but balances it with praise for performance in other areas and encouragement.

4. **Remember not to be trite.** If you use this technique, make sure it is relevant. It would be inappropriate to tell a terminated employee that he or she now has the opportunity to work on a novel or another lifetime goal. However, this could be an excellent response in consoling a spouse.

5. **Offer a solution.** Offering a solution and agreeing to work with the person is an excellent technique. It addresses the problem and shows the person that you are committed to moving forward rather than holding a grudge.

6. **Be objective.** Sometimes you can't minimize the blow. If you rely on facts, however, you aren't inserting any personal judgment; there still may be pain and hurt feelings, but at least you won't be the cause of it.

PRESENTING YOUR INFORMATION

Whenever you plan to present information, you need to present it in a logical fashion. Organized information is more readily absorbed because people don't have to try to sort out the facts and figures.

USE AN OUTLINE

No matter what you're doing, an outline will help you present your information in the most effective way.

Outlines don't have to be large undertakings to be effective. Even handwritten notes about a project or a presentation can be enough to keep you on task. Listing your major points will help you see the finished product in your mind and will provide you with the opportunity to refine and reorganize those points.

JUST A MINUTE

Rearranging an outline is considerably less work than trying to redo a 12-page report.

STRUCTURE YOUR DATA

When presenting data, you can choose from a few different methods of organization:

1. **Order of importance.** If you're listing sales figures, you may want to list the best-selling items first. If you're emphasizing products that are not meeting sales quotas, you may want to begin with the least satisfactory.

2. **Chronological order.** When referring to events, starting off with the earliest is usually the best bet. When you want to emphasize more recent events first, you can use a reverse-chronological list.

3. **Alphabetical order.** Unless another form is more appropriate, an alphabetical list is an excellent way to present information because it is easily accepted and understood.

4. **Numerical order.** When listing percentages or sales figures, you may want to list information in an ascending or descending order unless another form, such as alphabetical order or order of importance, is more appropriate.

5. **Conventional order.** Some companies have standard ways of reporting information, and these standard ways don't always follow a logical pattern. If your company prefers its information presented by sales area, for example, you should follow that format.

You may have to try one or more approaches before you hit on the one that works best for the particular presentation.

BUSINESS WRITING

In today's business world, employers demand versatility. Companies can require employees to perform many different tasks, and almost every one of them involves conversation in some form.

The following are various tasks an employee may face in the course of his or her duties, and we've included tips for how to produce them more effectively.

FYI For examples of business writing, see *Writing That Works: How to Improve Your Memos, Letters, Reports, Speeches, Resumes, Plans, and Other Business Papers* by Kenneth Roman and Joel Raphaelson, New York: Harper Mass Market Paperbacks, 1995 (ISBN: 0061093815). You can also find sample documents in most word-processing programs. Consult your Help documentation for more information.

INTEROFFICE MEMOS AND ELECTRONIC MAIL

Interoffice memos are used for a variety of reasons ranging from retirement party announcements to project-development updates.

Since interoffice memos don't leave the company, a conversational tone is often desirable, but you should choose your tone carefully. A formal tone can alienate the reader and sounds ridiculous when inviting staff to a company picnic; a conversational tone, however, is not appropriate in a layoff notice.

Here are some tips to consider when you're drafting a memo:

- When you write your memo, get to the point as quickly as you can. A long memo only wastes time—both when you write it and when others read it.

- Before you start drafting your memo, identify your main point. If you have more than two, you may want to consider splitting them into different memos. Subpoints are okay, but remember that too many of them will defeat your purpose.

- Many companies encourage their employees to use electronic mail instead of memos. Electronic messaging systems have existed for years, but they tended to be available only within the company before the advent of the Internet. Now employees can easily send electronic messages to clients and customers. It is a fast and economical method of communication.

- Because it is so convenient, many people find it tempting to reply very quickly to a message. Before you reply, consider your response. Remember that humor and sarcasm can be easily misinterpreted when a person's tone of voice and joking manner can't be easily conveyed. Take your time and avoid any potential misunderstandings.

- Most e-mail software allows you to "comment out" the original text of a message when you reply to it. This means you can quote the original

message, with each line beginning with an identifying symbol (such as
>). That way, you can respond directly to specific points in a message
by inserting your answers directly after them.

>Have you received the most recent inventory list from Denver?

Not yet. We are expecting it to be compiled by the beginning of next
week, and will forward it once it arrives.

>We have finished the sales reports for two of the five regions. The
final three should be complete by the end of next week.

If you can send the two finished reports, my department will begin
working on the shareholders' report. The others can be submitted as
they are completed.

JUST A MINUTE

Be considerate when using e-mail. Delete the quoted text that isn't directly relevant to your response and don't send a two-word reply (such as "I agree!")
followed by an entire copy of the original 1,200-word message. If you're for-
warding a message, delete any extraneous e-mail addresses or signature lines
that might have been included on previous forwards. This is not only a waste
of time, it's also a waste of space on your and your recipient's hard drives.

- If you correspond with someone regularly, make sure the subject line
  of your e-mail accurately reflects the content. Many people fall into the
  trap of simply hitting the Reply button and then typing in the text. If
  you do this, you run the risk of having your message lost in a sea of
  other messages with similar subject lines. Rather than risk it not being
  read, take a moment to update your subject line. The recipient will
  appreciate it because it helps keep message "threads" organized.

- Most important, remember to review your company's policy on electronic mail. Some companies allow their employees to use e-mail for
  personal use; others prohibit it. Your company may also have strict
  rules regarding protocol, such as not directly e-mailing a department
  head but passing it through your supervisor first. Since legal issues can
  arise from the improper use of e-mail, don't take chances. Even home
  users are governed by the Acceptable Usage Policy established by their
  Internet service providers. Find out if there's a policy governing you
  and, if there is, follow it.

As a final caution, remember that a computer network is an employer's
property, and other people have the ability to read your electronic

correspondence. E-mail is not secure, so it should not be used for confidential information. Your system administrator has access to all areas of the network including your e-mail. Don't let him or her find a message in which you wrote complaints about your boss.

PROCEED WITH CAUTION

Don't begin an interoffice memo with a header that reads "To: Jim, Paula, Dean, Alice, and Brian." Use a memo-type header such as "To: All Department Heads." Unless they have to respond, don't use a long list of recipients' e-mail addresses. Use the "blind cc" option, which hides everyone else's e-mail address. They'll know to whom the message is directed if you begin it with "All Department Heads."

BUSINESS LETTERS

Over the past 30 years, the approach to business letters has changed dramatically. Stilted and officious phrases such as "in the event that" are now seen as wordy and unnecessary, especially since "if" will usually suffice.

Business letters still take a more formal tone than memos or e-mail messages, but clear and concise is the current objective. Letters should be easy to understand and easy to follow. Clarity is key. Avoid using any phrases that sound old-fashioned or trite.

The following are some archaic phrases that still find their way into business communication. Instead of using them, use the shorter alternative.

Alternatives to Wordy Expressions

Wordy	Concise
as per your request	as you requested
as to whether	whether
at a later date	later
at this point in time	now, right now
at such time as	when
by means of	by
despite the fact that	although
enclosed, please find	enclosed is
in receipt of	received

continues

Alternatives to Wordy Expressions   (continued)

Wordy	Concise
please do not hesitate	please
pursuant to your request	as you requested
thanking you in advance	thank you
the manner in which	how
under separate cover	separately
until such time as	until
with reference to	regarding; about

Also watch for extraneous words—empty expressions that do nothing but take up space. Refer to Hour 21, "Getting Beyond Your First Draft," for more on this topic.

Since business letters are usually directed to people outside the company, more information is needed than in a simple memo. The following are important parts that should be included in all business letters:

- **The inside address** is your company's address. If your company does not have a preprinted letterhead, the inside address should be typed at the top of the letter.

- **The date** should be under the inside address, either three spaces below the letterhead or on the line directly adjacent to the completed inside address.

- **The recipient's name and address** tells to whom the letter is being directed and at what address.

- **The reference line** is a brief statement of the subject of the letter, referring to a previous letter, meeting, telephone conversation, file number, or anything that will give the recipient an idea of the reason for the letter. This is only required when the letter is written in response to another matter.

- **The greeting (or salutation)** is a greeting such as "Dear" followed by the recipient's name or title. Be careful not to be gender-exclusive by saying "Dear Sir" or "Dear Gentlemen." It is also very impersonal to say "To whom it may concern."

- **The body of the letter** contains all the questions, information, and other relevant material.

- **The complimentary closing** is the closing remark such as "Respect-fully yours," "Sincerely," or "Yours truly." The first word is capitalized but not the second word.
- **The signature block** contains your name and title.

TASK: PREPARING REPORTS

Reports are used for a variety of functions. Reports can be regular, such as quarterly sales reports, or can be created for a specific purpose, such as an evaluation of the operations of a department.

No matter what the subject or the purpose, there are steps you can take to put you on the right track.

1. **Ask for direction.** If you don't know the specific reason for the report, ask your supervisor. Asking questions will help you identify the focus or the important points to emphasize.
2. **Study samples.** Obtain similar reports from previous years, both within your department and outside of it. If the kind of report you are compiling has never been done within your company, consider obtain-ing reports from other organizations.
3. **Organize your information.** Use an outline and present your data in the most logical format.
4. **Write for your audience.** Use jargon when appropriate.
5. **Use tables to organize your data.** Tables provide a nice, clear reference-point for your reader.
6. **Use charts or diagrams to emphasize key points.** Organizational structures or sales figures can provide clear representations of the data you're describing in the text.

PROPOSALS

A proposal is similar to a report, but reports usually are aimed at describing the work a company is performing. Proposals are aimed at obtaining some-thing.

Proposals are often used by companies to secure additional business from outside the company. Departments may also be required to submit proposals for new projects or purchases. No matter what the purpose, all proposals have one thing in common—they all have to be approved.

The tips for report writing will also assist you in creating proposals. In addition, keep the following in mind:

1. **Be persuasive.** Your objective is to convince someone that the proposal should be approved. Use positive and persuasive language.

2. **Include all information and anticipate questions.** The best proposal is one that provides answers to any questions that may arise. Show what you plan to accomplish and how you plan to accomplish it. If all the information is present, a decision can be reached faster than if additional material has to be requested.

3. **Provide appendices.** Budgets, cash-flow projections, company profiles, and newspaper clippings can provide supporting documentation to back up your proposal.

4. **Know your criteria.** Proposals usually have to meet certain objectives to be approved. Understand these objectives and design the outline of your proposal to show how it meets them.

   When giving an oral proposal presentation, incorporate some sales psychology into your choice of words. Most people like to share their opinions. Therefore, a question such as, "Are you ready to reach a decision?" may be too blunt; however, asking someone "In your opinion, how do you feel about this?" will elicit a better response.

When the initial reaction to your proposal appears to be a negative one, don't be afraid to follow up by saying, "Other than that, is there any other reason why you feel we shouldn't proceed with what's been proposed?" Often, the first objection is the one that sounds good; if the second question receives a negative response, it's more likely to be the real reason why someone is opposed to the proposal, and you can respond accordingly.

MEETINGS

A meeting can be just as important as a report or a proposal, so just as much planning should go into it. The objectives are often the same, but the message is delivered face-to-face instead of on paper.

PROCEED WITH CAUTION

Never hold a meeting ...

1. When you cannot decide what the meeting is for or what its outcome should be.

2. If there is an easier way of handling the matter.

3. If you do not have adequate time to prepare and plan.

4. When key people cannot attend.

5. When the meeting's cost is not worth the outcome (include the hourly wage of employees attending).

To make the most effective use of meetings, keep the following points in mind:

- **Plan adequately.** Prepare an outline for your meeting. Make a list of the things you need to accomplish and the points you have to cover. Prepare an agenda to keep everyone on track. Identify any equipment you'll need such as overhead projectors or speakerphones for teleconferences. If you need to book meeting space, do it well in advance.

- **Inform everyone about the meeting.** Inform all participants of the meeting. Distribute your agenda and any supplementary materials that should be reviewed before the meeting.

- **Conduct the meeting in a professional manner.** Start on time. Review the agenda at the beginning of the meeting to allow for any additions and then follow it closely. Limit discussion to a certain length for each topic if time is a concern.

- **Manage the discussion.** Keep participants on topic at all times. At the conclusion of each agenda item, decide on a specific course of action, who will be responsible, and what the time expectations will be.

  Have someone transcribe minutes for the meeting. Minutes should reflect the proceedings and the general discussion, including any action decided at the meeting.

- **Follow up.** Distribute the minutes in a timely fashion after you've had time to review them for accuracy. If you are assigned a task, make sure it is completed in the time allotted. If you are to provide information so that someone else can complete a task, do it in a timely fashion.

PROCEED WITH CAUTION

Don't let anyone (including yourself) hog the meeting time. Remember to let ideas flow. Protect people from being criticized for their views and suggestions. If the meeting is for developing ideas and formulating plans, ask direct questions to draw people into the conversation. Don't manipulate the group with leading questions such as, "I can't see why anyone would be against this project, right?"

If you want to be a good participant in a meeting …

- **Come prepared.** Know the agenda, read the material sent to you in advance, bring your calendar, give careful thought to the meeting's topic before you show up, and arrive with a positive attitude.

- **Help the team.** Don't attack other people. Be cooperative in helping the leader keep the meeting on task and bring it to the desired results.

ORAL PRESENTATIONS

Creating the content of a presentation is much like compiling a report. Instead of writing it, however, you'll be delivering it orally.

In addition to adapting the preceding suggestions for compiling reports, see the section "Task: Evaluate Your Audience" in Hour 13, "The Importance of Knowing the Rules."

BROCHURES AND AD COPY

Brochures and ad copy are designed to grab people's attention. Use the following tricks to increase their effectiveness:

- Use words that will make your reader want to learn more.

- Use the active voice. Try not to make your statements passive. You want people to act—usually by buying a product. Using the passive voice appears weak.

- Use short sentences. Short sentences are more easily understood and grab attention better than long ones.

- Anticipate questions. Just as with a proposal, the most effective ad copy answers any questions the reader may have.

- Be positive and direct. Make strong and emphatic statements that will make people want to act.

PRESS RELEASES

Press releases can be used in a variety of functions such as announcing fund-raisers, seminars, mergers, or even changes in management. You can create strong press releases with the following techniques:

1. Grab attention with the opening. Start off with something that will pique curiosity and make people want to read more.

2. Answer questions. Once again, anticipating questions is important.

3. Put your important information close to the beginning.

JUST A MINUTE

Press release information is sometimes used as filler in newspapers and periodicals. *Filler* is used to "fill" leftover space. A hurried editor is more likely to chop off end paragraphs that don't fit in the available space than to rewrite your press release material to fit. That's why it's important for you to keep your best information at the top of the press release.

4. Keep it short.

5. Keep your copy clean. Typos and other mistakes detract from your message.

Refer to Hour 15, "Getting the Job Done," for more on prepairing press releases.

PREPARING A RESUMÉ OR CURRICULUM VITAE

When applying for jobs, a resumé is your most important tool. It introduces you to the human resources officer; it should also make that person interested enough in your abilities to call you in for an interview.

STRICTLY DEFINED

The terms *resumé* (French for "summary") and *vita* (Latin for "life") are terms used for fact sheets about who you are and what sort of academic, occupational, military, and community achievements you have gained.

Your resumé should focus on the aspects of your life that have a direct application to the position you are seeking. For instance, if you are applying to be a teacher's aide at a preschool, it is important to list all your experiences with children including baby-sitting, teaching Sunday school, doing volunteer work at the children's library, and working with the local PTA.

As you piece together the parts of your resumé, ask yourself if each part is relevant to the job for which you're applying. If the answer is yes, put it in; if the answer is no, delete it.

Employers appreciate a resumé that outlines the specific skills they are seeking. Only include information that is directly applicable to the job at hand.

TASK: USING ACTION WORDS IN YOUR RESUMÉ

When you create a resumé, you want to call attention to your abilities. Using active verbs will point out the key duties you want to emphasize.

Review your current resumé and check the words you used against the action words in this list:

- **Leadership verbs:** achieved, expanded, pioneered, reduced, resolved, restored, spearheaded, transformed
- **Research verbs:** clarified, collected, critiqued, composed, diagnosed, evaluated, examined, identified, inspected, interpreted, interviewed, investigated, organized, summarized
- **Communication verbs:** addressed, arranged, collaborated, composed, convinced, developed, drafted, edited, explained, formulated, negotiated, persuaded, promoted, publicized, wrote

 For resumé samples, see *Writing That Works* (listed in Appendix B, "Resources") and *The Complete Idiot's Guide to the Perfect Resume,* by Susan Ireland, Indianapolis: Alpha Books, 2000 (ISBN: 0028639946).

- **Management verbs:** administered, analyzed, consolidated, coordinated, delegated, developed, directed, evaluated, improved, increased, organized, oversaw, planned, prioritized, recommended, scheduled, strengthened, supervised
- **Financial verbs:** administered, allocated, analyzed, appraised, audited, balanced, budgeted, calculated, computed, developed, forecasted, managed, marketed, planned, projected
- **Technical verbs:** assembled, built, calculated, computed, designed, devised, engineered, executed, fabricated, maintained, operated, overhauled, programmed, remodeled, repaired, solved, upgraded

- **Creative verbs:** acted, composed, conceptualized, created, customized, designed, developed, directed, established, founded, illustrated, initiated, instituted, introduced, invented, originated, performed, planned, revitalized
- **Supporting verbs:** assessed, assisted, clarified, coached, counseled, demonstrated, diagnosed, educated, expedited, facilitated, familiarized, guided, motivated, referred, represented

PROCEED WITH CAUTION

Be honest in your resumé. Falsifying information is dishonest and can be grounds for immediate dismissal when discovered.

Although misrepresenting dates or job titles may seem like a small offense, most human resources professionals take the issue very seriously, and most companies are quick to act on such matters.

- **Performance verbs:** approved, catalogued, classified, collected, compiled, generated, inspected, monitored, operated, organized, prepared, processed, purchased, recorded, screened, specified, systematized, tabulated

The organization and style of your resumé depends on the type and level of work you do and are seeking. Look at resumés of friends or colleagues in the same field, and see Appendix B for books that can help you produce a resumé that will present your abilities and qualifications in the best way.

HOUR'S UP!

1. Which of the following is not a good word choice for a resumé?
   - a. developed
   - b. initiated
   - c. demonstrated
   - d. broke

2. Which of the following is not an effective tool when delivering bad news?
   - a. finding a positive to emphasize
   - b. being blunt
   - c. being objective
   - d. offering a solution

3. Which of the following is not a good choice for a resumé?

    a. collaborated

    b. composed

    c. consolidated

    d. capsized

4. A great way to organize your presentation is to

    a. pay someone to do it

    b. use an outline

    c. shorten the presentation

    d. create a filing system

5. Which of the following is not an effective way to organize data?

    a. alphabetical order

    b. numerical order

    c. chronological order

    d. random order

6. Which of the following is not a good thing to include with proposals?

    a. all information

    b. bankruptcy statements

    c. persuasive language

    d. visual aids

7. Which of the following is not an important consideration when drafting a memo?

    a. identifying your main point

    b. getting to the point

    c. the recipient's tie

    d. none of the above

8. Never hold a meeting when

    a. you have no reason

    b. key people cannot attend

    c. there are more effective ways of handling the matter

    d. a, b, and c

9. Which verb is not a good choice for a resumé?

    a. coordinated

    b. managed

    c. forecasted

    d. bungled

10. When using e-mail, always remember to

    a. wear a tin-foil hat to protect you from the rays

    b. change the subject line to reflect the content

    c. scrub your computer's recycle bin

    d. cc everyone you've ever met

ANSWERS

1. d		**6.** b	
2. b		**7.** c	
3. d		**8.** d	
4. b		**9.** d	
5. d		**10.** b	

RECAP

This Hour covered different forms of business communication. You should now understand how to deliver your point in the most effective manner and how to use general techniques to achieve your goal. Now that you have learned about some basic forms of business writing, in the next hour you'll learn about other forms of writing.

HOUR 23

Putting Your Style into Practice II

By now you know that you add style to your written and oral presentations when you put the words in your voice. Unless you're writing experimental fiction or poetry (with no high expectations of selling your work), however, your *voice* doesn't mean "no rules." Even Picasso's training included a period of imitating the masters so he could learn the rules to see how he wanted to break them. Your voice will emerge in a similar manner. You learn by doing, adapting, improvising, and evolving.

If you've progressed this far into the hours in this book, however, there's one thing you have probably observed by now: There are rules, but that doesn't mean the rules can't or don't change. There are basic questions you need to have answered before beginning any project:

- Are there specific guidelines or a style sheet?
- Which style guide is appropriate or required?
- Which dictionary is appropriate or required?

STRICTLY DEFINED

A publication's style preferences are sometimes referred to as the *house style* or *press style,* and they usually are enumerated in a *style sheet.*

Once you've ascertained the answers to these questions, you can plan and prepare your project using the appropriate resources, doing your work within the parameters set forth by whoever commissioned the project.

CHAPTER SUMMARY

LESSON PLAN:

In this Hour, you will learn how to write for specialized areas ranging from science to humor. The point of this session is to show you how to direct your information to a targeted audience, how to use the correct vocabulary and examples, and how to choose the right format for the material.

Among the things we'll cover are

- How to write about science for the lay audience.
- How to write reviews and criticism.
- How to prepare academic writing.
- How to write about sports events and athletes.

An excellent general guide is *How to Write It: A Complete Guide to Everything You'll Ever Write* by Sandra E. Lamb (Ten Speed Press, 1999. ISBN: 1580080014).

WRITING THE ESSAY

When it comes to writing formats, while an article is generally unbiased or neutral in tone, the essay by its very nature usually has a distinct slant. You use essay format when you write about *your personal* opinions and thoughts on a topic.

An essay is developed around a central thesis or theme. There are three primary essay types:

1. **The Formal Essay:** used to present the rational understanding of a topic. The formal essay is the structured format used for many college writing assignments.

 Fundamentals of Essay Writing: An Orientation Manual by Erskine Peters (Regent Press, 1990. ISBN: 0916147053) covers such subjects as the importance of the essay introduction and conclusion.

Other useful volumes are *Ready to Write More: From Paragraph to Essay* by Karen Blanchard and Christine Root (Addison-Wesley Publishing Co., 1997. ISBN: 0201878070) and *Schaum's Quick Guide to Writing Great Essays* by Molly McClain and Jacqueline D. Roth (McGraw-Hill, 1998. ISBN: 0070471703).

2. **The Personal Essay:** used to present the writer's personal feelings and opinions about a topic.

 Writing Personal Essays: How to Shape Your Life Experiences for the Page by Sheila Bender (Writers Digest Books, 1995. ISBN: 0898796652).

3. **The Functional Essay:** used to serve a specific function, such as an entrance application essay for college, law school, and so forth.

 For help with college application essays, we suggest *Essays That Worked: 50 Essays from Successful Applications to the Nation's Top Colleges* by Boykin Curry and Brian Kasbar (Fawcett Books, 1990. ISBN: 0449905179) and *Writing a Successful College Application Essay: The Key to College Admission* by George Ehrenhaft (Barrons Educational Series, 1993. ISBN: 0812014154).

No matter what kind of essay you are writing, all forms will have simple elements in common.

Your *introduction* prepares the reader for the points you will be making. It's the initial presentation of your subject material, and briefly sums up your objective in writing the piece.

PROCEED WITH CAUTION

Many educators have encouraged the use of first-person statements at the beginning of essays; however, remember that in formal writing, the first person should only be inferred and never used directly.

The introduction often includes a *thesis statement,* which is a one-sentence summation of the objective you are trying to accomplish or the point you are trying to prove. You can think of this as the essay's premise—the basic underlying principle of the essay, and the thing that will be proven once the essay is complete.

In a personal essay, the thesis statement is often a reflection on how events served to change the author's life. However, in a personal essay, a thesis statement or similar construction is not required.

In the *body* of your essay, you expand upon your introduction and thesis statement and provide the material that illustrates your point. It is the body of the piece that proves your argument, or the point raised by your introduction and thesis statement.

FYI Two of the many specialized guides are *Essays That Will Get You into Business School* by Daniel Kaufman, Amy Burnham, and Chris Dowhan (Barrons Educational Series, 1998. ISBN: 0764106139) and *Essays That Will Get You into Law School* by Daniel Kaufman, Amy Burnham, and Chris Dowhan (Barrons Educational Series, 1998. ISBN: 0764106120).

At the end of your essay, your *conclusion* states the answers you have found, based on your analysis of the argument in the body of the essay. Your conclusion should leave the reader feeling that all main points have been addressed, and that the points you conclude are solid.

Writing About Law

Anyone who has ever looked over a legal document will probably remember the language being unwieldy and complicated. Legal writing is often confusing because it employs "terms of art"—words and phrases that have come to mean certain things within the legal profession. That's why contracts and other legal documents always look so daunting and hard to understand.

Law is about rules, and legal writing is about conveying those rules. When laws are passed by statute, the legislatures are trying to define what is acceptable and what is not. The only tool available to do this is language. However, you have seen that language is not precise; it can be interpreted in different ways, since different words carry different nuances and can be used to mean different things. In the past, in an attempt to be precise, more terms were added, further defining the intended meaning. Between the qualifications and the terms of art, you'd often end up with something that only a lawyer could understand.

In recent years, however, the trend has been shifting toward simplified writing in the world of law. Judges no longer encourage long and drawn-out motion briefs or other documents. They now expect lawyers to be clear, concise, and succinct—much like the direction in which the rest of the business world has been heading. Instead of making their writing more precise by adding limiting statements and qualifiers, lawyers are now encouraged to get the point across in the most simple and economical fashion.

If you find yourself writing something relating to the law, don't think that you should be wordy or complicated. Nowadays, instead of using officious language, legal writing should use simple language. Your goal in legal writing, as with all other forms of writing, is to be understood. Using words that only lawyers will understand won't help that goal.

 FYI *The Elements of Legal Style* by Bryan A. Garner (Oxford University Press, 1991. ISBN: 0195058607) is a no-nonsense legal writing guide.

WRITING ABOUT SCIENCE

Whether you are already in the writing field, you want to establish yourself as a writer, or you're just interested in improving your writing skills, if you're looking for a rich area to explore, consider science. There are six specific reasons why science is of interest to everyone:

1. Science is part of the general cultural knowledge, and good communicators help bridge the gap of understanding between the arts and science.

2. Research and grant application funds at the national, state, and city levels create curiosity about the types of research under consideration, the potential benefits of such research, and the negative effects if such research is *not* conducted.

Human curiosity is such that there is always interest in learning about scientific advances—whether it's the cure of a disease, the development of a new fertilizer, or the invention of an automobile engine that reduces pollution.

STRICTLY DEFINED

Science refers to anything scientists discover about nature—the physical world and its phenomena, sometimes referred to as **natural science.**

Pure science deals in scientific minutiae about the entire universe.

Applied science refers to attempts to exert controls over certain aspects of nature.

Technology is the narrowing of categories (scientific method, educational method) that define the technical process by which research is conducted or scientific knowledge is applied.

3. An understanding of the total costs of scientific advances and the research involved—as well as the justifications for such expenditures, benefits, and consequences—leads to better appreciation for scientific developments.

 Your style and approach depends on the guidelines under which you're commissioned to do the work. However, you can find style suggestions at The University of Chicago Press (publishers of *The Chicago Manual of Style*) Science Links page (www.lib.uchicago.edu/LibInfo/SourcesBySubject/Science/style.html) or at the American Psychological Association's APA-Style Helper site (www.apa.org/apa-style).

TASK: IS IT TIMELY, INTERESTING, AND UNDERSTANDABLE?

As a general rule, you should name the scientists responsible for a breakthrough, the scientists' company or research facility affiliations, the scientific name of any new drug (or product), and a layperson's definition of any scientific terminology or experiments. Follow the usual pattern of informative writing by covering the five W's and two H's:

1. **When** was the breakthrough made and how soon will it be available to the public?

2. **Who** discovered it and who plans to market it?

3. **What** is the new discovery and what are its various applications?

4. **Where** will people be able to obtain this drug or product?

5. **Why** was this company or research facility concentrating its efforts on this area of science?

6. **How** will the drug or product be produced and distributed?

7. **How much** will this cost the consumer?

After you've assembled the basic information about the subject, you can go on to transform it into a piece of writing.

PROCEED WITH CAUTION

When writing for a general audience, round off numbers or present them in terms that anyone can understand; you'll compound confusion exponentially otherwise.

SPECIALIZED SCIENCE WRITING

Certain realms of science are usually set apart from generic science writing. All of the preceding rules still apply, but other factors come into play when writing about the environment, medicine, and technology.

FYI If you want to get the latest information from prominent professionals in a field, go to www.exp.com, a database of "experts" that also allows you to post public questions to which the experts can respond.

THE ENVIRONMENT

Writing about the environment doesn't just mean "the great outdoors"—the ozone layer, global warming, extinction of species, oil spills, population expansion, land revitalization, and conservation of natural resources. The "environmental" study of ergonomics concerns itself with the indoor working or living environments of people: furniture, equipment, and office supplies arrangements; lighting placement; noise pollution reduction; workplace-induced conditions such as carpal tunnel syndrome and multiple chemical sensitivities; and air-quality concerns.

JUST A MINUTE

Your style comes into play when you take a broad topic, such as one of those mentioned here, and narrow the focus to adapt it so it applies to your audience and is told in your voice. Your audience determines to what extent "your terms" are layman's terms.

MEDICINE

Medical writing includes a number of specialized areas:

1. **Preventive medicine** involves the steps taken to preserve good health and prevent disease.

2. **Sports medicine** concerns itself with the ways to maximize professional, amateur, and casual sports activity while avoiding injury.

3. **Natural medicine** is the holistic approach of involving both the mind and the body and using natural and herbal remedies to treat and prevent illness.

 An excellent guide to science writing is *Scientific Style and Format: The CBE Manual for Authors, Editors, and Publishers* (6th Ed) by Edward J. Huth (Cambridge University Press-Trade, 1994. ISBN: 0521471540).

Look for "Eureka!" moments in science.

For example, an article online at home.vicnet.net.au/~mecfs/general/lactic.html describes how scientists at Australia's Adelaide University studied the metabolism of lactic acid during exercise and inadvertently discovered that people with chronic fatigue syndrome (CFS) released far more lactic acid into their blood than the healthy test subjects did. (Lactic acid is the exercise byproduct that causes pain in muscles and therefore is of vital concern to athletes, who want to reduce lactic acid production and increase their exercise endurance.)

The discovery regarding the CFS–lactic acid–pain connection opened up an entirely new path for researchers to take in subsequent studies related directly to what may be the cause of CFS.

TECHNOLOGY

Be consistent when you write about technology. Standard practice, when you introduce a new term, is to define it within the context of the sentence. Likewise, whenever a new term is also known by a common acronym or abbreviation, first spell out the term and then show the acronym or abbreviation in parentheses. After the common abbreviation or acronym is shown in parentheses, it is acceptable to use that shortened form of the word or words throughout the balance of your text.

e.g.

> Most laser printers now print at a minimum resolution of 600 dots per inch **(dpi)** in normal mode and 300 **dpi** in draft mode.

Do not switch between technical synonyms without first establishing the related meanings of the words.

PROCEED WITH CAUTION

 Although some abbreviations, such as mph, are considered to be common usage or standard, it's best to err on the side of caution and define them. In such instances, however, it is acceptable to put the definition for the abbreviation in parentheses behind the abbreviation, such as **mph (miles per hour).**

Someone whose first language is not English might find it confusing to distinguish between common synonyms such as "policeman," "cop," and "officer"; unless you first establish the meanings of technical synonyms, it can be equally confusing to someone when you switch labels for aspects of technology.

It is sometimes acceptable to follow the most common technical term with a technical synonym in parentheses; however, you need to use some discernment when you do so. Otherwise, because it's the style used with abbreviations and acronyms, the reader will expect to see the substitute word throughout the balance of the technically written piece. With complete words, it is far better to use the "define within the context of the paragraph" method for introducing new terms.

e.g.

> Many offices now use **electronic mail** for interoffice communications. **E-mail** has replaced routing interoffice memos as the preferred means to send notifications to employees.

CRITICISM AND REVIEWING

This specialized form of writing—book, movie, software, hardware, art, or drama reviews—must be written in a format required by the periodical or other volume for which the work is commissioned. First study the publication so you can adapt your piece to the style required. Most offer written guidelines that specify the preferred number of words, the submission method, and other important details.

BOOK REVIEWS

Whenever possible, review a book by an author whose works are already familiar to you. In this way, you can use your previous experience as a comparison when reviewing the new book. Don't trust your memory. Take notes as you are reading.

JUST A MINUTE

One reviewing method is to begin writing the review without first consulting any notes. In this way, you see which parts of the book remain vivid and then use those key points or scenes as the basis for your review. You can refer to your notes or the book itself later to confirm facts and to verify other details in your review.

Be informative but not concerned with trivial details unless that is of importance to your audience. (*People Weekly* magazine is more likely to include a sprinkling of gossip as part of a review than *The New Republic* is.) Include the basic information: book title, author name, publisher, date of publication, price, and genre (business, science, western novel, romance); the manner in which you state this information will vary according to the publication's guidelines. Most prefer that you provide a short summary of the book's content, mention any pertinent data (this is book two of a series, this book is a reissue), and then provide your impressions and opinion of the book's content. Don't be influenced by other reviewers' opinions or by publicity sheets.

FYI Two good guides to writing reviews are *Writing Reviews: How to Write About Arts & Leisure for Pleasure & Profit* by Carole Baldock (How To Books Ltd, 1996. ISBN: 1857034414) and *The Elements of Writing About Literature and Film* by Elizabeth McMahan, Robert Funk, and Susan Day (Allyn & Bacon, 1988. ISBN: 0023279540).

STAGE AND SCREEN REVIEWS

An effective film or stage review evaluates the acting (original, natural, forced), the direction (scenes, action, focus), and the writing (dialogue, setting, plot tension). Do these elements work well together? Does one element stand out above the others or does one element seem out of sync with the others? Was anyone miscast? Was the original version of this production modified in any way and, if so, was it a good change? Is any specific performer worthy of mentioning? If you're reviewing a play, include the dates and times of additional performances; if you're reviewing a movie, mention whether this is a sequel or part of a series.

FYI For film reviewing, we recommend *Critical Approaches to Writing About Film* by John E. Moscowitz (Prentice Hall, 1999. ISBN: 0130837075).

JUST A MINUTE

 Experts in a given field most often do specialized reviews such as evaluations of computer programs, architecture, and works of art. Such reviews usually require a knowledge base on which to formulate the opinion of the review.

SERIOUSLY FUNNY

Humor is used to relieve tension in a sales presentation. As you saw in Hour 18, "Managing Your Research," it's an effective way to grab attention when used in a lead. For humor to work, it must be based on a truth—albeit an exaggerated one.

e.g.

Laugh and the world laughs with you; giggle maniacally and you get to go to the front of the line.

 FYI A guide you may find useful is *Business Humor: Jokes & How to Deliver Them* by Gene "*Using Humor for Effective Business Speaking*" Perret (Sterling Publications, 1998. ISBN 0806999047).

ACADEMIC WRITING

The function of academic writing is to add new insight or interpretation to the general pool of knowledge that will bring additional enlightenment to the study of original material. Academic writing is generally considered to be original in its research, thorough in its documentation, and complete in its analysis. Although format and presentation styles vary according to the field for which you write (many of which have detailed style guides), all academic writing employs formal English usage.

 FYI If the discipline for which you're writing does not have its own style guide, follow the guidelines in *A Manual for Writers of Term Papers, Theses, and Dissertations* by Kate L. Turabian, John Grossman, and Alice Bennett (The University of Chicago Press, 1996. Hard-cover. ISBN: 0226816265, Trade ISBN: 0226816273).

Sports Writing

Sports writing requires that you become familiar with the sporting event on which you are reporting; you must know the game's

- Rules and traditions.
- Terminology, including its slang.
- Most intriguing aspects to its followers.

 FYI For sports writing, see *Sports Style Guide & Reference Manual: The Complete Reference for Sports Editors, Writers, and Broadcasters* by Jennifer Swan, Editor (Triumph Books, 1996. ISBN: 1572431016).

You must first know a sport inside and out before you can write about it.

Hour's Up!

1. The question you're not required to answer before beginning any project is

   a. Are there specific guidelines or a style sheet?

   b. Which style guide is appropriate or required?

   c. Which dictionary is appropriate or required?

   d. Do you want fries with that?

2. A publication's style preferences, enumerated in a style sheet, are sometimes referred to as the press style or

   a. the house style

   b. the house dressing

   c. the window treatment

   d. the house cluster of picky rules

3. Which is not an essay style?

   a. formal essay

   b. functional essay

   c. impervious essay

   d. personal essay

4. Nowadays, effective legal writing is

    a. a judge's dream come true

    b. a copy editor's nightmare

    c. simplified, straightforward, and concise

    d. a choice between boxers or briefs

5. Scientific writing does not involve details about

    a. applied science

    b. domestic science

    c. natural science

    d. pure science

6. Informative writing should cover

    a. the birds and the bees

    b. the five W's and the two H's

    c. 500 words or more

    d. all of the above

7. When writing for a general audience

    a. elaborate using your extensive, abstruse vocabulary so that you sound like an expert

    b. use military terms

    c. include pictures

    d. round off numbers or present them in terms that anyone can understand

8. Specialized areas of medical writing include

    a. preventive medicine

    b. natural medicine

    c. sports medicine

    d. all of the above

9. In technical writing, whenever a new term is also known by a common acronym or abbreviation, you should

    a. first spell out the term and then show the acronym or abbreviation in parentheses.

    b. include a toll-free, tech support number.

    c. include the URL for a tech support Web site.

    d. avoid using any technical terms.

10. The three primary areas of science do not include

   a. applied science

   b. pure science

   c. echinacea

   d. technology

Answers

1. d	**6.** b
2. a	**7.** d
3. c	**8.** d
4. c	**9.** a
5. b	**10.** c

Recap

This Hour showed you how to write for science, criticism and reviews, humor, and other narrowly focused types of writing. You now know that the choice of words, the range of research, and the focus of the writing should all be topic-specific. Now that you have finished two special hours of training in how to put your writing style into practice, you're ready to continue to the next hour on problem words and expressions.

Hour 24

Problem Words and Expressions

Chapter Summary

LESSON PLAN:

In this Hour, you'll learn about problem words and expressions and some exceptions to some of the rules you've already learned.

Among the things we'll cover are

- Some things are just downright wrong.
- Other things may be wrong.
- Sometimes the rule is that there is no rule.

Despite these times of cultural diversity, political correctness, and expanded awareness, since the advent of the Internet, American English is becoming the international standard. It's not so much a matter of conformity as a matter of establishing a common standard. Rules are needed if everyone wants to communicate effectively.

Face it! Language is one of the ways we impress others. That impression can just as easily be a negative one as a positive one. The latter is the objective.

There is no definitive authority on English; therefore, there is no ultimate standard of absolute correctness. There are, however, common usage rules you should know. That way, when you use nonstandard usage, it's intentional— not because of an error.

The goal of this hour is to help you get rid of any inadvertent misuse of the problem words and expressions you'll find on these pages so you can meet your objective and make a positive impression.

Styles Change

In any language, you adapt your style to what is appropriate for the circumstance, which many people distinguish as either formal or informal. We like to expand these two categories to include a third: casual. Here are some styles and their accepted structures:

- Formal written
    1. Uses inanimate nouns as subjects of a sentence
    2. Tends to use passive structures
    3. Uses more gerunds (verbal nouns)
    4. Tends to use more words in Latin or of other foreign origin
- Informal written
    1. Uses humans as the subjects of sentences
    2. Uses active verb structures (when a choice is possible)
    3. Uses passive structures less often
    4. Uses more words of Germanic origin
- Casual written (slang or colloquial)
- Formal spoken
- Informal spoken
- Casual spoken (slang)

Consider the topic for this section of the book; based on the three style types, possible written adaptations could be …

e.g.

Formal: Proper style is adapted to serve each appropriate instance of usage.

Informal: Styles change.

Casual: You've gotta have style.

Examples that evolve through the formal written to the spoken casual styles are …

Formal written: Please maintain the appropriate style usage so as to comply with those instructions given in the class syllabus.

Informal written: You should follow the style guidelines included with the class syllabus.

Casual written: Write your report according to the class syllabus style guidelines.

Formal spoken: Please maintain the appropriate style usage that complies with the instructions you were given in the class syllabus.

Informal spoken: Write your report according to the style guidelines you received in the class syllabus.

Casual spoken: Use the style guidelines I gave you in the class syllabus when you do your report.

JUST A MINUTE

Jargon is often associated with formal written and spoken presentations when its use is appropriate for the audience. Such usage includes official reports, technical studies, and other audience-specific commentary.

PROBLEMS WHEN THE RULES KEEP CHANGING

You won't find finite rules in a language that devises abbreviations such as "No." for "number" and "lb." for "pound" when there isn't an "o" in "number" or an "l" or a "b" in pound. In many cases, memorization will serve you much better than attempting to arrive at any type of logical conclusion.

ACCENTS AND OTHER DIACRITICAL MARKS

Wire services don't use special accents or other diacritical marks. Some computer fonts do not include these special characters either. You could argue that not including accent marks in some words can cause confusion— "resume" when it means "curriculum vitae," for example. If you're writing for yourself or for an organization that does not have a policy on using special accents or marks, this is the best rule: When in doubt, leave them out. Accept that English is a language without accent marks, even when it borrows words from other languages that have them.

It is acceptable, however, to include any necessary accent marks if you are using a foreign word that hasn't been formally adopted into English. Most word-processing programs have special fonts that include most of the symbols you might need.

APOSTROPHES FOR PLURALS

In Hour 3, "Elementary Sentence Components I: Nouns," we stated the following rule:

Add an 's to make a number or letter plural.

Not everyone agrees with this rule, however, especially when it's expanded to include *acronyms*—words created by using the initials of a company or the major parts of an expression. Because many acronyms are written in all capital letters, some people prefer to form the plural by adding an *'s* after the capital letters of the acronym; because many acronyms can be treated as nouns, others add only the *s* when doing so will not create confusion.

To 's or Not to 's

Acronym	's Plural	Acceptable Plural
AK-47	AK-47's	AK-47s
CD	CD's	CDs
DVD	DVD's	DVDs
MIA	MIA's	MIAs
POW	POW's	POWs

PROBLEMS THAT MAY NOT BE PROBLEMS

Over the past 24 hours, you've been learning very intricate rules regarding English grammar. As you'll learn in the following pages, sometimes it's okay to break a rule or two.

TO SPLIT OR NOT TO SPLIT AN INFINITIVE

You've heard it before, and now we'll say it again: Avoid splitting infinitives. Now that you recall the rule, make a note: There will be times when this rule doesn't apply.

It's an artificial rule and was actually brought into English later than most of the other rules you've learned. In formal writing, the rule should be observed. In other writing, a split infinitive is often seen as adding emphasis since the word usually amplifies the verb.

e.g.

Muriel told me **to** *only* **buy** one.

In the preceding, the emphasis is placed on purchasing the product rather than on the quantity, as in the following:

Muriel told me **to buy** *only* one.

In conversation, the rule barely seems to exist at all. Most speakers invariably split one infinitive after another. Remember, however, that some people always adhere to this rule even in speech; when dealing with such people, trying not to split any infinitives might be the best thing.

TURNING NOUNS INTO VERBS

The practice of converting a noun into a verb should be avoided, especially in formal usage.

e.g.

Incorrect: Stephen King has **authored** many novels.
Correct: Stephen King has **written** many novels.

Pay close attention when dealing with copyrighted or trademarked proper nouns.

e.g.

Incorrect: Beatrice, will you **Xerox** this for me?
Correct: Beatrice, will you **copy** this for me?
Correct: Beatrice, will make a **photocopy** of this for me?

When you refer to the brand name, use it with the appropriate modifier:

e.g.

Beatrice, will you make a **Xerox**-*brand copy* of this for me?

IMPLIED INFINITIVES

You've already learned that prepositions require something after them, which is why you should never use one to end a sentence.

Sometimes, though, the preposition is part of a verb used in the infinitive, and the verb is often dropped:

e.g.

It's my party and I'll cry if I want **to**.
This sentence actually means:
It's my party and I'll cry if I want **to cry**.

You should avoid using an implied infinitive in formal writing; however, it has become widely accepted in general usage.

PROBLEM WORDS

Some words in English are very similar to other words, and this often causes confusion in the way they are used. Others have a subtle meaning that often becomes muddled in everyday usage.

Here are some problematic words that cause difficulty for many people.

A WHILE VERSUS AWHILE

"A while" means a short period of time:

I'll sit and wait **a while.**

"Awhile" is a colloquial expression joining the two words, and it is usually not appropriate in formal usage:

She'll be here after **awhile.**

ALL READY VERSUS ALREADY

To have something "all ready" indicates that it is prepared:

The sales reports are **all ready** for the meeting.

"Already" is an adverb that means "by this time":

He's closed four major sales **already.**

APPENDIX VERSUS GLOSSARY

An "appendix" is the section of a book or report that provides additional material; its plural is "appendices," but it also can be "appendixes."

A "glossary" is a list of words with their definitions.

 You can find explanations about other problem words and expressions on the Common Errors in English Web page at www.wsu.edu:8080/~brians/errors/errors.html. Also, entire books are devoted to helping you build a better, correct vocabulary. You can find information about some of those titles in Appendix B, "Resources."

COMPLEMENT VERSUS COMPLIMENT

A "complement" is something that completes or adds to something else.

e.g.

Our staff **complement** has grown 15 percent.

The scarf will **complement** that sweater nicely.

To "compliment" is to flatter or give praise.

e.g.

To hear that he liked my speech was a nice **compliment**.

DIALOGUE VERSUS DIALOG

Although both forms are technically acceptable, "dialogue" is preferred when referring to conversations of people:

The **dialogue** in the play is very realistic.

"Dialog" is preferred when used as an adjective:

Click "OK" in the **dialog** box to continue.

FARTHER VERSUS FURTHER

When referring to distance, "farther" is often used, but either word is acceptable:

It's only a mile **farther.**

"Further" can also refer to quantity rather than just distance.

e.g.

They had to sell a **further** 2,000 shares to survive.

We need to delve **further** into this matter before we can reach a decision.

FORMER AND LATTER

"Former" indicates the first of two nouns, and "latter" indicates the second.

e.g.

> Our choices today are roast beef or salmon; the **former** comes with horseradish and the **latter** with a lemon sauce.
>
> "Roast beef" is the **former** and will be served with horseradish. Salmon, the **latter,** will be served in a lemon sauce.

FEWER VERSUS LESS

When referring to numbers, "fewer" is used:

Phyllis wished that **fewer** people had come to the party.

"Less" is used to indicate a general amount of something that isn't easily counted:

The lottery is worth **less** money this week.

ITS VERSUS IT'S

One of the most common mistakes is to use "it's" when "its" is the proper choice.

Although "it's" appears to conform with the 's rule to indicate possession, "it's" is actually a conjunction of "it" and "is" or "it" and "has."

e.g.

> **It's** raining. (**It [i]s** raining.)

"Its" is a personal possessive pronoun, so it doesn't need an apostrophe.

e.g.

> The dog wagged **its** tail.

LAY VERSUS LIE

This is a very confusing combination because the present and past participles don't make very much sense.

"Lay" is a transitive verb and must have a direct object:

> You may **lay** your head on my shoulder.

"Your head" is the direct object of "lay."

The present participle for the verb is "laying":

> She is **laying** her head on my shoulder.

The past tense and past participle is "laid":

> He **laid** his head on her shoulder.

The verb "to lie" is intransitive and does not require an object. Rather, it describes the state of the subject.

> If you **lie** awake at night, you may suffer from insomnia.

The present participle is "lying":

> John is **lying** down for a nap.

The past tense is "lay," which causes the most confusion because it is often confused with the verb "to lay."

> Edna **lay** in the tanning bed, enjoying the warmth.

The past participle is "lain":

> Edna would not have a sunburn if she hadn't **lain** in the tanning bed so long.

MOOT VERSUS MUTE

A "moot" point can be one that is arguable and open to discussion, but it is more often one that is pointless to discuss.

e.g.

Angela, what everyone else is doing is a **moot** point; you are not going to the concert.

"Mute" means "not making sound," which may be why the two words are so often confused. "Mute" originally referred to people who were incapable of speech, but the meaning has become extended to people who remain silent, or even to things.

e.g.
_____

The suspect was **mute** about the robbery.

Some people **mute** the television while they talk on the phone.

THAN VERSUS THEN

"Than" is a conjunction that is usually used to compare things:

Purple is a darker color **than** lilac.

"Then" is an adverb and adds a quality of time:

Tama agreed and **then** laughed.

THEIR, THEY'RE, AND THERE

"Their" is a personal possessive pronoun and is used only to indicate possession.

The band members played **their** instruments as they marched.

"They're" is a contraction of "they" and "are."

They're planning to attend the concert together.

(**They [a]re** turning the corner.)

"There" is an adverb that adds a quality of location or existence.

There is a lot of noise coming from **there.**

The first "there" is used to indicate that the rest of the sentence exists in a general sense. The second "there" is indicating a location.

TO, TOO, AND TWO

"To" is a preposition and is used to introduce prepositional phrases or infinitives.

To speak correctly, a person has **to** know the rules of a language.

"Too" is an adverb that means "also" or "excess."

She has missed **too** many days of school to graduate this year.

He has missed a lot of days, **too.**

"Two" is a number.

It's cheaper if you buy **two.**

PROBLEM EXPRESSIONS

Sometimes, groups of words can cause problems. Informal meanings of phrases can muddle the meaning of an otherwise correct statement. Two of the most common problem areas are slang and ambiguity.

SLANG

A *slang* expression is one that's usually unique to a geographic area or a group of persons. As such, slang should always be avoided in formal English usage; it is often not understood by people outside of the "group" using the expression.

 See the table of Common Slang Expressions in Appendix C.

AMBIGUITY AT WORK

Well, okay. Maybe we don't mean ambiguity where you work or while you're at work. We're referring to the ways ambiguity sneaks into general conversation or even into print. We've gathered some cute examples from the Internet to show how ambiguity can manifest itself within sentences.

Consider the following, billed as actual newspaper headlines from around the world:

e.g.
_____

Farmer Bill Dies In House

This headline reads as if a farmer named Bill passed away. More likely, it probably refers to a bill relating to farmers being considered by Congress.

e.g.

Iraqi Head Seeks Arms

Ambiguity can also be caused when a word can carry two meanings. In this sentence, "arms" means weapons; however, following "head," the meaning is ambiguous.

e.g.

Eye Drops Off Shelf

This headline seems like a perfectly reasonable account of a company recalling bottles of eye drops; however, it leaves many people asking what the eye was doing on a shelf in the first place.

e.g.

Miners Refuse to Work After Death

Either the miners work for a very demanding company or a fatal industrial accident is causing mine workers to abandon their posts under protest.

Each headline has two meanings—one true and one absurd. Newspaper headlines aren't necessarily indicative of problems you'll face with ambiguity because many words are left out of headlines. Here are some examples taken from church bulletins:

For those of you who have children and don't know it, we have a nursery downstairs.

This sentence is directed at people who are unaware of the church's nursery, not to people who might not realize that they have children.

This being Easter Sunday, we will ask Mrs. Lewis to come forward and lay an egg on the altar.

Although the form of the verb is correct, another verb would be more appropriate:

This being Easter Sunday, we will ask Mrs. Lewis to come forward and **place** an egg on the altar.

Hour's Up!

1. When is it okay to end a sentence with a preposition?

    a. implied infinitives

    b. on Tuesdays

    c. informal communication

    d. a and c

2. Choose the most appropriate sentence:

    a. The staff compliment agreed.

    b. The award was a great complement.

    c. The mints are complementary.

    d. The applause was a nice compliment.

3. Choose the most appropriate sentence:

    a. We went to the park, than we went to the store.

    b. I'm closer then you.

    c. It's warmer than I thought.

    d. a and b

4. Choose the most appropriate sentence:

    a. Their are four left.

    b. There lawn is overgrown.

    c. Harry decided to go they're.

    d. none of the above

5. Choose the most appropriate sentence:

    a. I have too cats.

    b. Two many people came to lunch.

    c. I want two go.

    d. To err is human.

6. Choose the most appropriate sentence:

    a. Its a wonderful song.

    b. The dog wagged it's tail.

    c. Its only a paper moon.

    d. It's a lovely day today.

7. Choose the most appropriate sentence:

    a. There are to many eggs in your basket.

    b. Seven to eight guests will attend.

    c. I don't spell to well.

    d. I had too pay extra.

8. Choose the most appropriate sentence:

    a. She smiled, and than walked away.

    b. I don't know what I'd do than.

    c. I'll buy two, then.

    d. Than I don't want to go.

9. Choose the most appropriate sentence:

    a. I have never been there.

    b. I went to there wedding.

    c. You don't want to know they're answer.

    d. Their are only two left.

10. Choose the most appropriate sentence:

    a. I figure that it's only money.

    b. It's not ready yet.

    c. The company surpassed its quota.

    d. a, b, and c

QUIZ

ANSWERS

1. d	**6.** d
2. d	**7.** b
3. c	**8.** c
4. d	**9.** a
5. d	**10.** d

RECAP

Now that you have mastered problem words and expressions, and all of the other important issues in this book, we recommend that you keep the book close by for a handy reference. You might also want to refer to the appendixes for suggestions on other books that will also help you teach yourself grammar and style.

APPENDIX A
Glossary

absolute phrase   A noun phrase and participle combined, giving complete meaning to the phrase but without a complete verb.

action verb   A verb that relates what action the subject is performing.

active voice   When the subject of a sentence actively performs the action of the verb.

adjective   A word that modifies or qualifies a noun or a pronoun.

adjective clause   A clause used to modify a noun or a pronoun.

adjective phrase   A noun and a modifier used to modify other parts of a sentence.

adverb   A word or group of words that modifies a verb, adjective, another adverb, clause, or sentence.

adverbial clause   A subordinate clause that modifies a verb, adverb, adjective, or entire main clause, joined to the main clause using a subordinator.

alliteration   Repeating the first consonant of a series of words to draw attention.

allusion   An indirect reference that is presumed to be understood.

antecedent   The word or words to which a pronoun refers.

anthropomorphism   Attributing human characteristics to a nonhuman object.

antonym   A word whose meaning is the opposite of another word.

apostrophe   Punctuation (') used to indicate possession or the exclusion of letters in a contraction.

appositive phrase   A noun phrase used directly beside a noun, separated by commas.

article   A word that precedes a noun to qualify it.

auxiliary verb   A verb that can stand with its own meaning or serve to help other verbs within a sentence.

cardinal   A number expressed as a word (*one, two,* and so on).

case   The form a noun takes to indicate its meaning within a sentence. See *direct object, indirect object, subject.*

clause   A group of words that contains both a subject and a verb and expresses a complete thought.

cliché   A word or phrase that has become dated, common, and unoriginal.

collective noun   Refers to a group as a unit and most often takes a singular verb.

collocation   When the meaning of a word must be derived from its context. See *homonym.*

colloquialism   A phrase that carries meaning within a specific group or geographic area.

colon   Punctuation (:) used to direct attention to the information that follows it.

comma   Punctuation (,) used to indicate a slight separation of the information or a slight pause in speech.

comma splice error   The improper use of a comma between two main clauses.

common noun   Refers to a person, place, thing, idea, or activity in general terms.

comparative   An adjective used to compare two things or people.

comparison   Used to show a greater degree of a characteristic or quality. See *positive, comparative, superlative.*

complete predicate   The verb and any objects, complements, and adverbial modifiers that tell what the complete subject does or is.

complete subject   The subject of a sentence, comprising a noun or a pronoun plus any modifiers.

complex sentence   One main clause and one or more subordinate clauses.

compound noun   Words that function together as a single unit but have a different meaning together than each word has on its own.

compound sentence   Two or more main clauses joined by a coordinating conjunction or a semicolon.

compound subject   Two or more subjects, joined by a conjunction, using the same verb.

compound-complex sentence   Two or more main clauses and one or more subordinate clauses.

conjunctive adverb   Connects independent clauses.

context   The facts surrounding a comment that must be taken into consideration to interpret the comment's meaning.

contraction   The omission of letters between two words, indicated by an apostrophe.

coordinating adjectives   Two or more adjectives receiving the same rank within a sentence.

coordinating conjunction   A word used to join parts of a sentence together (*and, but, or, nor, yet, for, so*).

coordination   Joining parts of a sentence with coordinating conjunctions.

correlative conjunction   A series of conjunctions used together to indicate the relationship between words (*as ... as, either ... or*).

count noun   A noun that can be quantified or counted.

cultural context   The context within a society; the underlying belief systems that define society.

dash Punctuation (—) used to add special emphasis or to set off parenthetical remarks.

declarative sentence A sentence that makes a statement.

definite article Used to indicate a specific item or person.

demonstrative article Indicates distance between the speaker and the object (*that, this*).

demonstrative pronoun Directs attention to its antecedent (*this, that, these, those*).

dependent clause See *subordinate clause.*

descriptive adjective Shows a characteristic, condition, or quality.

descriptive grammar How people speak and the patterns they use.

determiner See *article.*

direct object The noun being directly affected by the verb.

distributive article Shows how something is distributed, divided, or shared (*all, both, double, each, either, every, half, neither*).

ellipsis Punctuation (…) used to indicate omitted text.

euphemism A word or phrase that represents another phrase, often used for taboo subjects.

exclamation point Punctuation (!) used to emphasize an exclamatory remark.

exclamative article Introduces an expression of admiration, surprise, or other strong emotion or reaction (*such, what*).

function The way words are used in a sentence and the grammatical meanings they convey.

fused sentence error Joining two or more main clauses that are not separated by any form of punctuation.

future perfect progressive tense Continuing action that will take place at a later time but before another action.

future perfect tense A condition or an action that will be completed before another one.

future progressive tense Continuing action that will take place at a later time.

future tense An action or a condition that will take place at a later time.

gender The masculine, feminine, or neuter characteristics of a noun.

gerund A verb form ending in *-ing* that's used within a sentence as a noun.

gerund phrase A phrase that uses a gerund.

gist The basic meaning of a statement.

grammar The rules that govern a language.

helping verb A verb added to another verb to add clarification to the meaning.

homonym A word that is spelled the same as another word but carries a different meaning.

hyperbole A figurative exaggeration for emphasis or effect.

hyphen Punctuation (-) used between words or parts of words.

idiom An expression unique to a language that does not translate directly into other languages.

idiomatic translation A translation that preserves the original meaning of a text.

imperative mood Used to convey commands or to make requests.

imperative sentence A sentence that issues a command or makes a request.

indefinite article Used to indicate any one of a general group without being specific.

indefinite pronoun Refers to nonspecific persons or things.

independent clause See *main clause.*

indicative mood Used for statements and questions about actual events and things.

indirect object The noun being indirectly affected by the verb.

infinitive The pure form of a verb, appearing with no subject or object.

infinitive phrase   A phrase that uses an infinitive.

intensive pronoun   A pronoun ending in -*self* or -*selves* used to directly emphasizes a noun.

interrogative adverb   An adverb that forms a question (*when*).

interrogative pronoun   A pronoun that introduces questions or noun clauses (*who, what*).

interrogative sentence   A sentence that asks a question.

intransitive verb   A verb that does not require a direct object.

irony   Subtle criticism or ridicule that means the opposite of what is being said.

irregular verb   A verb that does not follow conventional rules for creating its forms.

jargon   Specialized vocabulary unique to a certain segment of a population for reasons such as trade, occupation, technology, medical science, and academic discipline.

lexicon   The dictionary and vocabulary used by the speakers of a particular language.

limiting adjective   Indicates number or quantity or highlights an identifiable characteristic.

linguistics   The scientific study of language.

linking verb   A verb that joins the subject to the predicate.

main clause   A group of words that contains both a subject and a verb and expresses a complete thought.

malapropism   A word used in error that carries a different meaning than originally intended.

mass noun   A word that can't be identified with a number.

metaphor   A grammatical structure that suggests that someone or something has the qualities of something else.

metonymy   The use of a word in place of something it symbolizes.

modality   The mood of a verb.

mood   The mindset surrounding the performance of a verb.

morpheme   The smallest unit of meaning in a language.

noun   A word that indicates a person, place, thing, idea, or activity.

noun clause   A clause that functions as a noun and can be used as a subject, object, or complement.

noun phrase   Nouns and the words added to them, used within a sentence.

numeral   A number expressed in numeric format (*1, 2,* and so on).

object   The noun being affected by the action of the verb.

object complement   The noun appearing with a linking verb.

onomatopoeia   The sound of a word reflecting its meaning.

ordinal   A number expressed by relative rank (*first, second,* and so on).

parallel structure   The use of the same pattern in words, phrases, or clauses to show that two or more concepts are similar or have the same level of importance.

parallelism   See *parallel structure.*

participial phrase   Uses a participle and always acts as an adjective.

participle   A verbal phrase that acts as an adjective, usually ending in *-ing.*

passive voice   When the subject of a sentence receives the action of the verb.

past perfect tense   Compares an action that was completed before another action.

past progressive tense   An ongoing action in the past or one that occurred over time in the past.

past tense   A completed action or condition.

pedagogical grammar   A systematic set of instructions for the usage of a language.

period   Punctuation (.) used to mark the end of a declarative or imperative sentence or an indirect question.

personal pronoun   Replaces a noun and indicates gender, number, and person (point of view).

phonetics   The study of how sounds are used to convey meaning.

phonology   A subcategory of phonetics; the study of the sounds and sound changes humans make to convey meaning.

phrasal verb   A verb and a preposition used as a unit.

phrase   A collection of words that carries a meaning but contains no subject or verb.

plural noun   A noun used to indicate more than one person, place, thing, idea, or activity.

positive   The original form of an adjective or adverb.

possessive noun   A noun that indicates ownership, usually indicated by adding an apostrophe plus an "s" to the original form of the noun.

possessive pronoun   A pronoun that indicates possession or ownership.

pragmatics   The study of language in context.

prepositional phrase   A part of a sentence introduced by a preposition.

preposition   A word that introduces a prepositional phrase (*about, above, across, after, against, along, among, around, as, behind, below, beneath, beside, between, by, despite, down, during, except, for, from, in, inside, near, next to, of, off, on, out, over, past, to, under, until, up, with*).

prescriptive grammar   The rules that govern how people should speak and the principles they should follow.

present perfect tense   An action or condition that began in the past and continues on into the present.

present progressive tense   A temporary condition or action that is currently taking place.

present tense   Taking place at the current time.

pronoun   A word that stands in place of a noun.

proper noun   The name of a specific person, place, thing, idea, or activity.

pun   Using words to emphasize a double meaning or to infer similarities to another word.

question mark   Punctuation (?) used to mark the end of a question.

reciprocal pronoun   A pronoun that indicates a reciprocal relationship (*each other, one another*).

reference grammar   Grammar rules listed in a dictionary format.

reflexive pronoun   Reflects the action back to a noun or pronoun and ends in *-self* or *-selves.*

regular verb   A verb that can be changed from the singular present tense to the plural present tense by adding *-s* or *-es* and to the past tense by adding *-d, -ed,* or *-t.*

relative pronoun   Joins a subordinate clause to a main clause (*that, which, who, whose*).

restrictive clause   A clause required in a sentence because it limits the meaning of the sentence.

restrictive modifier   See *restrictive clause.*

rhyme   Word endings that repeat the same or similar sounds.

rhythm   Emphasized repetition of stressed and unstressed syllable patterns rather than sounds.

run-on sentence   Joining more than one complete sentence to read as an improperly punctuated single sentence.

semantics   The study of individual words and how they interrelate.

semicolon   Punctuation (;) used to divide independent parts of a sentence.

sentence fragment   An incomplete sentence.

serial comma   Used to separate the nouns in a series.

series   A list of nouns followed by a proper conjunction and separated by commas.

simile   A figure of speech that indicates a comparison using "like" or "as."

simple adverb   An adverb used as a simple modifier to convey degree, manner, number, place, or time.

simple sentence   Has only one main clause, contains no subordinate clauses, and is limited to one subject and one predicate.

simple subject   See *complete subject.*

social context   The circumstances surrounding an exchange, such as the social status of the participants and the purpose of the speaker.

subject   The noun in a sentence that performs the action of the verb.

subject complement   A word that follows a linking verb and completes the meaning of the subject.

subjunctive mood   Used in formal usage to indicate hopes, desires, and statements contrary to fact.

subordinate clause   A group of words that contains a subject and an incomplete verb but does not express a complete thought.

subordination   Using subordinators to link two related sentences to each other so that one becomes dependent on the other.

subordinator   A word used to introduce subordinate clauses (*after, although, as, as if, because, before, even if, even though, if, if only, rather than, since, that, though, unless, until, when, where, whereas, wherever, whether, which, while*).

superlative   An adjective used to compare more than two nouns or to give a noun an absolute quality.

synonym   A word that has the same meaning as another word.

syntax   The rules that govern sentence structure and word usage.

tense   The form of a verb used to show when the action took place.

theoretical grammar   The analysis of a language's necessary components.

traditional grammar   The traditional approach to grammar, based on the approaches of classical languages.

verb   Describes the action within a sentence.

vocative phrase   A noun used for emphasis at the beginning of a sentence, indicating someone being addressed.

APPENDIX B

Resources

DICTIONARIES

Maggio, Rosalie. *Dictionary for Bias-Free Usage: A Guide to Nondiscriminatory Language.* Phoenix: Oryx Press, 1991 (out of print).

———. *The Nonsexist Word Finder.* Boston: Beacon Press, 1989 (out of print).

———. *Talking About People: A Guide to Fair and Accurate Language.* Phoenix: Oryx Press, 1997 (ISBN: 1573560693).

GRAMMAR GUIDES

Bernstein, Theodore M. *The Careful Writer: A Modern Guide to English Usage.* New York: Atheneum, 1977 (ISBN: 0689100388).

Follett, Wilson, and Erik Wensberg. *Modern American Usage: A Guide.* New York: Hill & Wang, 1998 (ISBN: 0809069512).

Harris, Muriel. *Prentice Hall Reference Guide to Grammar and Usage.* Paramus: Prentice Hall, 1999 (ISBN: 0130210226).

Princeton Language Institute, Joseph Holland (Editor), Barbara Ann Kipfer. *21st Century Grammar Handbook.* New York: Dell Pub Company, 1993 (ISBN: 0440215080).

Rozakis, Laurie E. Ph.D. *The Complete Idiot's Guide to Grammar and Style.* New York: Alpha Books, Macmillan USA, 1997 (ISBN: 0028619560).

STYLE GUIDES

Amato, Carol J. *The World's Easiest Guide to Using the MLA: A User-Friendly Manual for Formatting Research Papers According to the Modern Language Association Style.* Westminster, CA: Stargazer, 1999 (ISBN: 0964385376).

American Psychological Association. *Publication Manual of the American Psychological Association (Publication Manual of the American Psychological Association, 4th Ed).* Washington, DC: American Psychological Association, 1994 (ISBN: 1557982414).

The Associated Press. *The Stylebook and Libel Manual: Fully Revised and Updated.* Cambridge: Perseus Books, 2000 (ISBN: 0738203084).

Connolly, William G., and Allan M. Siegal. *The New York Times Manual of Style and Usage.* New York: Times Books, 1999 (ISBN: 0812963881).

Gibaldi, Joseph, and Herbert Lindenberger. *MLA Style Manual and Guide to Scholarly Publishing (2nd Ed).* New York: Modern Language Association of America, 1998 (ISBN: 0873526996).

Strunk, William Jr., and E.B. White. *The Elements of Style.* Needham Heights, MA: Allyn & Bacon, 1999 (ISBN: 020530902X).

Trimmer, Joseph F. *The Essentials of MLA Style: A Guide to Documentation for Writers of Research Papers.* New York: Houghton Mifflin, 1998 (ISBN: 0395883164).

The University of Chicago Press. *Chicago Guide to Preparing Electronic Manuscripts: For Authors and Publishers (Chicago Guides to Writing, Editing, and Publishing).* Chicago: The University of Chicago Press (Trade), 1987 (ISBN: 0226103935).

The University of Chicago Press. *The Chicago Manual of Style: The Essential Guide for Writers, Editors, and Publishers (14th Edition).* Chicago: The University of Chicago Press (Trade), 1993 (ISBN: 0226103897).

VOCABULARY GUIDES

Bromberg, Murray. *1100 Words You Need to Know*. Hauppauge, NY: Barron's Educational Series, Inc., 1993 (ISBN: 0812016203).

Cornog, Mary Wood. *Merriam-Webster's Vocabulary Builder*. Springfield, MA: Merriam Webster Mass Market, 1994 (ISBN: 0877799105).

Funk, William and Norman Lewis. *30 Days to a More Powerful Vocabulary*. New York: Galahad Books, 1998 (ISBN: 1578660300).

Lewis, Norman. *Word Power Made Easy*. New York: Pocket Books, 1995 (ISBN: 067174190X).

WRITING GUIDES

Goldberg, Natalie. *Writing Down the Bones: Freeing the Writer Within*. Boston: Shambhala Publications, 1998 (ISBN: 1570624240).

Lamott, Anne. *Bird by Bird: Some Instructions on Writing and Life*. New York: Anchor Books/Doubleday, 1995 (ISBN: 0385480016).

Roman, Kenneth, and Joel Raphaelson. *Writing That Works: How to Improve Your Memos, Letters, Reports, Speeches, Resumes, Plans, and Other Business Papers*. New York: HarperPaperbacks, 1995 (ISBN: 0061093815).

Zinsser, William. *Writing to Learn*. New York: HarperCollins, 1989 (ISBN: 0062720406).

————. *On Writing Well: The Classic Guide to Writing Nonfiction*. New York: HarperReference, 1998 (ISBN: 0062735233).

ONLINE RESOURCES

If you prefer to do your research online, here are some of the Web sites we recommend.

DICTIONARIES

A Web of Online Dictionaries and Others
http://www.yourdictionary.com

Computer Currents High-Tech Dictionary
http://www.currents.net/resources/dictionary/index.html

The Jargon Dictionary
http://www.netmeg.net/jargon/

The Semantic Rhyming Dictionary
http://www.link.cs.cmu.edu/dougb/rhyme-doc.html

WWWebster: Merriam-Webster Dictionary Online
http://www.m-w.com/netdict.htm

GENERAL REFERENCE

Facts on File
http://www.facts.com/

Reference Desk
http://www.refdesk.com/

GRAMMAR GUIDES

A Blue Book of Grammar and Punctuation
http://www.grammarbook.com/

An Online English Grammar
http://www.edunet.com/english/grammar/fram-gr.html

Common Errors in English
http://www.wsu.edu:8080/~brians/errors/errors.html

Grammar Bytes! Interactive Grammar Review
http://www.chompchomp.com/menu.htm

Grammar Handbook, University of Illinois at Urbana-Champaign
http://www.english.uiuc.edu/cws/wworkshop/grammarmenu.htm

Guide to Grammar and Writing
http://cctc.commnet.edu/HP/pages/darling/grammar.htm

STYLE GUIDES

The Curmudgeon's Stylebook
http://www.theslot.com/contents.html#start

The Elements of Style, 1918
http://www.bartleby.com/141/index.html

APPENDIX C
Tables

IRREGULAR VERBS WITH SPELLING CHANGES

Use the base form present tense with **I, you, we, they,** and **plural nouns.**

Use the +s and +es forms of the present tense with **he, she, it,** and **singular nouns.**

Common Irregular Verbs

Base Form Present	Present (+s or +es)	Simple Past	Past Participle
arise	arises	arose	arisen
awake	awakes	awoke	awoken
bear	bears	bore	born
beat	beats	beat	beaten
become	becomes	became	become
befall	befalls	befell	befallen
begin	begins	began	begun
bend	bends	bent	bent
bind	binds	bound	bound
bite	bites	bit	bitten
bleed	bleeds	bled	bled
blow	blows	blew	blown
break	breaks	broke	broken
breed	breeds	bred	bred
bring	brings	brought	brought
build	builds	built	built

continues

Common Irregular Verbs (continued)

Base Form Present	Present (+s or +es)	Simple Past	Past Participle
burn	burns	burned/burnt	burned/burnt
buy	buys	bought	bought
catch	catches	caught	caught
choose	chooses	chose	chose
cling	clings	clung	clung
come	comes	came	come
creep	creeps	crept	crept
deal	deals	dealt	dealt
dig	digs	dug	dug
dive	dives	dived	dove
do	does	did	do
draw	draws	drew	drawn
dream	dreams	dreamed/dreamt	dreamed/dreamt
drive	drives	drove	driven
drink	drinks	drank	drunk
eat	eats	ate	eaten
fall	falls	fell	fallen
feed	feeds	fed	fed
feel	feels	felt	felt
fight	fights	fought	fought
find	finds	found	found
fit	fits	fit/fitted	fit/fitted
flee	flees	fled	fled
fling	flings	flung	flung
fly	flies	flew	flown
foretell	foretells	foretold	foretold
forbid	forbids	forbade	forbidden
forgive	forgives	forgave	forgiven
forget	forgets	forgot	forgotten
freeze	freezes	froze	frozen
get	gets	got	gotten

Base Form Present	Present (+s or +es)	Simple Past	Past Participle
give	gives	gave	given
go	goes	went	gone
grind	grinds	ground	ground
grow	grows	grew	grown
hang	hangs	hung	hung
have	has	had	had
hear	hears	heard	heard
hide	hides	hid	hidden
hold	holds	held	held
keep	keeps	kept	kept
kneel	kneels	knelt	knelt
knit	knits	knit/knitted	knit/knitted
know	knows	knew	known
lay	lays	laid	laid
lead	leads	led	led
leap	leaps	leaped/leapt	leaped/leapt
learn	learns	learned/learnt	learned/learnt
leave	leaves	left	left
lend	lends	lent	lent
lie	lies	lay	lain
light	lights	lit	lit/lighted
lose	loses	lost	lost
make	makes	made	made
mean	means	meant	meant
meet	meets	met	met
mislay	mislays	mislaid	mislaid
mislead	misleads	misled	misled
mistake	mistakes	mistook	mistaken
overcome	overcomes	overcame	overcome
pay	pays	paid	paid
ride	rides	rode	ridden

continues

Common Irregular Verbs   (continued)

Base Form Present	Present (+s or +es)	Simple Past	Past Participle
ring	rings	rang	rung
rise	rises	rose	risen
run	runs	ran	run
saw	saws	sawed	sawed/sawn
say	says	said	said
see	sees	saw	seen
seek	seeks	sought	sought
sell	sells	sold	sold
send	sends	sent	sent
sew	sews	sewed	sewed/sewn
shake	shakes	shook	shaken
shear	shears	sheared	sheared/shorn
shine	shines	shone	shone
shoe	shoes	shoed	shoed/shod
shoot	shoots	shot	shot
show	shows	showed	showed/shown
shrink	shrinks	shrank	shrunk
sing	sings	sang	sung
sink	sinks	sank	sunk
sit	sits	sat	sat
sleep	sleeps	slept	slept
slide	slides	slid	slid
sling	slings	slung	slung
sow	sows	sowed	sowed/sown
speak	speaks	spoke	spoken
speed	speeds	sped	sped
spend	spends	spent	spent
spill	spills	spilled/spilt	spilled/spilt
spin	spins	spun	spun
spit	spits	spat	spit
split	splits	split	split

Base Form Present	Present (+s or +es)	Simple Past	Past Participle
spring	springs	sprang	sprung
stand	stands	stood	stood
steal	steals	stole	stolen
stick	sticks	stuck	stuck
sting	stings	stung	stung
stink	stinks	stank	stunk
stride	strides	strode	stridden
strike	strikes	struck	struck
strive	strives	strove	striven
swear	swears	swore	sworn
sweep	sweeps	swept	swept
swim	swims	swam	swum
swing	swings	swung	swung
take	takes	took	taken
teach	teaches	taught	taught
tear	tears	tore	torn
tell	tells	told	told
think	thinks	thought	thought
throw	throws	threw	thrown
tread	treads	trod	trodden
undergo	undergoes	underwent	undergone
uphold	upholds	upheld	upheld
understand	understands	understood	understood
underwrite	underwrites	underwrote	underwritten
wake	wakes	woke	woken
wear	wears	wore	worn
weave	weaves	wove	woven
wed	weds	wedded/wed	wedded/wed
weep	weeps	wept	wept
wind	winds	wound	wound
win	wins	won	won

continues

Common Irregular Verbs   (continued)

Base Form Present	Present (+s or +es)	Simple Past	Past Participle
withdraw	withdraws	withdrew	withdrawn
withhold	withholds	withheld	withheld
withstand	withstands	withstood	withstood
wring	wrings	wrung	wrung
write	writes	wrote	written

SLANG

A *slang* expression is usually unique to a geographic area or a group of persons. As such, slang should always be avoided in formal English usage; it often is not understood by those outside of the "group" using the expression.

Some slang does make its way into common informal usage, however. Some examples follow.

Common Slang Expressions

Slang Word or Expression	Definition
blown away by	very impressed by (not to be confused with "blow," which has sexual connotations)
broke	without any money
bucks	dollars
bum around	hang around doing nothing
chill	calm down
crack up	go crazy
(that) cracks me up	makes me laugh
crap	something with no value
crash	go to bed, go to sleep
cut it out	stop
dope	drugs
dough	money
dude	man
grass (noun)	marijuana

Slang Word or Expression	Definition
grub	food
guy	man, boy, person
hang on	wait
hell of a (expression used as an adjective)	huge
high	under the influence of drugs
hit the sack	go to bed
miffed	angry
nerd	person of high intelligence (and no fashion sense) or interested in computers
nick	Internet term for "nickname"
puke	vomit
rat (verb)	to divulge information about someone to the police
sad	pathetic
score	have sex with
(have a) screw loose	crazy, not logical
screw	cheat someone; (impolite) have sex with a person
screw it up	fail at something
screwball	idiot
shack up with	live with
shoot down	reject someone's idea
shoot up	inject a drug
sleep over	spend the night at someone else's house
stoned	under the influence of marijuana or other drugs
strapped	short of cash
throw up	vomit
tie the knot	get married
twisted	strange
twit	stupid person
yucky	disgusting, unpleasant

Index

Symbols

1100 Words You Need to Know,
   book, 387
*21st Century Grammar
   Handbook*, book, 386
*30 Days to a More Powerful
   Vocabulary*, book, 387

A

a while versus awhile, 366
abbreviated titles, italics, 290
absolute phrases, 130-131
academic, writing, 356-357
accents, 363
acronyms, rules, 363-364
actions
   predicates, 23
   scenes, leads, 243
   sequences, leads, 244
   verbs, 71-72, 80-82
      intransitive, 80
      irregular, 78-80
      mood, 72
      regular, 77-78
      rules, 208
      tenses, 72-77
      transitive, 80
active voice
   rules, 213
   verbs, 81-82

activities, writing categories,
   258
ad copy, 340-341
addresses
   business letters, 336
   direct, commas, 167
   geographical, commas, 169
   Internet, 273
addressing audiences, 221
   presentations, 221-222
   vocative phrases, 133
adjectives, 87, 92-94, 200
   -al endings, 95-96
   -ar endings, 95
   -en endings, 95-96
   -ish endings, 95
   -like endings, 95
   -ly endings, 95, 166
   -ory endings, 95
   -y endings, 95
   adverb comparisons, 97-100
   articles, 87
   clauses, 151
      complements, 152-153
      objects, 152
      subjects, 151
      subordinators, 154-156
   commas, 166
   common, 93
   compound, 93
   descriptive, 93-94
   endings, 95-96
   forms, 94-95
   functions, 94-95
   indefinite, 93

interrogative, 61
invariable, 94-95
limiting, 93-94
nouns, 93
objects, 94
participles, 122, 134-135
past participle verbs, 94
phrases, 130-135
position, 92-93
prepositional phrases, 94
present participle verbs, 94
proper, 94
quizzes, 101-102
types, 93-94
adverbial modifiers, complete
predicates, 23
adverbs, 87, 96, 121, 200
-ly endings, 97, 187
adjective comparisons,
97-100
agreements, 111
clauses, 153
subordinators, 154-156
comparisons, 112
conjunctive, 96, 147
endings, 111
interrogative, 96
position, 97
quizzes, 101-102
simple, 96
advertisements, press releases,
228-230
advice columns, idea
stimulators, 264
agreements
adverbs, 111
clauses
tasks, 152
closings, 248
indefinite pronouns,
104-106
lesson plans, 103
pronouns and antecedents,
62-64, 103-104
Q & A, 111-112
quizzes, 112-114
subjects and verbs, 107
collective nouns,
108-109
compound subjects,
107-108

confusing nouns, 109
quantity expressions,
109-110
word pattern difficulties,
110
all ready versus already, 366
alliterations, 7-8
allusions, 8
alphabetical order, 332
already versus all ready, 366
AltaVista, Web site, 274, 324
altered word meanings,
195-196
ambiguity, 318
grammar, 200
indefinite pronouns,
104-106
problems, 371-373
pronouns, 62, 106-107
American Psychological
Association's APA-Style
Helper site, Web site, 351
analogies, metaphors, 12-13
anecdotes, Kid Report, The, 299
angles, presentations, 202-203
announcements, 226, 333-335
annual reports, ticklers, 262
answers
questions, pronouns, 69
quizzes, 128
agreements, 114
articles, adjectives, and
adverbs, 102
business communication,
345
business writing and
speaking, 235
clauses, 159
commas and semicolons,
175
communicating, 313
grammar, 18
sentence structures, 19
ideas, 268
leads and closings, 251
nouns, 53
phrases, 143
problems, 374
proofreading and
editing, 327
punctuation, 190, 302

research, 287
rules, 205
sentences, 33
verbs, 85
writing rules, 220
writing styles, 359
antecedents, 59
compound agreements,
103-104
pronoun agreement, 62-64,
103-104
pronouns, unclear, 106-107
anthropomorphisms, 8-10
antonyms, 8-9
apostrophes, 182-184, 363-364
contractions, 59, 118-119,
182-184
nouns, 182-184
plurals, 182-184
possession, 182-184
possessive nouns, 46-47
pronouns, 182-184
punctuation, 182-184
rules, 182-184
appendices
proposals, 338
versus glossaries, 366
applications, grants, 351
applied sciences, 351
appositives
parentheses, 290-293
phrases, 131-133
commas, 131-135
parentheses, 131-133
articles, 37-38, 87, 93. See
also determiners
capitalizing, 39
definite, 88
demonstratives, 88-89
distributives, 89
exclamatives, 89
indefinite, 87
lesson plans, 87
numbers, 90
possessive pronouns, 90-91
quantifiers, 91-92
quizzes, 101-102
assonance, 9
attention grabbers, 225,
243-246
attention spans, tasks, 238-239

audiences, 197-199
  adapting, tasks, 221-222
  business communication, 329
  establishing voices, 232
  identifying, 221
  presentations, 221-222
  prethinking, 269-270
  simplicity, 232-233
  speeches
    closings, 246-249
    leads, 238-246
  verbalizing nouns, 199
audio tapes, 235
auxiliary verbs, 140-141
Avery Label Company, 263
awhile versus a while, 366

B

backslashes, 293-294
bad news, business communication, 330-331
benefits, 226
Bible verses, colons, 180-182
bibliographies
  personal, 230-231
  recording sources, 275-276
Bird by Bird: Some Instructions
  on Writing and Life, book,
  387
Blue Book of Grammar and
  Punctuation, Web site, 388
blueprints, workshop, 307-309
body
  business letters, 337
  essays, 349
  language, interviews, 278
bold type, emphasis, 289
books
  1100 Words You Need to
    Know, 387
  21st Century Grammar
    Handbook, 386
  30 days to a More Powerful
    Vocabulary, 387
  Bird by Bird: Some
    Instructions on Writing
    and Life, 387

Business Humor: Jokes &
  How to Deliver Them, 356
Careful Writer: A Modern
  Guide to English Usage,
  385
Chicago Guide to Preparing
  Electronic Manuscripts:
  For Authors and
  Publishers (Chicago
  Guides to Writing,
  Editing, and Publishing),
  386
Chicago Manual of Style:
  The Essential Guide for
  Writers, Editors, and
  Publishers (14th Ed), 186,
  387
Complete Idiot's Guide to
  Grammar and Style, The,
  78, 386
Complete Idiot's Guide to
  the Perfect Resume, The,
  342
Craft of Research, The, 275
Critical Approaches to
  Writing About Film, 356
Dictionary for Bias-Free
  Usage: A Guide to
  Nondiscriminatory
  Language, 385
Elements of Legal Style,
  The, 350
Elements of Style, The, 386
Elements of Writing About
  Literature and Film, The,
  355
Essays That Will Get You
  into Business School, 349
Essays That Will Get You
  into Law School, 349
Essays That Worked: 50
  Essays from Successful
  Applications, 348
Essentials of MLA Style: A
  Guide to Documentation
  for Writers of Research
  Papers, The, 386
Fundamentals of Essay
  Writing: An Orientation
  Manual, 348

How to Write It: A
  Complete Guide to
  Everything You'll Ever
  Write, 348
italics, 289
Jargon Dictionary, The, 388
Macmillan Teach Yourself
  Grammar and Style in 24
  Hours, 283
Manual for Writers of Term
  Papers, Theses, and
  Dissertations, A, 357
Merriam-Webster's
  Vocabulary Builder, 387
MLA Handbook for Writers
  of Research, 275
MLA Style Manual and
  Guide to Scholarly
  Publishing (2nd Ed.), 386
Modern American Usage: A
  Guide, 385
New Publicity Kit, The, 230
New York Times Manual of
  Style and Usage, The, 386
Nonsexist Word Finder, The,
  385
On Writing Well: The
  Classic Guide to Writing
  Nonfiction, 387
One True Thing, 266
Prentice Hall Reference
  Guide and Usage, 385
Publication Manual of the
  American Psychological
  Association (Publication
  Manual of the American
  Psychological Association,
  4th Ed.), 386
Reader's Guide to
  Periodical Literature, 271
Ready to Write More: From
  Paragraph to Essay, 348
reviews, 355
Schaum's Quick Guide to
  Writing Great Essays, 348
Scientific Style and Format:
  The CBE Manual for
  Authors, Editors, and
  Publishers, 353
Semantic Rhyming
  Dictionary, The, 388

Six Steps to Free Publicity: And Dozens of Other Ways to Win Free Media Attention for You and Your Business, 230
Sports Style Guide & Reference Manual: The Complete Reference for Sports Editors, Writers, and Broadcasters, 357
Stylebook and Libel Manual: Fully Revised and Updated, The, 386
Talking About People: A Guide to Fair and Accurate Language, 385
Wall to Wall, 283
Word Power Made Easy, 387
World's Easiest Guide to Using the MLA: A User-Friendly Manual for Formatting Research Papers According to the Modern Language Association Style, The, 386
Write on Target: A Five-Phase Program for Nonfiction Writers, 279
Writing a Successful College Application Essay: The Key to College Administration, 348
Writing Down the Bones: Freeing the Writer Within, 387
Writing Personal Essays: How to Shape Your Life Experiences for the Page, 348
Writing Reviews: How to Write About Arts & Leisure for Pleasure & Profit, 355
Writing That Works: How to Improve Your Memos, Letters, Reports, Speeches, Resumés, Plans, and Other Business Papers, 333, 387
Writing to Learn, 387

brackets, 293
brainstorming, mind mapping, 255
breaking ground, presentations, 310
brochures, 262, 340-341
Business Humor: Jokes & How to Deliver Them, book, 356
businesses
  cards, ticklers, 261
  communication, 329
    ad copy, 340-341
    audiences, 329
    bad news, 330-331
    brochures, 340-341
    electronic mail, 333-335
    interoffice memos, 333-335
    letters, 335-337
    meetings, 339-340
    oral presentations, 340
    presenting information, 331-332
    press releases, 228-230, 341
    proposals, 337-338
    quizzes, 344-345
    resumés, 341-342
    tasks, 330
    writing, 332-335
  letters, 222-223, 335-337
    addresses, 336
    body, 337
    closings, 337
    dates, 336
    reference lines, 336
    sales, 224-227
    salutations, 336
    signatures, 337
    writing rules, 223-224
  press releases, 228-230, 341
  sales letters, 224
    fundraising, 227
    preparing, 224-226
  speaking
    lesson plans, 221
    quizzes, 233-235
  writing
    lesson plans, 221
    quizzes, 233-235

C

capitalizing, 39
  articles, 39
  conjunctions, 39
  corporation names, 40
  product names, 40
  proper nouns, 38-41
Capitol Community College, Web site, 317
cards (business), ticklers, 261
Careful Writer: A Modern Guide to English Usage, The, book, 385
cases
  nominative, 64-65
  nouns, 64-65
  objective, 64-65
  possessives, 64-65
  pronouns, 64-65
  subjective, 64-65, 136-137
casual language, 361-363
categories, writing
  activities, 258
  crime, 258
  entertainment, 258
  events, 258
  lifestyles, 257
  mental health, 257
  money, 257
  personal-advancement ideas, 257
  physical fitness, 257
  school, 258
  topics, 257-258
cause and effect
  formats, 281
  organizing research, 281
certainty, 303
changes, rules of style, 361-364
characters, 242, 303
charts, pronouns, 67
chat rooms, 274
checking revisions
  rules, 323
  spotting problems, 323
  workshops, 323
checklists
  grammar logic, 200-202
  oral presentations, 197-198

Chicago Guide to Preparing Electronic Manuscripts: For Authors and Publishers (Chicago Guides to Writing, Editing, and Publishing), book, 386
Chicago Manual of Style: The Essential Guide for Writers, Editors, and Publishers (14th Edition), The, book, 186, 387
chronological order, 332
    leads, 245
    presentation, 311
    research, 281
    sequencing events, 311
    writing, 311
clarity (presentations and writing), 200-202, 303-307
classified-ad sections, idea stimulators, 259
classifying mass nouns, 41-42
clauses
    adjectives, 151
        complements, 152-153
        objects, 152
        subjects, 151
        subordinators, 154-156
    adverbs, 153
        subordinators, 154-156
    agreements
        tasks, 152
    colons, 180-182
    coordinating, 146
    dependent, 23, 147
    independent, 22-23
    lesson plans, 145
    main, 22-23, 145-147
        comma splice errors, 28
        commas, 162
        complex sentences, 25, 147-148
        compound sentences, 25, 146-147
        compound-complex sentences, 25-26, 148
        fused sentence errors, 28
        relative pronouns, 58
        run-on sentences, 28
        simple sentences, 24-25
    nouns, 148-149
        direct objects, 150
        indirect objects, 150

        interrogative pronouns, 61
        object complements, 150-151
        subjects, 149-150
    parallel structures, 27-28
    prepositional phrases, 30-31
    Q&As, 156-157
    quizzes, 158-159
        answers, 159
    restrictive, 153
    subordinates, 23, 30
        adjective clauses, 151-153
        adverbial clauses, 153-156
        commas, 163
        complex sentences, 25, 147-148
        compound-complex sentences, 25-26, 148
        noun clauses, 148-151
        Q&As, 157
        relative pronouns, 58
        restrictive clauses, 153
        sentence fragments, 26-27
    weak, commas, 164
clichés, 9, 124-125
    metaphors, 124-125
    rules, 209
    similes, 124-125
closings, 237, 246-247, 310-311
    agreement affirmation, 248
    business letters, 337
    echo effects, 247
    ironic twists, 248
    jokes, 248
    lesson plans, 237
    puns, 248
    quizzes, 249-251
    quotations, 249
    sales, 310-311
    techniques, 247-249
collective nouns, 48
    rules, 48
    subject and verb agreements, 108-109
collocation, 124
colloquialisms, 9-10

colons, 180-182
    Bible verses, 180-182
    clauses, 180-182
    fused sentence errors, 28
    magazines, 180-182
    punctuation, 180-182
    quotations, 180-182
    ratios, 180-182
    salutations, 180-182
    series, 180-182
    time, 180-182
    titles, 180-182
columns (advice), idea stimulators, 264
comic strips, idea stimulators, 264-265
comma splice errors, 28
commands, imperative sentences, 21-22
commas, 94, 161, 291
    -ly adjectives, 166
    adjective phrases, 133, 135
    adjectives, 166
    appositive phrases, 131-135
    clauses
        main, 162
        subordinate, 163
        weak, 164
    dates, rules, 168
    emphasizing words in a direct address, 167
    essential elements, 170-171
    expressions, 166
    geographical names and addresses, 168-169
    introductory words and phrases, 164
    lesson plans, 161
    phrases, 162
    position, 171
    Q&As, 173
    quizzes, 173-175
    quotations (direct), 168
    rules, dates, 168
    separating coordinate adjectives before a noun, 165
    separating nonessential words, 166-167
    serial, 164-165
    simple sentence divisions, 161

splices, 169-170
titles, 169
comments, sincere, 223
common adjectives, 93
Common Errors in English,
    Web site, 366, 388
common irregular verbs,
    389-392, 394
common nouns, 38
common sense, 200-202
communication
    adjectives, 200
    adverbs, 200
    business, 329
        ad copy, 340-341
        audiences, 329
        bad news, 330-331
        brochures, 340-341
        lesson plans, 329
        meetings, 339-340
        oral presentations, 340
        presenting information,
            331-332
        press releases, 341
        quizzes, 344-345
        resumés, 341-342
        tasks, 330
        writing, 332-338
    closings, 237, 246-249
    common sense, 200-202
    grammar rules, 200
    leads, 237-238
        attention grabbers,
            243-246
        fiction writing, 241-243
        nonfiction writing,
            239-241
    lesson plans, 303
    quizzes, 312-313
    rules, 207
        active voices, 213
        clichés, 209
        conversational narra-
            tives, 215
        edits, 218
        everyday language, 208
        nouns and verbs, 208
        originality, 216-217
        paragraphs, 211
        punctuation, 218
        research, 215
        sentences, 210-211

terminology, 217
    words, 210, 212, 214
seven c's, 303
speeches, audiences,
    197-198
verbs, 342
words, 304
comparative forms, 97-100
comparisons
    adverbs, 112
    similes, 123
    subordinators, 154
    well and good, 111
comparisons and contracts
    formats, 282
    organizing research, 282
complements
    complete predicates, 23
    versus compliment, 367
Complete Idiot's Guide to
    Grammar and Style, The,
    book, 78, 386
Complete Idiot's Guide to the
    Perfect Resume, The, book,
    342
complete predicates, 23-24
complete sentences, run-ons, 28
complete subjects, 20-21
completeness, 303
complex sentences, 25, 147-148
compliment versus comple-
    ment, 367
complements
    adjective clauses, 152-153
    objects
        noun clauses, 150-151
        phrases, 139-140
    subjects, pronouns, 65-66
compound sentences, 25, 66
    main clauses, 146
        conjunctive adverbs, 147
        coordinating conjunc-
            tions, 146-147
compounds
    adjectives, 93
    antecedent agreements,
        103-104
    nouns, 47-48
    predicates, 24
    prepositional phrases,
        116-117
    pronouns, 66

sentences, 25, 66
subjects, 24, 107-108
words
    hyphens, 188
    quantifiers, 91
compound-complex sentences,
    25-26, 148
Computer Currents High-Tech
    Dictionary, Web site, 388
concerns, 303
concessions, subordinators, 154
conciseness, 303
conclusions, 310-311, 349
conditions, subordinators, 155
conflicts (leads), fiction
    writing, 243
confusing nouns, subject and
    verb agreements, 109
conjunctions, 94, 119-121
    capitalizing, 39
    coordinating, 29, 146-147
        compound sentences, 25
        parallel structures, 27-28
    correlative, 119-121
    parallelism, 121-122
    subject and verb agree-
        ments, 107-108
    subordinating, 119-121
conjunctive adverbs, 96, 147
consonant sounds, alliteration,
    7-8
context, 6
continuous tenses, 74
contractions, 118-119
    apostrophes, 59, 182-184
    coordinating, 119-121
    pronouns, 59
    verbs, 59
conventional order, 332
conversational narrative, rules,
    215
coordinating adjectives, com-
    mas, 165
coordinating clauses, 146
coordinating conjunctions, 29,
    146-147
    compound sentences, 25
    parallel structures, 27-28
coordinating contractions,
    119-121
corporation names, capitalizing,
    40

correlative conjunctions, 119-121
count nouns, 45-46
counterpoints and rebuttals
  formats, 282
  organizing research, 282
Craft of Research, The, book, 275
creative verbs, 343
creativity, 269-270, 303
crimes, writing, 258
Critical Approaches to Writing About Film, book, 356
criticisms, 355
  book reviews, 355
  screen reviews, 356
  stage reviews, 356
crude phrases, 318
cultural context, 6
Curmudgeon's Stylebook, The, Web site, 388
cutting tasks, 214

D

dangling participles, 122
dashes, 188, 291
data, organizing, 332
dates
  business letters, 336
  comma rules, 168
declarative sentences, 22
define and exemplify
  formats, 282
  organizing research, 282
definite articles, 88
definitions, altered words, 195-196
degrees
  commas, 169
  subordinators, 155
demonstrative articles, 88-89
demonstrative pronouns, 59
Department of Applied Linguistics & ESL, Georgia State University, Web site, 78
dependent clauses, 23, 147

depth
  sentences, 209
  writing, 209
descriptive adjectives, 93-94
descriptives
  grammar, 4
  metaphors, 123
  passage leads, 243
  powerful leads, 241
  similes, 123
determiners, 37-38, 61, 87-90. *See also* articles
diagramming sentences, 3-4
dialog versus dialogue, 367
dialogue versus dialog, 367
dialogues (opening), leads, 243
dictionaries, 385
  online, 388
  plural nouns, 45
Dictionary for Bias-Free Usage: A Guide to Nondiscriminatory Language, book, 385
direct addresses, commas, 167
direct objects
  noun clauses, 150
  phrases, 137-138
  transitive verbs, 80
direct quotations, commas, 168
direct statements, leads, 240
discrepancies, 318
distributive articles, 89
divisions (sentences), commas, 161
DNS (Domain Name System), 273
documentation, 283-284
Domain Name System. *See* DNS
dots per inch. *See* dpi
dpi (dots per inch), 354
drafts (first), lesson plans, 315

E

e-mail, 222-224, 333-335, 354
echo effects, closings, 247

editing, 319-322, 324-325
  ambiguous construction, 319-322
  illogical phrases, 319-322
  metaphors, 319-322
  mixed metaphors, 319-322
  phrases, 319-322
  pretentious language, 319-322
  procedures, 319-322
  pronouns, 319-322
  quizzes, 326-327
  rules, 218
  thoughts, 319-322
  words, 319-322
electronic mail. *See* e-mail
elements, essential, 170-171, 201
Elements of Legal Style, The, book, 350
Elements of Style, 1918, The, Web site, 388
Elements of Style, The, book, 386
Elements of Writing About Literature and Film, The, book, 355
ellipses, 184-185
emphasis
  bold type, 289
  dashes, 188
  exclamation marks, 180
  italics, 289
  parentheses, 291
  vocative phrases, 133
  word positions, 212
  words in a direct address, commas, 167
emphatic tense, 83
encyclopedias, 275
endings
  adjectives, 95-96
    -al, 95-96
    -ar, 95
    -en, 95-96
    -ish, 95
    -like, 95
    -ly, 95
    -ory, 95
    -y, 61

adverbs, -ly, 97, 111, 187
commas, -ly, 166
gerunds, -ing, 49, 135
nouns, -ics, 109
parallel structure, -ing,
    27-28
participles, -ing, 122
pronouns, intensive
    -self, 61
    -selves, 61
English
    mutable meanings, 195-196
    spell check, 193-195
enhanced proofreading,
    324-325
entertainment writing cate-
    gories, 258
environment, writing, 352-353
errors
    comma splices, 28
    fused sentences, 28
    proofreading, 318
    writing, 318
essays
    body, 349
    conclusions, 349
    formal, 348
    functional, 348
    introductions, 349
    personal, 348
    thesis statements, 349
    writing, 348-349
*Essays That Will Get You into
    Business School*, book, 349
*Essays That Will Get You into
    Law School*, book, 349
*Essays That Worked: 50 Essays
    from Successful Applications*,
    book, 348
essential elements, commas,
    170-171
*Essentials of MLA Style: A
    Guide to Documentation for
    Writers of Research Papers,
    The*, book, 386
establishing voices, 232
euphemisms, 16, 201
events
    chronological sequence, 311
    writing categories, 258

everyday language, rules, 208
exclamation marks, 180
exclamative articles, 89
exercises, prethinking, 269-270
experts
    interviews
        idea stimulators,
            260-261
        research, 276-279
    Web site, 352
expletives, 22
expressions
    clichés, 124-125
    commas, 166
    hackneyed, 9
    idioms, 11, 123-124
    interrogative, question
        marks, 178-180
    mathematical parentheses,
        290-293
    parenthetical, 290-293
    problems, 371
        ambiguity, 371-373
        lesson plans, 361
        slang, 371
    quantity, subject and verb
        agreements, 109-110
    rules, 209
    slang, 371, 394-395

F

Facts on File, Web site, 388
FAQ (Frequently Asked
    Questions), 274
farther versus further, 367
faulty parallelism, 121-122
feminine gender, pronouns,
    55-56
fewer versus less, 368
fiction writing, 266
    idea stimulators, 264-266
    leads, 241
        characters, 242
        conflicts, 243
        locale, 241-242
        setting, 242
        tone, 242-243

figures of speech, 10
    metaphors, 12-13
    similes, 15
file folders, ticklers, 262
files
    FAQ, 274
    ticklers, idea stimulators,
        261-264
fillers, newspapers, 341
films, italics, 289
financial verbs, 343
first drafts, lesson plans, 315
first person pronouns, 55-56
fitness (physical), writing cate-
    gories, 257
flaws, sentences
    fragments, 26-27
    tasks, 26
folders (files), ticklers, 262
foreign words, italics, 290
foreward slashes, 293-294
formal essays, 348
formal language, 361-363
formats, 239, 359
    cause and effect, 281
    comparisons and contrasts,
        282
    counterpoints and rebuttals,
        282
    define and exemplify, 282
    leads, 280-281
    process analysis, 282-283
    sequential order, 281
    soapboxes, 282
former versus latter, 368
forms
    adjectives, 94-95
    comparative, 97-100
        positive, 97-100
        superlative, 97-100
    pronoun charts, 67
    verb tenses, 72-73
        future, 76, 79-80
        future perfect, 76
        future perfect progres-
            sive, 77
        future progressive, 76-77
        past, 74-75, 78-80
        past participle, 78-79
        past perfect, 75
        past perfect progressive,
            76

past progressive, 76
present, 73-74, 77-80
present perfect, 75
present perfect progressive, 76
present progressive, 74
progressive, 74
fragments, sentences, 26-27
free write
organizing, 310-311
presentations, 310-311
topics, 310-311
Frequently Asked Questions.
See FAQ
functional essays, 348
functions
adjectives, 94-95
grammar, 6
pronoun charts, 67
Fundamentals of Essay Writing: An Orientation Manual, book, 348
fundraising letters, 227
further versus farther, 367
fused sentence errors, 28
future perfect progressive tense verbs, 77
future perfect tense verbs, 76
future progressive tense verbs, 76-77
future tenses, verbs, 72-73, 76, 79-80

G

gender
nouns, 48-49
personal pronouns, 55-56
pronouns, 48-49
gender-sensitive writing, 196-197
geographical addresses, commas, 169
geographical names, commas, 168-169
gerunds, 134
-ing endings, 49-50, 135
nouns, 49-50
phrases, 134

possessives, 49-50
pronouns, 49-50
tasks, 49-50
verbs, 49
getting started, 310-311
gist, 10
glossary versus appendix, 366
good versus well, 111
Google, Web site, 274, 324
graded quantifiers, 91
grammar, 3-4, 238. *See also* language
ambiguity, 200
checks, 315-317
context, 6
functions, 6
guides, 386
logic, 5-6
online resources, 387-388
dictionaries, 388
grammar guides, 388
style guides, 388
parallelism, 121-122
pragmatics, 6-7
quizzes, 16-18
resources, 385
dictionaries, 385
grammar guides, 386
style guides, 386-387
vocabulary guides, 387
writing guides, 387
semantics, 7
senses, 4-5
descriptive, 4
pedagogical, 4
prescriptive, 4
reference, 5
theoretical, 5
traditional, 5
sound patterns, 7
styles, 7
alliteration, 7-8
allusion, 8
anthropomorphism, 8
antonyms, 8-9
assonance, 9
clichés, 9
colloquialisms, 9-10
figures of speech, 10
gist, 10
homonyms, 10
hyperbole, 10-11

idiomatic translations, 11
idioms, 11
irony, 11-12
jargon, 12
lexicons, 12
malapropisms, 12
metaphors, 12-13
metonymy, 13
morphemes, 13
onomatopoeia, 13-14
puns, 14
rhymes, 14-15
rhythm, 15
sarcasm, 15
similes, 15
synonyms, 16
wording, 7
Grammar Bytes! Interactive Grammar Review, Web site, 388
Grammar Handbook, University of Illinois at Urbana-Champaign, Web site, 388
grant applications, 351
guarantees, take-away value, 305-307
Guide to Grammar and Writing, Web site, 388
guidelines, writing, 239, 355. *See also* formats, style
book reviews, 355
screen reviews, 356
stage reviews, 356
guides
grammar, 386-388
style, 386-388
vocabulary, 387
writing, 387

H

hackneyed expressions, 9
headlines, 225
health (mental), writing categories, 257
help-wanted listings, idea stimulators, 259

helping verbs, 81
historical present tense, 73-74
history, language, 196
homonyms, 10, 193-195
horoscopes, idea stimulators, 265
house style, 347
How to Write It: A Complete Guide to Everything You'll Ever Write, book, 348
humor
    leads, 244, 280-281
    meanings, 318-319
    words, dual meanings, 318-319
    writing, 356
hyperbole, 10-11
hyphens, 185-188
    compound sentences, 188
    modifiers, 186
    prefixes, 185-188
    rules, 185-188
    sounds, 187
hypothesis, 5-6

I

iambic sentences, 14
ideas, 256-257
    categories, 257-258
    leads, 280-281
    lesson plans, 255
    mind mapping, 255-256
    organizing research
        cause and effect, 281
        comparisons and contrasts, 282
        counterpoints and rebuttals, 282
        define and exemplify, 282
        process analysis, 282-283
        sequential research, 281
        soapboxes, 282
    prethinking, 269-270
    quizzes, 266-268

research, 270-273
    Internet searches, 273-274
    interviews, 276-279
    libraries, 274-275
    media merit, 275
    narrowing the topic, 271
selling, business letters, 222-224
stimulators, 258-259
    advice columns, 264
    comic strips, 264-265
    fiction writing, 264-266
    horoscopes, 265
    interviews, 260-261
    letters to the editor, 265
    movie reviews, 265
    storyboards, 263
    ticklers, 261-264
    yellow pages, 259-260
identifying audiences, 221
idiomatic translations, 11
idioms, 11, 123-124
imperative mood verbs, 72
imperative sentences, 21-22
impressions, 223
inadvertent errors, 318
incomplete sentences, 26-27
indefinite adjectives, 93
indefinite articles, 87
indefinite pronouns, 59-60, 104-106
independent clauses, 22-23
indicate dialogue, quotation marks, 294-298
indicative mood verbs, 72
indirect objects
    intransitive verbs, 80
    noun clauses, 150
    phrases, 138-139
infinitives, 117-118
    implied, 365-366
    parallel structures, 27-28
    perfect, 117-118
    phrases, 135-136
    present, 117-118
    split, 118, 364-365
inflection, voice, 5-6, 11-12
informal language, 361-363
information, presenting, 331
    organizing, 332
    outlines, 331-332

inspirations, ideas, 256-259
    categories, 257-258
    fiction writing, 264-266
    interviews, 260-261
    storyboards, 263
    ticklers, 261-264
    yellow pages, 259-260
intensive pronouns, -self endings, 61
Internet
    addresses, 273
    research, 273-274
interoffice memos, 333-335
interrogative adjectives, 61
interrogative adverbs, 96
interrogative expressions, question marks, 178-180
interrogative pronouns, 61
interrogative sentences, 28-29, 178-180
interviews
    body language, 278
    idea stimulators, 260-261
    notes, 277
    questions, 278
    research, 276-279
    restaurants, 277
    tape recorders, 277
    tasks, 216
intransitive verbs, 80
introductions, essays, 349
invariable adjectives, 94-95
investigating, research projects, 284
irony, 11-12, 248
irregulars
    noun plurals, 44
    verbs, 78-79, 389-392, 394
        past participle, 389-394
        past tense, 389-394
        present tense, 389-394
        spelling, 79
        to be, 79-80
it's versus its, 368
italics, 289-290, 299-300
    books, 289
    emphasis, 289
    films, 289
    magazines, 290
    plays, 290
    titles, 289-290

underlining, 290
words
  foreign, 290
  scientific, 290
  unfamiliar, 290
its versus it's, 368

J

jargon, 12, 217, 223, 363
Jargon Dictionary, The, book, 388
jobs listing, idea stimulators, 259
jokes, closings, 248
journal research, 274-275

K

Kid Report,The, anecdote, 299

L

language, 238. *See also* grammar
adjectives, 92
  endings, 95-96
  invariable, 94-95
  position, 92-93
  types, 93-94
adverbs, 96-97
agreements
  adverbs, 111
  pronouns and
    antecedents, 103-106
  subjects and verbs, 107-110
articles, 87
  definite, 88
  demonstratives, 88-89
  distributives, 89
  exclamatives, 89
  indefinite, 87

numbers, 90
possessive pronouns, 90-91
quantifiers, 91-92
auxiliary verbs, 140-141
body, interviews, 278
business communication, 329
  ad copy, 340-341
  audiences, 329
  bad news, 330-331
  brochures, 340-341
  meetings, 339-340
  oral presentations, 340
  presenting information, 331-332
  press releases, 341
  resumés, 341-342
  writing, 332-338
clauses
  adjectives, 151-153
  adverbial, 153-156
  main, 145-147
  nouns, 148-151
  restrictive, 153
  subordinate, 147-148
clichés, 124-125
collocation, 124
comparisons, adjectives and adverbs, 97-100
conjunctions, 119-121
contractions, 118-119
editing, 319-322
gender-sensitive, 196-197
grammar, 4-6
  context, 6
  descriptive, 4
  functions, 6
  parallelism, 121-122
  pedagogical, 4
  pragmatics, 6-7
  prescriptive, 4
  reference, 5
  semantics, 7
  sound patterns, 7
  styles, 7-16
  theoretical, 5
  traditional, 5
  wording, 7
history, 196
idioms, 123-124

infinitives, 117-118
metaphors, 123
nouns, 37-38
  collective, 48
  common, 38
  compound, 47-48
  count, 45-46
  gender, 48-49
  gerunds, 49-50
  mass, 41-42
  plural, 42-45
  possessive, 46-47
  proper, 38-41
participles, 122
persuasion, proposals, 338
phrases, 129, 136
  absolute, 130-131
  adjectives, 130
  appositives, 131-133
  direct objects, 137-138
  indirect objects, 138-139
  nouns, 129-130
  object complements, 139-140
  subjective cases, 136-137
  verbs, 134-136
  vocative, 133
prepositions, 115-117
presentations, 305-307
pronouns, 55, 62
  ambiguity, 62
  antecedent agreements, 62-64
  cases, 64-65
  charts, 67
  contractions, 59
  demonstrative, 59
  gerunds, 49-50
  indefinite, 59-60
  intensive, 61
  interrogative, 61
  numbers, 56
  personal, 55-56
  possessives, 56-57
  reciprocal, 62
  reflexive, 60-61
  relative, 57-58
  rules, 65-66
  unclear, 106-107
  workshops, 66

rules, 208
similes, 123
style
    changes, 361-363
    rules, 363-364
subjunctives, 125-126
verbs, 71-72
    actions, 80
    gerunds, 49
    helping, 81
    irregular, 78-80
    linking, 80-81
    mood, 72
    regular, 77-78
    tenses, 72-77
    voices, 81-82
words
    mutable meanings,
        195-196
    spell check, 193-195
latter versus former, 368
laws, writing, 200, 349-350
lay versus lie, 369
leadership verbs, 342
leads, 237-238, 280-281
    action scenes, 243
    attention grabbers, 243-246
    chronological order, 245
    descriptive passages, 243
    direct statements, 240
    fiction writing, 241
        characters, 242
        conflicts, 243
        locale, 241-242
        setting, 242
        tone, 242-243
    formats, 280-281
    humor, 244, 280-281
    lesson plans, 237
    nonfiction writing, 239-241
    opening dialogues, 243
    pending action sequences,
        244
    pensive, 241
    plots, 245
    powerful descriptions, 241
    quizzes, 249-251
    quotations, 240
    senses, 245
    shocking statements, 239
    suspense, 244

learning, writing, 323-324
legal writing, 349-350
less versus fewer, 368
lesson plans
    agreements, 103
    articles, 87
    business communication,
        329
    business writing and speak-
        ing, 221
    clauses, 145
    commas and semicolons,
        161
    communicating, 303
    developing ideas, 255
    first drafts, 315
    leads and closings, 237
    phrases, 129
    problem words and expres-
        sions, 361
    pronouns, 55
    punctuation, 177, 289
    research, 269
    rules, 193
    sentence structure, 20
    style, 347
    verbs, 71
    writing rules, 207
letters
    business, 222-223, 335-338
        addresses, 336
        body, 337
        closings, 337
        dates, 336
        proposals, 337-338
        reference lines, 336
        salutations, 336
        signatures, 337
        writing rules, 223-224
    capitals, proper nouns,
        38-41
    fundraising, 227
    italics, 289-290
    sales, 224
        announcements, 226
        attention grabbers, 225
        benefits, 226
        businesses, 224-226
        fundraising, 227
        headlines, 225
        preparing, 224-226

    sales pitch, 226
    time-frame notices, 225
    writing rules, 223-224
letters to the editor, idea stimu-
    lators, 265
lexicons, 12
libraries
    encyclopedias, 275
    research, 274-275
lie versus lay, 369
lifestyles, writing categories,
    257
limiting adjectives, 93-94
lingo, rules, 217
linguistics, 4
    context, 6
    phonology, 7
linking verbs, 80-81, 139-140
    adjective clauses, comple-
        ments, 152-153
listening, 249
lists, mind mapping, 255
locale (leads), fiction writing,
    241-242
logic, 5-6, 200-202
long-form pronouns, 56-57

M

Macmillan Teach Yourself
    Grammar and Style in 24
    Hours, book, 283
magazines
    ads, ticklers, 262
    colons, 180-182
    italics, 290
    press releases, 228-230
    research, 274-275
    Sheriff and Deputy
        Quarterly, 284
mail, electronic, 333-335
main clauses, 22-23, 145-147
    comma splice errors, 28
    commas, 162
    complex sentences, 25,
        147-148

compound sentences, 25, 146
  conjunctive adverbs, 147
  coordinating conjunctions, 146-147
compound-complex sentences, 25-26, 148
fused sentence errors, 28
relative pronouns, 58
run-on sentences, 28
simple sentences, 24-25
malapropisms, 12, 318
management verbs, 342
manners, subordinators, 155
Manual for Writers of Term Papers, Theses, and Dissertations, A, book, 357
mapping, mind, 255-256
markers, nouns, 37-38, 88
marks
  accents, 363
  exclamation, 180
  hyphens, 185-188
  questions, 178-180
  quotation, 299-300
masculine gender pronouns, 55-56
mass nouns, 41-42
math, 201
mathematical expressions, parentheses, 290-293
meanings
  altered words, 195-196
  humorous, 318-319
measurements, mass nouns, 41-42
media merit research, 275
medicine, 353
meetings, 339-340
memos, interoffice, 333-335
mental health, writing categories, 257
merit, media research, 275
Merriam-Webster's Vocabulary Builder, book, 387
metaphors, 10-13, 123, 320
  clichés, 124-125
  editing, 319-322
  phrases, 123
metonymy, 13

Microsoft Word 2000, 170
miles per hour. *See* mph
mind mapping, 255
  brainstorming, 255
  lists, 255
  tasks, 256
misused words, 304
MLA Handbook for Writers of Research Papers, book, 275
MLA Style Manual and Guide to Scholarly Publishing (2nd Ed), book, 386
models, writing, 323-324
Modern American Usage: A Guide, book, 385
modifiers
  hyphens, 186
  participles, 49
money, writing categories, 257
mood, verbs, 72
  imperatives, 72
  indicatives, 72
  subjunctives, 72, 125-126
moot versus mute, 370
morphemes, 13
morphology, 13
movie reviews, idea stimulators, 265
movies, tasks, 238-239
mph (miles per hour), 354
mutable meanings, words, 195-196
mute versus moot, 370

N

names (geographical), commas, 168-169
narratives, conversational, 215
natural medicine, 353
natural science, 351
negative realities, 309
neuter language, 196-197
neuter gender pronouns, 55-56
neuters, 48-49
New Publicity Kit, The, book, 230

New York Times Manual of Style and Usage, The, book, 386
news, bad, 330-331
newsgroups, 274
newsletters, ticklers, 262
newspapers, 82
  idea stimulators, 259, 264-266
  press releases, 228-230, 341
nominative cases, 64-65
nonessential words
  commas, 166-167
  tasks, 167
nonfiction writing, 239-241, 266
Nonsexist Word Finder, The, book, 385
notes
  interviews, 277
  thank-yous, 262
notices, time-frame sales letters, 225
nouns, 37-38, 94, 134
  -ics endings, 109
  adjectives, 92-96
  apostrophes, 182-184
  articles, 87
  capitalizing, 39
  cases, 64-65
    nominative, 64-65
    objective, 64-65
    possessives, 64-65
    subjective, 64-65
  clauses, 148-149
    direct objects, 150
    indirect objects, 150
    interrogative pronouns, 61
    object complements, 150-151
    subjects, 149-150
  collective, 48, 108-109
  commas, 165
  common, 38
  compound, 47-48
  compound subjects, 24
  confusing subject and verb agreements, 109
  count, 45-46

depth, 209
gender, 48-49
gerunds, 49-50
indefinite articles, 87
markers, 37-38, 88
mass, 41-42
parallelism, 121-122
phrases, 129-130
plurals, 42-45, 389-392, 394
possessive, 46-47
presentations, 198-199
proper, 38-41
quizzes, 51-53
simple subjects, 20-21
singulars, 389-392, 394
turning into verbs, 365
verbalizing, 199
visual, rules, 208
writing, depth, 209
numbers, 90
    articles, 90
    mass nouns, 41-42
    order, 332
    personal pronouns, 55-56
    pronouns, 56

O

object complements, noun
    clauses, 150-151
objective cases, 64-65
objectives, timetable, 308-309
objects
    adjective clauses, 152
    adjectives, 94
    auxiliary verbs, 140-141
    complement phrases,
        139-140
    complete predicates, 23
    direct
        noun clauses, 150
        phrases, 137-138
        transitive verbs, 80
    indirect
        intransitive verbs, 80
        noun clauses, 150
        phrases, 138-139
    prepositions, 115-116

*On Writing Well: The Classic
    Guide to Writing Nonfiction,*
    book, 387
On-Line English Grammar, An,
    Web site, 388
One True Thing, book, 266
online resources, 273-274,
    387-388
    dictionaries, 388
    grammar guides, 388
    style guides, 388
onomatopoeia, 13-14
open-minded questions,
    277-278
opening dialogue, leads, 243
oral presentations, 197-198,
    340
order, 332
    alphabetical, 332
    chronological, 245, 332
    conventional, 332
    numerical, 332
    sequential, organizing
        research, 281
    words, 201
ordinary verbs, 82-83
organizing, 332
    free writes, 310-311
    research
        cause and effect, 281
        comparisons and con-
            trasts, 282
        counterpoints and rebut-
            tals, 282
        define and exemplify,
            282
        process analysis,
            282-283
        sequential order, 281
        soapboxes, 282
        tasks, 279
originality, rules, 216-217
outlines
    cause and effect, 281
    comparisons and contrasts,
        282
    counterpoints and rebuttals,
        282
    define and exemplify, 282
    presenting information,
        331-332

    process analysis, 282-283
    sequential order, 281
    soapboxes, 282
ownership
    possessive nouns, 46-47
    possessive pronouns, 56-57

P

paragraphs, rules, 211, 214
parallel structures, 27-28
parallelism, 121-122
paraphrasing, 283-284
parentheses, 290-293, 299-300
    appositive phrases, 131-133
    appositives, 290-293
    emphasis, 291
    mathematical expressions,
        290-293
    parenthetical expressions,
        290-293
    question marks, 178-180
    rules, 290-293
parenthetical expressions,
    290-293
parenthetical phrases, 131-133
parenthetical questions,
    178-180
participles, 49, 122
    -ing endings, 122
    dangling, 122
    phrases, 134-135
    present, 30
parts of speech, presentations,
    198-199
passages, descriptives, 243
passive voice verbs, 81-82
past participle tense verbs,
    78-79, 94, 389-394
past perfect progressive tense
    verbs, 76
past perfect tense verbs, 75
past progressive tense verbs, 76
past tense verbs, 72-75, 78-80,
    389-392, 394
pasting, tasks, 214
patterns
    parallel structure, 27-28
    sound, 7

syllables, rhythm, 15
words, subject and verb
agreements, 110
pedagogical grammar, 4
pending action sequences,
leads, 244
pensive leads, 241
perfect infinitives, 117-118
performance verbs, 343
periodicals
press releases, 341
research, 274-275
periods, 177-178, 184-185
personal
bibliographies, 230-231
essays, 348
portfolios, ticklers, 262
pronouns, 55-56
style, 257
personal-advancement ideas,
writing categories, 257
personality, reflecting tasks,
231-232
perspectives, 202-203
persuasive
proposals, 338
words, 304
phone books (yellow pages),
idea stimulators, 259-260
phonics, 7
phrases, 129, 136
absolute, 130-131
adjectives, 130-135
appositives, 131-133
commas, 131-135
parentheses, 131-133
clichés, 9
colloquialisms, 9-10
commas, 162, 164
crude, 318
direct objects, 137-138
editing, 319-322
euphemisms, 16
exclamation marks, 180
gerunds, 134
idioms, 123-124
indirect objects, 138-139
infinitives, 135-136
lesson plans, 129
metaphors, 12-13, 123

metonymy, 13
nouns, 129-130
object complements,
139-140
parenthetical, 131-133
participles, 30, 134-135
patterns, parallel structure,
27-28
prepositions, 30-31, 94,
116-117
adjectives, 94
indirect objects, 138-139
quizzes, 141, 143
rules, 209
subjective cases, 136-137
verbs, 117, 134
gerunds, 134
infinitives, 135-136
participles, 122, 134-135
prepositions, 117
vocative, 133
physical fitness, writing categories, 257
pitches (sales) attention grabbers, 226, 243-246
places, subordinators, 155
planning research tasks,
271-272
plans, lessons
agreements, 103
articles, 87
clauses, 145
business communication,
329
business speaking and writing, 221
commas and semicolons,
161
communicating, 303
developing ideas, 255
expressions, 361
first drafts, 315
leads and closings, 237
phrases, 129
pronouns, 55
punctuation, 177, 289
research, 269
rules, 193
style, 347
writing rules, 207
verbs, 71

plays, italics, 290
plots, leads, 245
plurals
apostrophes, 182-184,
363-364
demonstrative articles,
88-89
nouns, 42-45, 389-392, 394
pronouns, 56, 65-66,
103-106
verbs
present tense, 77-78
subjunctive mood,
125-126
points of view, 202-203
police reports, 82
portfolios, ticklers, 262
positions
adjectives, 92-93
adverbs, 97
commas, 171
subjects, 22
words, 212
positive comparative forms,
97-100
possessives
apostrophes, 182-184
cases, 64-65
gerunds, 49-50
nouns, 46-47
pronouns, 56-57, 90-91
powerful descriptions, leads,
241
powerful words, 304
pragmatics, 6-7
predicates
complete, 23-24
complex sentences, 25
compound sentences, 24-25
compound-complex sen-
tences, 25-26
linking verbs, 80-81
main clauses, 145-146
simple sentences, 23-25
tasks, 23-24
verbs, 71-72
prefixes, hyphens, 185-188
*Prentice Hall Reference Guide
to Grammar and Usage*,
book, 385

preparing
  personal bibliographies,
    230-231
  reports, 337
  sales letters, 224-226
prepositions, 30-31, 115-116,
  121
  capitalizing, 39
  infinitive phrases, 136
  parallelism, 121-122
  phrasal verbs, 117
  phrases, 30-31, 94, 116-117
    adjectives, 94
    indirect objects, 138-139
Presbyterian College Writing
  Center, Web site, 317
prescriptive grammar, 4
present infinitives, 117-118
present participles, 30, 94
present perfect progressive
  tense verbs, 76
present perfect tense verbs, 75
present progressive tense verbs,
  74
present tense verbs, 72-74,
  77-80, 389-394
presentations. *See also*
speeches
  ad copy, 340-341
  angles, 202-203
  audiences, 221-222, 329
  bad news, 330-331
  breaking ground, 310-311
  brochures, 340-341
  chronological, 311
  clarity, 305-307
  documentation, 283-284
  electronic mail, 333-335
  establishing voices, 232
  evaluating audiences,
    197-198
  free writes, 310-311
  language, 305-307
  leads, 280-281
  meetings, 339-340
  organizing research, 332
    cause and effect, 281
    comparisons and con-
      trasts, 282
    counterpoints and rebut-
      tals, 282

    define and exemplify,
      282
    process analysis,
      282-283
    sequential research, 281
    soapboxes, 282
  oral, 197-198, 340
  outlines, 331-332
  press releases, 341
  research, 270-273
    Internet searches,
      273-274
    interviews, 276-279
    libraries, 274-275
    media merit, 275
    narrowing the topic, 271
  resumés, 341-342
  rules, 305-307
  sales letters, 224
    fundraising, 227
    preparing, 224-226
    writing rules, 223-224
  sequence, 311
  simplicity, 232-233
  style, 221-222, 347
    essays, 348-349
    laws, 349-350
    science, 350-354
  successful, 311
  take-away value, 305-307
  timetable, 308-309
  topics, 202-203
  value, 304-307
  verbalizing nouns, 199
  visualizing, 310-311
  writing, 332-333
    business letters, 335-338
    interoffice memos,
      333-335
press releases, 228-230, 341
press styles, 347
prethinking, 269-270
preventive medicines, 353
problems, 364
  expressions, 371-373
  implied infinitives, 365-366
  quizzes, 373-374
  slang, 371
  splitting infinitives, 364-365
  turning nouns into verbs,
    365

  words, 366
    a while versus awhile,
      366
    all ready versus already,
      366
    appendix versus glos-
      sary, 366
    complement versus com-
      pliment, 367
    dialogue versus dialog,
      367
    farther versus further,
      367
    fewer versus less, 368
    former versus latter, 368
    its versus it's, 368
    lay versus lie, 369
    moot versus mute, 370
    than versus then, 370
    their, they're, and there,
      370
    to, too, and two, 371
procedures, editing, 319-322
processes
  analysis, 282-283
  writing
    lists, 255
    mind mapping, 255-256
product names, capitalizing, 40
profiles, personal bibliographies, 230-231
ProfNet, Web site, 261
ProFusion, Web site, 274
progressive tense verbs, 74
projects, research, 284
pronouns, 55, 62, 94
  adjectives, 92-93
  ambiguity, 62
  antecedent agreements,
    62-64, 103-104
  apostrophes, 182-184
  cases, 64-65
    nominative, 64-65
    objective, 64-65
    possessives, 64-65
    subjective, 64-65
  charts, 67
  compound sentences, 66
  contractions, 59
  demonstrative, 59
  editing, 319-322
  first person, 55-56

gender, 48-49, 55-56
gerunds, 49-50
indefinite, 59-60, 104-106
intensive, 61
   -self endings, 61
   -selves endings, 61
interrogative, 61
   noun clauses, 61
   questions, 61
lesson plans, 55
long-form, 56-57
numbers, 56
personal, 55-56
plurals, 56-67, 103-104
position, 92-93
possessives, 56-57, 90-91
quizzes, 67-69
reciprocal, 62
reflexive, 60-61
relative, 30, 57-58
rules, 65-66
second person, 55-56
short-form, 56-57
simple subjects, 20-21
singular, 56, 65-66
subject complements, 65-66
third person, 55-56
unclear, 106-107
workshops, 66
proofreading
   enhanced, 324-325
   errors, 318
   grammar check, 315-317
   inadvertent errors, 318
   quizzes, 326-327
   rules, 315-317
   techniques, 315-317
proofreading techniques, 317
proper adjectives, 94
proper nouns, 38-41
proposals
   appendices, 338
   persuasion, 338
   writing, 337-338
Publication Manual of the
American Psychological
Association (Publication
Manual of the American
Psychological Association,
4th Ed), book, 386

punctuation
   apostrophes, 182-184
   backslashes, 293-294
   brackets, 293
   colons, 180-182
   commas, 161
      adjectives, 166
      dates, 168
      degrees, 169
      emphasizing words in
        a direct address, 167
      essential elements,
        170-171
      expressions, 166
      geographical addresses
        and names, 168-169
      introductory words and
        phrases, 164
      main clauses, 162
      phrases, 162
      position, 171
      quotations (direct), 168
      separating coordinate
        adjectives before a
        noun, 165
      separating nonessential
        words, 166-167
      serial, 164-165
      simple sentence divi-
        sions, 161
      splices, 169-170
      subordinate clauses, 163
      titles, 169
      weak clauses, 164
   dashes, 188
   ellipses, 184-185
   exclamation marks, 180
   forward slashes, 293-294
   hyphens, 185-188
   italics, 289-290
   lesson plans, 177, 289
   parentheses, 290-293
   periods, 177-178
   question marks, 178-180
   quizzes, 189-190, 301-302
   quotation marks, 294-298
   rules, 218
   semicolons, 171-173
   slashes, 293-294
puns, 14, 248, 318-319

Purdue University's OWL
   (Online Writing Lab)
   Handouts, Web site, 317
pure science, 351
purposes, subordinators, 155

Q

Q & A
   agreements, 111-112
   clauses, 156-157
   commas and semicolons,
      173
   subordinate clauses, 157
   subordinators, 157
quantifiers, 37-38
   articles, 91-92
   graded, 91
quantities, count nouns, 45-46
quantity expressions, subject
   and verb agreements, 109-110
question marks, 178-180
questions
   direct, 178-180
   interrogative pronouns, 61
   interviews, 278
   open-minded, 277-278
   parenthetical, 178-180
   simple, 28-29
quizzes, 67, 83, 101, 112,
   126-128, 141, 284
   agreements, 112-114
   answers, 18, 33, 53, 69, 85,
      102, 114, 128, 143, 175,
      190, 205, 220, 235, 251,
      268, 287, 302, 313, 327,
      345, 359, 374
   articles, adjectives and
      adverbs, 101-102
   business communication,
      344-345
   business writing and speak-
      ing, 233-235
   clauses, 158-159
      answers, 159
   commas and semicolons,
      173-175

communicating, 312-313
editing, 326-327
grammar, 16-18
ideas, 266-268
leads and closings, 249-251
nouns, 51-53
phrases, 141, 143
problems, 373-374
pronouns, 67-69
proofreading, 326-327
punctuation, 189-190,
    301-302
research, 285-286
rules, 203-205
sentences, 32-33
verbs, 83-85
writing, 326-327
writing rules, 218-220
writing styles, 358-359
quotation marks, 294-300
    formats, 294-298
    indicate dialogue, 294-298
    rules, 294-298
    single, 299
quotations
    closings, 249
    colons, 180-182
    commas, 168
    leads, 240
quotes, 298-299

R

ratios, colons, 180-182
*Reader's Guide to Periodical
    Literature*, book, 271
reading purposes, 324-325
*Ready to Write More: From
    Paragraph to Essay*, book,
    348
realities, negatives, 309
reciprocal pronouns, 62
recorders (tape) interviews, 277
recording sources, 275-276
redundancies, 318
Reference Desk, Web site, 388
reference grammar, 5
reference lines, business letters,
    336

references, online, 273-274,
    388
reflecting, personality, 231-232
reflexive pronouns, 60-61
regular verbs, 77-78
relative pronouns, 30, 57-58
releases, press, 341
replacements, relative pro-
    nouns, 30
reports
    police, 82
    preparing, 337
research, 270-273
    bibliographies, 275-276
    chronological order, 281
    documentation, 283-284
    grant applications, 351
    Internet searches, 273-274
    interviews, 276-279
    journals, 274-275
    lesson plans, 269
    libraries, 274-275
    magazines, 274-275
    media merits, 275
    narrowing the topic, 271
    organizing
        cause and effect, 281
        comparisons and con-
            trasts, 282
        counterpoints and rebut-
            tals, 282
        define and exemplify,
            282
        process analysis,
            282-283
        sequential order, 281
        soapboxes, 282
        tasks, 279
    periodicals, 274-275
    planning, 271-272
    prethinking, 269-270
    projects, 284
    quizzes, 285-287
    rules, 215
    tasks, 216
    verbs, 342
resources, 385
    dictionaries, 385, 388
    grammar guides, 386, 388

online, 387-388
    dictionaries, 388
    grammar guides, 388
    style guides, 388
style guides, 386-388
vocabulary guides, 387
writing guides, 387
restaurant interviews, 277
restrictive clauses, 153
results, subordinators, 156
resumés, 341-342
    communication verbs, 342
    creative verbs, 343
    financial verbs, 343
    leadership verbs, 342
    management verbs, 342
    performance verbs, 343
    research verbs, 342
    supporting verbs, 343
    tasks, 342-343
    technical verbs, 343
    writing, 342-343
reviews
    books, 355
    movies, 265
    screen, 356
    stage, 356
rhymes, 14-15
rhythm, 15
rules, 364
    acronyms, 363-364
    action verbs, 208
    active voices, 213
    adjective and adverb com-
        parisons, 100
    apostrophes, 182-184
    capitalizing proper nouns,
        38-41
    checking revisions, 323
    clichés, 209
    collective nouns, 48
    colons, 180-182
    communicating, 207
        active voices, 213
        clichés, 209
        conversational narrative,
            215
        edits, 218
        everyday language, 208
        nouns and verbs, 208
        originality, 216-217

paragraphs, 211
punctuation, 218
research, 215
sentences, 210-211
terminology, 217
words, 210, 212, 214
compound nouns, 47-48
conversational narrative, 215
count nouns, 45-46
dashes, 188
dates, 168
edits, 218
ellipses, 184-185
everyday language, 208
expressions, 209
grammar, 3-5, 200
hyphens, 185-188
implied infinitives, 365-366
indefinite pronoun agreements, 104-106
jargon, 217
language, 208
lesson plans, 193
lingo, 217
mass nouns, 41-42
originality, 216-217
paragraphs, 211, 214
parentheses, 290-293
plural nouns, 42-45
possessive nouns, 46-47
presentations, 305-307
pronoun and antecedent agreement, 62-64
pronouns, 65-66
proofreading, 315-317
punctuation, 218
question marks, 178-180
quizzes, 203-205
quotation marks, 294-298
research, 215
sentences, 3-4, 31, 210-211, 214
speaking, pedagogical grammar, 4
spelling, 193-195
splitting infinitives, 364-365
style, 363-364
terminology, 217
turning nouns into verbs, 365

useless words, 214
visual nouns, 208
words, 210
    position, 212
writing, 207
    active voice, 213
    clichés, 209
    conversational narrative, 215
    edits, 218
    everyday language, 208
    lesson plans, 207
    nouns and verbs, 208
    originality, 216-217
    paragraphs, 211
    punctuation, 218
    quizzes, 218-220
    research, 215
    sales letters, 223-224
    sentences, 210-211
    terminology, 217
    words, 210, 212, 214
run-ons
    quotes, 298-299
    sentences, 28

S

sales
    attention grabbers, 243-246
    closings, 310-311
    letters, 224
        announcements, 226
        attention grabbers, 225
        benefits, 226
        fundraising, 227
        headlines, 225
        preparing, 224-226
        sales pitch, 226
        time-frame notices, 225
        writing rules, 223-224
    pitches, 226, 243-246
    press releases, 228-230
salutations
    business letters, 336
    colons, 180-182
sarcasm, 15

sayings
    clichés, 9
    colloquialisms, 9-10
scenes
    action leads, 243
    shocking leads, 245
Schaum's Quick Guide to Writing Great Essays, book, 348
school, writing categories, 258
sciences, 351
    applied, 351
    natural, 351
    pure, 351
    terminology, 351
    words, italics, 290
    writing, 350-352
        environment, 352-353
        medicines, 353
        tasks, 351-352
        technology, 354
Scientific Style and Format: The CBE Manual for Authors, Editors, and Publishers, book, 353
scientific words, italics, 290
screen reviews, 356
scripts, attention grabbers, 243-246
search engines, 273-274
second person pronouns, 55-56
selling ideas, business ideas, 222-224
Semantic Rhyming Dictionary, The, book, 388
semantics, 6-7
semicolons, 171-173
    compound sentences, 25
    fused sentence errors, 28
    lesson plans, 161
    Q&As, 173
    quizzes, 173-175
senses
    descriptive grammar, 4
    grammar, 4-5
    leads, 245
    pedagogical grammar, 4
    prescriptive grammar, 4
    reference grammar, 5
    theoretical grammar, 5
    traditional grammar, 5

sentences, 5-6, 24
    agreements
        adverbs, 111
        pronouns and
            antecedents, 103-106
        subjects and verbs,
            107-110
    apostrophes, 182-184
    commas
        adjectives, 166
        dates, 168
        degrees, 169
        emphasizing words in
            a direct address, 167
        essential elements,
            170-171
        expressions, 166
        geographical addresses
            and names, 168-169
        introductory words and
            phrases, 164
        main clauses, 162
        phrases, 162
        position, 171
        quotations (direct), 168
        separating coordinate
            adjectives before a
            noun, 165
        separating nonessential
            words, 166-167
        serial, 164-165
        simple sentence divi-
            sions, 161
        splices, 28, 169-170
        subordinate clauses, 163
        titles, 169
        weak clauses, 164
    complete predicates, 23-24
    complete subjects, 20-21
    complex, 25, 147-148
    compound, 25, 66
        main clauses, 146-147
    compound predicates, 24
    compound subjects, 24
    compound-complex, 25-26,
        148
    conjunctions, 120
    declarative, 22
    dependent clauses, 23
    depth, 209
    fragments, 26-27

fused sentence errors, 28
iambic, 14
imperative, 21-22
incomplete, 26-27
independent clauses, 22-23
interrogative, 28-29,
    178-180
main clauses, 22-23
parallel structure, 27-28
parentheses, 290-293
pedagogical grammar, 4
periods, 177-178
quizzes, 32-33
rules, 31, 210-211, 214
run-ons, 28
semicolons, 171-173
simple, 24-25
simple predicates, 23-24
simple subjects, 20
structure, 3-4, 19-20
subjects, 21-22
subordinate clauses, 23
tasks, 26
variations, 29-31
wording, 7
sequels, presentations, 311
sequencing
    events, 311
    formats, 281
    organizing research mater-
        ial, 281
    pending action leads, 244
    presentations, 311
    time, 201
series, 121-122
    colons, 180-182
    commas, 164-165
    ellipses, 184-185
setting leads, fiction writing,
    242
seven c's, 303
sexism, writing, 196-197
Sheriff and Deputy Quarterly,
    magazine, 284
shocking scene leads, 245
shocking statement leads, 239
short-form pronouns, 56-57
signatures, business letters, 337
similes, 10, 15, 123-125
simple adverbs, 96
simple past tense, 74-75

simple predicates, 23-24
simple present tense, 73-74
simple questions, structure,
    28-29
simple sentences, 24-25, 161
simple subjects, 20
simplicity, 232-233
sincere comments, 223
single quotation marks, 299
singulars
    demonstrative articles,
        88-89
    indefinite pronouns,
        104-106
    nouns, 389-392, 394
    present tense regular verbs,
        77-78
    pronouns, 56-66
*Six Steps to Free Publicity: And
    Dozens of Other Ways to Win
    Free Media Attention for You
    or Your Business*, book, 230
skeletons, writing, 232
slang expressions, 394-395
    colloquialisms, 9-10
    problems, 371
slashes, 293-294
soapboxes, 282
social context, 6
sounds
    alliteration, 7-8
    assonance, 9
    hyphens, 187
    onomatopoeia, 13-14
    patterns, 7
    rhymes, 14-15
sources, recording, 275-276
speaking
    alliteration, 7-8
    allusions, 8
    business
        lesson plans, 221
        quizzes, 233-235
    contexts, 6
    functions, 6
    irony, voice inflections,
        11-12
    language history, 196
    pedagogical grammar, 4
    pragmatics, 6-7
    semantics, 7

simplicity, 232-233
sound assonance, 9
sound patterns, 7
voices, 11-12, 232
speeches. *See also* presentations
audiences, 197-198, 329
audio tapes, 235
bad news, 330-331
closings, 237, 246-249
documentation, 283-284
leads, 237-238, 280-281
attention grabbers, 243-246
fiction writing, 241-243
nonfiction writing, 239-241
meetings, 339-340
organizing research, 332
cause and effect, 281
comparisons and contrasts, 282
counterpoints and rebuttals, 282
define and exemplify, 282
process analysis, 282-283
sequential research, 281
soapboxes, 282
outlines, 331-332
presentations, 198-199, 331-332, 340
research, 270-273
Internet searches, 273-274
interviews, 276-279
libraries, 274-275
media merit, 275
narrowing the topic, 271
style, 347
essays, 348-349
laws, 349-350
science, 350-354
verbalizing nouns, 199
writing, 332-333
spelling
checks, 193-195
irregular verbs, 79
rules, 193-195
Spillane, Mickey, 237

splices, commas, 169-170
split infinitives, 118
sports writing, 357
sports medicine, 353
Sports Style Guide & Reference Manual: The Complete Reference for Sports Editors, Writers, and Broadcasters, book, 357
stage reviews, 356
statements
declarative sentences, 22
direct leads, 240
shocking leads, 239
thesis, essays, 349
stationery, business letters, 222-224
stimulators, ideas, 258-259
advice columns, 264
comic strips, 264-265
fiction writing, 264-266
horoscopes, 265
interviews, 260-261
letters to the editor, 265
movie reviews, 265
storyboards, 263
ticklers, 261-264
yellow pages, 259-260
storyboards, idea stimulators, 263
structures
parallel, 27-28
questions, 28-29
sentences, 3-4, 19-20, 31
studies, business letters, 222-223
style, 347, 353. *See also* formats, guidelines
changes, 361-363
grammar, 7
alliteration, 7-8
allusions, 8
anthropomorphism, 8
antonyms, 8-9
assonance, 9
clichés, 9
colloquialisms, 9-10
figures of speech, 10
gist, 10
homonyms, 10
hyperbole, 10-11

idiomatic translations, 11
idioms, 11
irony, 11-12
jargon, 12
lexicons, 12
malapropisms, 12
metaphors, 12-13
metonymy, 13
morphemes, 13
onomatopoeia, 13-14
puns, 14
rhymes, 14-15
rhythm, 15
sarcasm, 15
similes, 15
synonyms, 16
guides, 386-388
lesson plans, 347
personal, 257
presentations, 221-222
rules, 363-364
sheets, 347
voice, 347
essays, 348-349
laws, 349-350
writing, 323-324
academic, 356-357
essays, 348-349
humor, 356
laws, 349-350
quizzes, 358-359
science, 350-354
sports, 357
Stylebook and Libel Manual: Fully Revised and Updated, The, book, 386
subject complements, pronouns, 65-66
subjective cases, 64-65, 136-137
subjects, 21
adjective clauses, 151
complete, 20-21
complex sentences, 25
compound sentences, 24-25, 107-108
compound-complex sentences, 25-26
declarative sentences, 22
imperative sentences, 21-22

linking verbs, 80-81
main clauses, 22-23, 145-146
noun clauses, 149-150
positioning, 22
simple sentences, 20, 24-25
subordinate clauses, 23, 147
tasks, 20-21
understood *you*, 21-22
verb agreements, 107
    collective nouns, 108-109
    compound subjects, 107-108
    confusing nouns, 109
    quantity expressions, 109-110
    word pattern difficulties, 110
subjunctive mood verbs, 72
subordinating clauses, 23, 29-30, 147
    adjective clauses, 151
        complements, 152-153
        objects, 152
        subjects, 151
    adverbial clauses, 153
        subordinators, 154-156
    commas, 163
    complex sentences, 25, 147-148
    compound-complex sentences, 25-26, 148
    noun clauses, 148-149
        direct objects, 150
        indirect objects, 150
        object complements, 150-151
        subjects, 149-150
    Q&As, 157
    relative pronouns, 58
    restrictive clauses, 153
    sentence fragments, 26-27
subordinating conjunctions, 119-121
subordinators, 154-156
    clause, 154
    comparisons, 154
    concessions, 154
    conditions, 155
    degrees, 155

manners, 155
places, 155
purposes, 155
Q&As, 157
results, 156
times, 156
successful presentations, 311
superfluous brackets, 293
superlative comparative forms, 97-100
supporting verbs, 343
suspense leads, 244
syllable patterns, rhythm, 15
synonyms, 16
syntax, 3-4, 7

T

take-away values, 304-307
    guarantee, 305-307
    presentations, 305-307
talking, language history, 196
Talking About People: A Guide to Fair and Accurate Language, book, 385
tape recorders, interviews, 277
tapes, audio, 235
tasks
    adapting to your audiences, 221-222
    attention spans, 238-239
    business communication, 330
    clauses, agreements, 152
    cutting, 214
    gerunds, 49-50
    interviews, 216
    lists, 255
    mind mapping, 255-256
    movies, 238-239
    nonessential words, 167
    organizing research material, 279
    pasting, 214
    predicates, 23-24
    preparing reports, 337
    preparing sales letters, 224-226

pronoun ambiguity, 62
pronoun and antecedent agreement, 62-64
quotes, 298-299
recording sources, 275-276
reflecting your personality, 231-232
reflexive pronouns, 60-61
research, 216, 271-272
resumés, 342-343
scientific writing, 351-352
sentence flaws, 26
subjects, 20-21
technical verbs, 343
technical terminology, 223
techniques
    attention grabbers, 243-246
    closings, 247-249
    proofreading, 315-317
    visualize, 310-311
technology
    spelling, 193-195
    writing, 354
telephone books (yellow pages), idea stimulators, 259-260
terminology, science, 351
tenses
    active and passive voices, 199
    continuous, 74
    emphatic, 83
    future, 72-73, 76, 79-80
    future perfect, 76
    future perfect progressive, 77
    future progressive, 76-77
    historical present, 73-74
    past, 72-75, 78-80, 389-394
    past participle, 78-79, 389-394
    past perfect, 75
    past perfect progressive, 76
    past progressive, 76
    present, 72-74, 77-80, 389-394
    present perfect, 75
    present perfect progressive, 76
    present progressive, 74
    progressive, 74

simple past, 74-75
simple present, 73-74
verbs, 72-73
terminology
  rules, 217
  technical, 223
than versus then, 370
thank-you notes, 262
their versus there and they're, 370
then versus than, 370
theoretical grammar, 5
theories, 5-6
there versus their and they're, 370
thesaurus, 273
thesis statements, essays, 349
they're versus their and there, 370
third person pronouns, 55-56
thoughts
  editing, 319-322
  leads, 280-281
  mind mapping, 255-256
  organizing research
    cause and effect, 281
    comparison and contrast, 282
    counterpoint and rebuttal, 282
    define and exemplify, 282
    process analysis, 282-283
    sequential research, 281
    soapboxes, 282
  prethinking, 269-270
  research, 270-273
    Internet searches, 273-274
    interviews, 276-279
    libraries, 274-275
    media merit, 275
    narrowing the topic, 271
ticklers
  annual reports, 262
  brochures, 262
  business cards, 261
  file folders, 262
  idea stimulators, 261-264
  magazine ads, 262

newsletters, 262
portfolios, 262
time
  colons, 180-182
  sequences, 201
time-frame notices, 225
times, subordinators, 156
timetable
  objectives, 308-309
  presentations, 308-309
  task, 308-309
titles
  abbreviated, 290
  colons, 180-182
  commas, 169
  italics, 289-290
to versus too and two, 371
to be verbs, 79-83
to do verbs, 82-83
to have verbs, 82-83
tone leads, fiction writing, 242-243
too versus to and two, 371
topics
  free writes, 310-311
  presentations, 202-203
  research, 270-273
    Internet searches, 273-274
    interviews, 276-279
    libraries, 274-275
    media merit, 275
    narrowing, 271
  writing
    categories, 257-258
    stimulators, 258-266
traditional grammar, 5
transitive verbs, 80
translations, idiomatic, 11
two versus to and too, 371

U

unclear pronouns, 106-107
underlining italics, 290
understood *you*, imperative sentences, 21-22
unfamiliar words, italics, 290

uniform resource locator. *See* URL
University of Chicago Press, Web site, 351
URL (uniform resource locator), 273
useless words, rules, 214

V

value, presentations, 304-307
variety, sentences, 29-31
verbalizing nouns, 199
verbs, 22, 71-72
  action, 80-82, 208
  active voices, 199
  auxiliary, 140-141
  communication, 342
  complete predicates, 23-24
  compound predicates, 24
  contractions, 59
  creative, 343
  depth, 209
  emphatic tenses, 83
  financial, 343
  formed from nouns, 365
  future perfect progressive tense, 77
  future perfect tense, 76
  future progressive tense, 76-77
  future tense, 72-73, 76
  gerunds, 49
  helping, 81
  infinitives, 117-118
  intransitive, 80
  irregular, 78-79, 389-394
    future tense, 79-80
    past participle, 389-394
    past participle tense, 78-79
    past tense, 78-80, 389-394
    present tense, 78-80, 389-394
    spelling, 79
    to be, 79-80
  leaderships, 342

lesson plans, 71
linking, 80-81
    adjective clauses,
        152-153
    object complements,
        139-140
    subject agreements,
        107-108
main clauses, 22-23,
    145-146
management, 342
mood, 72
    imperative, 72
    indicative, 72
    subjunctive, 72
ordinary, 82-83
passive, 81-82, 199
past participle, 94
past perfect progressive
    tense, 76
past perfect tense, 75
past progressive tense, 76
past tense, 72-75
performance, 343
phrases, 134
    gerunds, 134
    infinitives, 135-136
    participles, 122, 134-135
    prepositions, 117
plural subjunctive mood,
    125-126
predicates, 71-72
present participle, 94
present perfect progressive
    tense, 76
present perfect tense, 75
present progressive tense,
    74
present tense, 72-74
presentations, 198-199
progressive tense, 74
quizzes, 83-85
regular, 77-78
    plural present tense,
        77-78
    present tense, 77-78
    singular present tense,
        77-78
research, 342
resumés, 342-343
simple predicates, 23-24

subject agreements, 107
    collective nouns,
        108-109
    compound subjects,
        107-108
    confusing nouns, 109
    quantity expressions,
        109-110
subordinate clauses, 23, 147
supporting, 343
technical, 343
tenses, 72-73
    emphatic, 83
    future, 76
    future perfect, 76
    future perfect progres-
        sive, 77
    future progressive, 76-77
    past, 74-75
    past perfect, 75
    past perfect progressive,
        76
    past progressive, 76
    present, 73-74, 77-80
    present perfect, 75
    present perfect progres-
        sive, 76
    present progressive, 74
    progressive, 74
to be, 79-83
to do, 82-83
to have, 82-83
transitive, 80
verbalizing, 199
voices
    active, 81-82
    passive, 81-82
writing, depth, 209
videotapes, speeches, 235
virgules, 293-294
visual nouns, 208
visualizing presentations,
    310-311
vocabulary
    guides, 387
    lexicons, 12
vocative phrases, 133
voices
    active, 81-82, 199, 213
    establishing, 232
    inflection, irony, 11-12

passive, 81-82, 199
style, 347
    essays, 348-349
    laws, 349-350
science, 350-354

W-X

Wall to Wall, book, 283
weak clauses, commas, 164
Web of On-Line Dictionaries
    and Others, Web site, 388
Web sites, 274
    AltaVista, 274, 324
    American Psychological
        Association's APA-Style
        Helper site, 351
    Blue Book of Grammar and
        Punctuation, 388
    Capitol Community
        College, 317
    Common Errors in English,
        366, 388
    Computer Currents High-
        Tech Dictionary, 388
    Curmudgeon's Stylebook,
        The, 388
    Department of Applied
        Linguistics & ESL,
        Georgia State University,
        78
    Elements of Style, 1918,
        388
    experts, 352
    Facts on File, 388
    Google, 274, 324
    Grammar Bytes! Interactive
        Grammar Review, 388
    Grammar Handbook,
        University of Illinois at
        Urbana-Champaign, 388
    Guide to Grammar and
        Writing, 388
    On-line English Grammar,
        An, 388
    Presbyterian College
        Writing Center, 317
    ProfNet, 261

Purdue University's OWL
  (Online Writing Lab)
  Handouts, 317
Reference Desk, 388
University of Chicago Press,
  351
Web of On-Line
  Dictionaries and Others,
  388
WWWebster: Merriam-
  Webster Dictionary
  Online, 388
Yahoo!, 274
well versus good, 111
who, relative pronouns, 57-58
wish mood, 125-126
Word Power Made Easy, book,
  387
words, 5-6
  adjectives, 92, 97-100
    endings, 95-96
    forms and functions,
      94-95
    position, 92-93
    types, 93-94
  adverbs, 96-98
    agreements, 111
    comparatives and
      superlatives, 98-100
    position, 97
  altered, definitions, 195-196
  antonyms, 8-9
  articles, 87
    definite, 88
    demonstratives, 88-89
    distributives, 89
    exclamatives, 89
    indefinite, 87
    numbers, 90
    possessive pronouns,
      90-91
    quantifiers, 91-92
  auxiliary verbs, 140-141
  clauses
    adjectives, 151-153
    adverbial, 153-156
    main, 145-147
    nouns, 148-151
    restrictive, 153

subordinate, 147-148
clichés, 124-125
collocation, 124
commas, 164
compound
  hyphens, 188
  nouns, 47-48
  quantifiers, 91
conjunctions, 119-121
context, 6
contractions, 118-119
direct addresses, 167
editing, 319-322
euphemisms, 16
exclamation marks, 180
figures of speech, 10
foreign, 290
functions, 6
grammar, 7
homonyms, 10
idioms, 11, 123-124
infinitives, 117-118
inflections, 5-6
malapropisms, 12
meanings, altered, 195-196
metaphors, 12-13, 123
metonymy, 13
misused, 304
morphemes, 13
nonessential, 166-167
onomatopoeia, 13-14
order, 201
participles, 122
patterns
  parallel structure, 27-28
  subject and verb agree-
    ments, 110
persuasive, 304
phrasal verbs, 117
phrases, 129, 136
  absolute, 130-131
  adjectives, 130
  appositives, 131-133
  direct objects, 137-138
  indirect objects, 138-139
  nouns, 129-130
  object complements,
    139-140
  subjective cases,
    136-137

verbs, 134-136
vocative, 133
position, rules, 212
powerful, 304
pragmatics, 6-7
prepositions, 115-117
problems, 366
  a while versus awhile,
    366
  all ready versus already,
    366
  appendix versus glos-
    sary, 366
  complement versus com-
    pliment, 367
  dialogue versus dialog,
    367
  farther versus further,
    367
  fewer versus less, 368
  former versus latter, 368
  its versus it's, 368
  lay versus lie, 369
  lesson plans, 361
  moot versus mute, 370
  than versus then, 370
  their, they're, and there,
    370
  to, too, and two, 371
pronouns, unclear, 106-107
puns, 14
resumés, 342-343
rhymes, 14-15
rules, 210
scientific, 290
semantics, 7
similes, 123
sound patterns, 7
spell checks, 193-195
subjunctives, 125-126
synonyms, 16
unfamiliar, 290
useless, rules, 214
work, ambiguity, 371-373
workshops
  blueprints, 307-309
  checking revisions, 323
  pronouns, 66
  work permits, 307-309

World's Easiest Guide to Using the MLA: A User-Friendly Manual for Formatting Research Papers According to the Modern Language Association Style, The, book, 386

Write on Target: A Five-Phase Program for Nonfiction Writers, book, 279

Write-On Cling Sheets, 262

writing, 3-6, 324-325, 332-333
  academic, 356-357
  attention grabbers, 243-246
  bibliographies, personal, 230-231
  business
    lesson plans, 221
    letters, 335-337
    quizzes, 233-235
    proposals, 337-338
  categories
    activities, 258
    crime, 258
    entertainment, 258
    events, 258
    lifestyles, 257
    mental health, 257
    money, 257
    personal-advancement ideas, 257
    physical fitness, 257
    school, 258
  chronological, 311
  closings, 246-249
  depth, 209
  electronic mail, 333-335
  environment, 352-353
  errors, 318
  essays, 348-349
  fiction, 241, 266
    idea stimulators, 264-266
    leads, 241-243
  gender-sensitive, 196-197
  grant applications, 351

guidelines, 355
  book reviews, 355
  screen reviews, 356
  stage reviews, 356
guides, 387
humor, 356
ideas, 256-257
  categories, 257-258
  stimulators, 258-266
interoffice memos, 333-335
laws, 349-350
learning, 323-324
legal, 349-350
medicines, 353
mistakes, 318
models, 323-324
nonfiction, 239-241, 266
personality, 231-232
presentations, 198-199
press releases, 228-230, 341
process
  lists, 255
  mind mapping, 255-256
proposals, 337-338
quizzes, 326-327
resumés, 341-343
rules, 207
  active voice, 213
  clichés, 209
  conversational narrative, 215
  edits, 218
  everyday language, 208
  lesson plans, 207
  nouns and verbs, 208
  originality, 216-217
  paragraphs, 211
  punctuation, 218
  quizzes, 218-220
  research, 215
  sales letters, 223-224
  sentences, 210-211
  terminology, 217
  words, 210, 212, 214
sales letters, 224
  fundraising, 227
  preparing, 224-226

science, 350-352
  environment, 352-353
  medicines, 353
  tasks, 351-352
  technology, 354
simplicity, 232-233
skeletons, 232
speeches, 197-198
sports, 357
style, 347
  changes, 361-363
  quizzes, 358-359
  rules, 363-364
styles, 323-324
technology, 354
voices, establishing, 232

Writing a Successful College Application Essay: The Key to College Admission, book, 348

Writing Down the Bones: Freeing the Writer Within, book, 387

Writing Personal Essays: How to Shape Your Life Experiences for the Page, book, 348

Writing Reviews: How to Write About Arts & Leisure for Pleasure & Profit, book, 355

Writing That Works: How to Improve Your Memos, Letters, Reports, Speeches, Resumés, Plans, and Other Business Papers, book, 333, 387

Writing to Learn, book, 387

WWWebster: Merriam-Webster Dictionary Online, Web site, 388

Y-Z

Yahoo!, Web site, 274
yellow pages, idea stimulators, 259-260
you, imperative sentences, 21-22